AN ENGLISH DICTIONARY
OF JAPANESE CULTURE

日本文化を英語で説明する辞典

本名信行
ベイツ・ホッファ　編

有斐閣
YUHIKAKU PUBLISHING CO., LTD.

AN ENGLISH DICTIONARY OF JAPANESE CULTURE
by
Nobuyuki Honna & Bates Hoffer eds. 1986
First published in Japan
by
YUHIKAKU PUBLISHING CO., LTD., Tokyo

は じ め に

　私たちはいま国際社会のなかで生活し，多大な国際交流の恩恵
を受けています。貿易による物の交流はいうにおよばず，資本の
交流，マスコミやニューメディアによる情報の交流，あるいは旅
行や留学による人の交流など，あらゆる地域との政治的・経済
的・文化的な相互依存の関係を有しています。この相互依存関係
の進展は他方で，思いもかけぬ不協和音や摩擦を生みだしていま
す。このようなさまざまな問題を国際社会の中で解決し，相互依
存関係をさらに展開していくためには，人びとがおたがいによく
理解しあうという気持ちをもつようにならなければなりません。

　国際理解を進める最も有効な方法は，私たちひとりひとりが個
人的あるいは職業的な関係のなかで，外国の人びとと親しく交際
し，心のふれあうコミュニケーションをもつことでしょう。現在
の国際交流の姿をながめると，国際理解の基礎をなす異文化理解
は，あらゆる時・場所を通じて広がっているといえます。海外旅
行や研修を通じて，私たちは多くの友人をつくるでしょう。日本
にやってくる旅行者や留学生とおつきあいをすることにもなるで
しょう。また，仕事のうえで，外国の人と接する機会もふえるで
しょう。こういった環境のなかで，私たちひとりひとりが相手の
文化を学び，同時に日本の風習・文化を理解してもらうという有
意義な市民レベルの異文化間コミュニケーションを，より一層す
すめていくことができるのです。

　国際コミュニケーションで最も便利なことばは英語です。英語

は，英米人を中心とした民族言語の枠を越え，世界の人びとが国際交流のために使う国際言語になっています。私たちは英語を使って，英米人はもちろんのこと，世界中の人びとと交際することができるのです。世界の多くの人びととはこのような手段のために英語を勉強しています。一説によると，世界で20億の人びとの間で英語によるコミュニケーションが可能であるといわれています。当然のことながら，ネイティブスピーカーでない英語の話し手は，発音や文法，表現力にハンディがあります。しかし，おそれることはありません。英語の表現力に一日もはやく慣れ，英語を自己表現の道具としてもっともっと積極的に使い，国際コミュニケーションの場に参加すべきだと思います。外国の人たちも，以前にもまして日本のことを学びたいのですから……。

　私たちは長らく外国の文化から多くのことを学んできました。外国文化の吸収にたけた民族といえましょう。もちろん，それには歴史上の理由があって，日本が現在のような発展をとげる過程で，外国とくに欧米から多くのことを学ぶ必要があったわけです。ところが，最近では逆に，外国の多くの人びとが，現在の日本や日本の風習・文化に強い関心をよせるようになってきました。このことは，外国の人びとと交際する際に，日本の風習や文化について様々な質問がなされることからもうかがえます。私たちはこのような機会に，外国人の質問に適切に答えられるよう，英語の表現力を磨かなければなりませんし，日本の風習や文化について正確な理解をもつよう心がけておかなければなりません。せっかく語学の表現力がついても，説明すべき日本の文化について無知であるということは，まさしく恥ずべきことなのです。

　本書は，衣食住はもちろんのこと，人間関係，風俗・習慣，芸

術，スポーツ，精神と心などの分野から重要なもの300項目を厳選し，英語でどのように表現したらよいのか，どういうすじみちで説明したらよいのかを主眼に構成してあります。英語の表現力だけでなく，日本文化そのものについての理解も深まるように工夫してあります。英語の表現は簡明で的確を心がけ，日本語であらすじをそえました。読者の必要に応じて自由に英語のバリエーションを考えてください。日本人が外国人に日本文化を英語で説明する姿を念頭において書きましたが，外国の友人が直接読んでも興味深いでしょう。こういった人たちへのプレゼントにもご利用いただけると思います。

　本書の構想は，日米2人の編者が長年にわたって親しく交際し，日米の文化をおたがいに学びあうなかで生まれました。出版にいたるまでには，多くの友人のお世話になりました。この分野に深い経験をもつ寄稿者のかたがたは，編者の趣旨をよく理解して，充実したものを書いてくださいました。とくに，鈴木紀之さんは，すべての英文原稿を読み，内容のチェックと文体の統一などについて，編者を援助してくださいました。デイビッドとペギー・ケイ（David and Peggy Kehe）夫妻は，英語原稿に目を通し，有意義なコメントをくださいました。そして，有斐閣編集部の酒井久雄さんは，構想の段階から出版にいたるまで，よきアドバイザーとして全面的にご協力くださいました。あわせて感謝の意を表します。最後になりましたが，読者のご教示をまって更によりよいものにしたいと願っております。

　　1986年4月

本 名 信 行

ベイツ・ホッファ

We live in the midst of an internationalized society which has seen people from all over the world make a life for themselves among us. The cross-cultural exchange of ideas and points of view are a great strength of the English-speaking countries. More and more each year we see more interchange in international commerce, development of more multinational enterprises, as well as news from all over the world. We see rapidly a growing number of intercultural contacts which occur in travel and study abroad. As a result, we might expect a deepening of our mutual interdependence in such areas as government and economic policy, especially with our major friends in the international community such as the Japanese.

For this goal of international understanding to be realized, more of us need to be in a receptive frame of mind for mutual understanding, especially for those cultures which have such a different history than ours. Our way of thinking or feeling or acting is affected by the cultural environment which influences us from our birth and through our development as we grow. The first step in proper understanding of the people of a country could be an understanding of the cultural environment in which their civilization grew and how it affects them now. In the case of Japan, its history in the Far East, its development of its native religion of Shinto, its many contacts with China, its completely different types of language and writing system have combined with other elements so that its culture can be difficult to understand. It is the purpose of this book to try to help with an understanding of Japan and its culture which can be both puzzling and intriguing to the English-speaker. It is our hope that this book can be a foundation for cross-cultural understanding.

The most effective way of deepening cross-cultural understanding is friendship and experience in Japan, either as individuals or as part of our business or profession. Communication

on the personal level is always an effective way to learn. Unfortunately the time available for most of us in Japan is limited to tourist travel or business trips. A friendly relationship with a Japanese who can explain his culture to us on the personal level is not possible. Other means must be used to begin the cross-cultural journey.

This book is designed to be a first step in that journey to understanding. It is organized to show and explain some of the customs and cultural items which will help in developing an awareness of Japanese culture. It is written as if a Japanese who knows English well were talking about his country in a way best suited for an English-speaker's understanding. It includes a range of entries as various as interesting items of Japanese culture and the intricate patterns of formality in speech and behavior. It covers a multitude of topics, including Japanese food, clothing and shelter, the patterned social structure, interpersonal relations among the Japanese, manners, customs, the arts, elements of the Shinto and Buddhist religions, the importance of "the spirit of the Japanese", and many others.

In giving the explanations, we have tried to make each entry as self-explanatory as possible. In several cases there are cross-references to other entries, but these have been kept to the minimum possible. Some earlier dictionaries contained explanations about Japanese culture which required previous information about Japan. Here each entry is written as if a Japanese were telling you about his country on your first visit. It covers the items which most English-speakers have heard about, many items which he will probably encounter on a first visit, and some which might not be encountered but are important for understanding the culture.

The contributors to this book have extenisve experience in explaining things Japanese to English speakers. They have collectively spent many years in English-speaking countries and have built up many cross-cultural friendships. The editors of this volume first met at Aoyama Gakuin University some 20 years ago at the suggestion of Prof. Yasuo Isami. They have spent

many years working together on cross-cultural projects. The Japanese editor has been a visiting Japan Foundation scholar at Trinity Univesity in San Antonio, Texas, where he and the American editor taught a course on cross-cultural communication. The latter has lived in Japan and visited it often for a variety of studies of Japanese culture and communication. We do not have room here to thank by name all the people who have contributed to our understanding of each other's culture. We want to express our hope that this book will lead each reader to a better understanding of the Japanese culture and to the kind of deep appreciation each of us has developed for each other's culture.

April 1986

Bates Hoffer
Nobuyuki Honna

執筆者一覧（五十音順　＊編者）

Editors and Writers

近 藤 光 雄（Mitsuo Kondo）　　慶応義塾大学

鈴 木 紀 之（Toshiyuki Suzuki）　金城学院大学

高橋みな子（Minako Takahashi）　名古屋短期大学

橋 内　　武（Takeshi Hashiuchi）　ノートルダム清心女子大学

＊ベイツ・ホッファ（Bates Hoffer）　トリニティ大学

＊本 名 信 行（Nobuyuki Honna）　青山学院大学

ケイコ・O・メイズ（Keiko O. Mayse）カナダ在住・通訳業

山 口 常 夫（Tsuneo Yamaguchi）　山 形 大 学

Simplified Pronunciation Guide

Japanese words are easy to pronounce. For the purpose of this dictionary, following rules are important.

(1) A word is composed of more than one syllable.

(2) A syllable is chiefly composed of either (a) a single vowel or (b) a combination of a consonant and a vowel.

(3) There are five vowels. They are always pronounced in the same way:

"**a**" as in a̲loha̲   "**e**" as in be̲ll   "**i**" as in i̲nk
"**o**" as in o̲il   "**u**" as in fu̲ll

Note 1. When two vowels come together, read them separately:

kuiawase = ku + i + a + wa + se

Note 2. A bar mark above a vowel shows that the vowel sound is long:

ā, ē, ī, ō, ū

(4) There are nineteen consonants. They are presented alphabetically as follows:

b, ch, d, f, g, h, j (read as in Jack), **k, m, n, p, r, s, sh, t, ts, w, y, z**

Note 1. Consonants always precede vowels to form syllables:
ba, be, bi, bo, bu

Note 2. Postvocalic "n" forms a syllable alone:
hon = ho + n

(5) Double consonants are of the two kinds:

1. Consonant "**y**" following another consonant to make up a syllable such as **kya, kyo, kyu**.

2. Two identical consonants appearing in the middle of a word such as **kappa**. In this case a slight glottal constriction constitutes the pronunciation of the first consonant.

AN ENGLISH DICTIONARY
OF
JAPANESE CULTURE

ai-ai gasa   a man and a woman sharing an umbrella. In feudal times, men and women in intimate relations were not supposed to be close together in public, to say nothing of linking arms or holding hands.   One of the rare occasions this was permissible was a rainy day when they could enjoy intimacy and closeness by sharing an umbrella.   Therefore, if a man offered an umbrella to a woman, it was very often interpreted as an implicit expression of his love for her.   Since then a man and a woman in love have been described as sharing an umbrella.   It has even become a part of the street graffiti of youngsters.   When a boy is in love with a girl and he is too shy to say so to her, he is tempted to draw a picture of *ai-ai gasa* to express his feeling.   A mischievous friend of his could also draw one either to tease him or to let his potential girl friend know how he feels about her.   (HO)

ama   a shellfish-collecting woman diver. Japanese women working outside the home is not a new phenomenon, especially in farming and fishing villages.   Among them the most conspicuous workers, far more famous than men counter-parts, are women divers known as *ama*.   They dive into the depth of the sea to collect various kinds of shellfish such as *awabi* (abalone) and *sazae* (turban shell) or edible seaweed. When they appear from under the water, they let out a deep breath, making a whistle-like sound called *isobue* (beach whistle).   Ise-Shima National Park is best known for women divers, and tourists can watch them demonstrate their skill in diving for pearls.   (T)

2

相合傘　封建時代には親しい関係にある男女は，人前ではいっしょにいるべきではないとされていました。腕を組んだり，手をにぎったりすることはとてもできることではありませんでした。めったにないチャンスの一つは，雨の日に一つの傘をさすことでした。こうして親密に接近することの楽

しさを味わったのでした。だから，もし男性が女性に傘をさし出したら，それは彼の彼女に対する暗黙の愛情表現であると解釈されました。以来，愛しあう男女は一つの傘をさしているように描写されてきました。それは若者による壁の落書きにもみられます。男の子が女の子に恋をするが恥ずかしくてそのことを言えないとき，彼は自分の気持ちを表わすために相合傘の絵を書くことがあります。茶目っ気のある友達も，彼をからかうためとか彼女に彼の気持ちを知らせるために，相合傘を書くことがあります。

海　女　日本の女性が外へ働きに出ることは，とりわけ農漁村では，新しい現象ではありません。中でもその働きが最も目覚ましく，男性の同業者よりはるかに有名なのは，海にもぐって働く女性で，海女と呼ばれています。海女は海中にもぐって，あわびやさざえなどの貝類や食用の海藻類を採ってきます。水中から顔を出すと，大きく息をはきます。そのとき出す口笛のような音を磯笛といいます。伊勢志摩国立公園は海女で有名で，観光客は海女がもぐって真珠を採る実演を見ることができます。

amae   a desire for dependence.   It is often said that the Japanese "self", on the whole, is fragile and vulnerable, and it often needs the support of others in order to feel safe and strong.   Thus the desire to be loved or supported by others gains a special lexical entity, *amae*.   This everyday word also refers to a person's expectation that others will be patient and tolerant of his conduct.   Unlike the Western concept of "dependency", *amae* has a positive meaning, for it can develop the sense of solidarity among people.   A fully independent person who does everything for himself may appear unsociable and arrogant to the Japanese mind.   In its narrowest sense, *amae* refers to the child's desire to be loved by its mother. This parent-child relationship symbolized by *amae* is extended to various other relationships such as husband-wife, professor-student, and employer-employee in Japanese society.   In these relationships, the person who wishes to be cared for hopes that his dependency is simultaneously giving the other the delight of supporting him.   For further explanation, refer to Takeo Doi's *Amae no Kōzo* (1971), translated by John Bester as *Anatomy of Dependence* (1973).   (HA)

ayatori   cat's cradle.   *Ayatori* is a game that became popular mainly among girls in the Edo period (1603-1867). The original form of this game was seen not only in Japan but also in other countries where it was used in religious ceremonies.   The single component of the game is a string approximately three feet long the ends of which are tied together to form a loop.   To play, a player positions the loop over the wrists and/or fingers of both hands and attempts to produce a

甘 え　　日本人の自我は，一般に弱くて傷つき易いとされています。だから，安心して力強く生き抜いていくには，だれかの支えが必要です。だれかに愛されたい，支えてもらいたいという欲求は，甘えということばを生みました。これは日常だれもが使う語ですが，自分の行為に他人が我慢強く寛容であってほしいという期待も意味します。西洋人の「依存心」という概念とは異なり，甘えには肯定的な意味があり，人と人との結び付きを促進させる働きがあるのです。独立心が強く何でも自分でやり遂げてしまうような人は，日本人の目からは，人づきあいの悪い不遜な人に見えます。狭義の甘えは，母親に可愛がってもらいたがる子どもの気持ちによく現われています。このような甘えで象徴される親子関係は，さらに夫婦，教授・学生，上司・部下といった他の関係にも及びます。甘える人は，自分が頼りにしたということで，相手が喜んで助けてくれることを願うのです。詳しくは，土居健郎著『甘えの構造』（弘文堂，1971）を参照。

あや取り　　あや取りは江戸時代に主として女の子の間に流行した遊びです。この遊びの原型は日本にだけ見られるのではなく，他の国々でも宗教儀式に使用されていました。この遊びに使用される唯一の道具は，両端を結んで輪にした長さが約 90 cm のひも 1 本です。遊ぶには，両手の手首または指にひもをまき，指を動かしながら，さまざまな物の形を作るのです。この遊びは，1 人でも，相手がいてもできます。2 人が組になって遊ぶ時には，一方がひもで作った形を他方に渡します。そのつど，その

variety of shapes and figures by manipulating the string with the fingers. The game can be played individually or in pairs. Playing in pairs involves transferring a figure, intact, from one partner to the other. The figure is changed following each transfer. (O)

banshaku supper-time alcoholic drinking. One of the rituals that many men go through before they call it a day is *banshaku*. After coming home from work and taking a refreshing bath, they sit at a dining table and begin their daily amount of liquor. The purpose of this ritual is evidently to get rid of the stress from strenuous work and prepare for the next day. Their most favorite drinks are beer (in summer) and *sake* (in winter). Some are now taking a liking to *shōchū* (distilled spirits). The amount of consumption is not very much. They take a long time (more or less than an hour) to enjoy their self-imposed ration. During a *banshaku* feast, they also enjoy eating *tsumami*, something that goes well with their drinks, preferably *sashimi* (raw fish slices) and the season's vegetables. Previously only men were entitled to the *banshaku*. But the trend now is for husbands to invite their wives to enjoy the wonderful moment together. Most drinkers know that they should have a non-alcoholic day or two a week to give their liver a rest. But there are apparently not many who practice this advice of doctors. (HO)

banzai a cheer meaning "long life". Three cheers of *banzai* are given to express enthusiasm, applause, and favor on happy occasions. *Banzai* is usually accompanied with the

形は変化します。

晩 酌　　多くの男性は1日を終える前に晩酌という儀式を行います。仕事から家へ帰り、ひと風呂あびてから食卓にすわり、まずいっぱいやりはじめます。この儀式の目的は、仕事のストレスをとり去り、次の日にそなえるためです。最も人気のある飲物は、夏ならビール、冬ならお酒です。最近は焼酎を好む人もいます。飲む量は多くはありません。だいたい1時間ほどかけて自分で決めた分量をゆっくり楽しみます。晩酌にはつまみがつきものです。これは飲みものにあった食べもので、さしみや季節の野菜などが好まれます。以前は男性のみが晩酌をしていましたが、今では夫が妻にいっしょにやろうと言うようです。晩酌をする人は、肝臓を休めるために週に1日か2日アルコールぬきの日をつくらなければならないことを知っています。しかし、このお医者さんのアドバイスを実行する人はあまりいないようです。

万 歳　　めでたい席では、感激や賞賛や支援を示すために、長寿という意味の「万歳」が三唱されます。万歳にはたいてい、大きな喜びを示す（勢いよく両手を挙げる）動作が伴います。比

gesture of great joy—holding up of the hands in an animated manner. On a relatively ceremonious social occasion the cheer is led by an important person of the gathering. The phrase uttered in hailing the Emperor is *"Tennō-heika bazai"*, which means "Long live the Emperor". (S)

batsu   a clique. Modern Japan is generally regarded as a "classless" society. Instead of clearly defined social classes, however, there have arisen within various social organizations groups of persons having the same cultural background—exclusive groups of people from particular clans or alumni of particular colleges. These social cliques seek to protect and advance the interests of their members rather than to enhance good friendship. Employment and promotion by favoritism are prevalent in companies and government offices that have cliques of this kind. In pre-war Japan, for example, some economic cliques (*zaibatsu*) controlled most of the financial circles and business enterprises. During the occupation period these were dissolved into smaller groups, but there have recently been some tendencies for the former *zaibatsu* cliques to reorganize themselves. In politics, factionalism is dominant. The ruling Liberal Democratic Party, for example, is composed of several factions. Each faction is headed by a strong man who takes care of his group members financially and politically on a similar basis to the traditional *oyabun - kobun* (boss-and-his-henchmen) relationship. Al-

較的儀式ばった場合には，その席の重
要な人物が万歳の音頭をとります。天
皇に対しては「天皇陛下万歳」と唱え
ますが，それは「天皇が永く生き栄え
ますように」という意味です。

閥　近代化した日本には一般に，社会的な階級制度はないと
されています。しかし，階級制度とまではいかないものの，数あ
る組織体の中では，ある学校の同窓生仲間や，特別な関係で結ば
れている人々などからなる排他的集団が存在します。こういった
閥は，仲間同士の友情の強化などというよりも，仲間の利益を守
り，さらに追求するよう努力するのです。閥の存在する企業や公
共団体などでは，雇用から昇進に至るまで情実によって決められ
ているようです。戦前の日本では，いくつかの財閥がほとんどの
金融企業を支配していました。戦後の占領期にこれらの財閥は解
体されたものの，最近になり財閥復興の兆しがうかがえます。政
界においても派閥が勢力を占めています。例えば，自由民主党は
いくつかの派閥からなっています。それぞれの閥には，党員の面
倒を公私にわたってみる実力者がいて，昔流の親分・子分の関係
で結ばれているのです。閥の存在は一般に社会悪とされてはいる
ものの，日本の社会に深く根づいています。

though it is regarded as a social evil, the *batsu* clique system is a deep-rooted way of life in Japanese society.　(K)

bentō　lunch taken at offices and factories or food put in a lunch box a person carries when he is on a trip.　Today comparatively few people carry their lunches to their places of work, because many of the big companies are provided with refectories or because people have little time for packing a lunch before going to work.　Furthermore, some people prefer to have lunch at nearby restaurants.　For travelers and pic- nickers, rice balls (*o-musubi*) used to be the usual type of *bentō*.　Box-lunches sold at railway kiosks are called *ekiben*. One of the most popular types of *ekiben* is *makunouchi*, which is made up of rice supplemented with tidbits of many other kinds of food.　(S)

bon　the Bon Festival. It was originally held on July 15 by the lunar calendar.　Today it generally refers to the period from August 13 to 16.　In old times, ancestral spirits and depart- ed souls were believed to return to their families during this period.　It is a festival for welcoming them home, making offerings to them and holding memorial services.　People pay a visit to the family grave and pray for the repose of the dead, offering candles and bunches of flowers and burning incense sticks (*senkō*).　It is customary in many districts to make bonfires for welcoming (*mukae-bi*) the ancestral spirits.　On the last evening of the festival, bonfires for speeding them back (*okuri-bi*) to their world are also made in some districts.　In seaside districts, wooden or straw lanterns instead of *okuri-bi*

弁 当　今日では職場に昼食を持参する人は比較的少なくなりました。それは，大きな会社にはたいてい食堂がありますし，出勤前に弁当を詰める時間がなかったりするからです。また，近くのレストランで昼食をとるのを好む人もいます。昔は，旅行や遠足にはおむすびが主流でした。鉄道の売店で売っている弁当は駅弁といいます。駅弁で最も一般的なものは幕の内ですが，それは，御飯にいろいろな種類のおかずが少しずつついたものをいいます。

盆　盆の行事は，もとは太陰暦の 7 月15日を中心にに催されましたが，今日では一般に 8 月13日から16日までの期間を指します。昔は，この期間に先祖の霊や死者の霊がその家族のもとに帰ってくると信じられていました。盆は，それらの霊を家に迎え，供物を供えて，礼拝を行う祭りです。人々は墓に参り，花を供え，線香を焚き，死者の冥福を祈ります。多くの地方には，先祖の霊を迎える焚き火（迎え火）をする風習があります。盆の最後の夜には，霊をその世界へ送り返す焚き火（送り火）をする地方もあります。海岸地帯では，送り火のかわりに，木製または竹製の灯籠が水上に流されます（灯籠流し，または精霊流し）。盆踊りは全国各地で行われます。音頭とりや囃子方のための屋台が神社や寺院の境内，公園や広場や通りに組まれ，浴衣を着た人たちが，囃子方の歌や囃子に合わせて屋台の周囲で踊ります。

are offered afloat on the water (*tōrō-nagashi* or *shōrō-nagashi*). The Bon Festival folk dances (*bon-odori*) are held in various parts of the country. A scaffold for singers and musical bands is set up on the grounds of shrines and temples, or in parks and squares, or in the streets, and people dressed in informal cotton kimono for summer wear (*yukata*) dance around it to the folk songs sung and played by the folk musicians. (S)

bōnenkai a year-end party. To most Japanese, December, though it is the busiest month, is the time they enjoy *bōnenkai*, which literally means a party for forgetting the year. Various social groups or sections of companies and offices have their own *bōnenkai*. Some of them have *shinnenkai* (New Year party) instead of year-end parties, but it is far less common. Although more and more parties are held in Western-style restaurants or hotels, particularly in cities, *bōnenkai* are almost always Japanese-style gatherings in *tatami*-matted rooms in which all those present feel more relaxed. Forgetting all the unpleasant memories of the passing year, they spend a couple of happy hours eating and drinking, very often enlivened by their songs, magic tricks and other entertainments. Tremendously popular in recent years is singing to the accompaniment of *karaoke* (cassette-taped music). With all formality laid aside, *bōnenkai* is a good opportunity to strengthen the emotional solidarity of the participants. (T)

bonsai a potted dwarf tree as distinguished from potted plants in general. While the charm of a potted flower

忘年会　ほとんどの日本人にとって，12月は1年中で一番あわただしい月なのですが，忘年会をして楽しむ時期でもあります。忘年会とは，文字通りに，その年のことを忘れるためのパーティーを意味します。さまざまな社交グループや会社・役所などの部課がそれぞれ忘年会を開きます。忘年会はせずに，新年会をすることもありますが，忘年会をするほうがずっと一般的です。最近，各種のパーティーをレストランやホテルで洋式に行うことが多くなっています。特に都市部ではその傾向があります。しかし，忘年会はまずたいていの場合，畳敷きの部屋で行う日本式の集まりです。その方が出席者全員くつろいだ気分になれるのです。過ぎた1年の不快なことはすべて忘れ，飲んだり食べたりします。合間に歌や手品やその他の余興をいれて，にぎやかに楽しく2，3時間を過ごします。この数年，圧倒的に人気があるのはカラオケです。忘年会は，堅苦しいことはいっさいなくし，参加者全員の連帯感を強めるよい機会となっています。

盆　栽　鉢植の花や観葉植物の魅力は植物そのものの美にあるのですが，盆栽の魅力はそれが醸し出す自然の雰囲気にあると

or a foliage plant lies in its own beauty, that of *bonsai* is said to consist in the natural atmosphere it creates. *Bonsai* culture dates back to the Heian period (794-1185), and it became the fashion as the southern school of Chinese painting (*nanga*) gained popularity in the late Edo period (1603-1867). A dwarf tree planted in a pot is trained and trimmed into a graceful shape so that it may represent a beautiful landscape in miniature. Although great care and artificial aid are given in raising it, a dwarf tree is expected to appeal to the viewer's imagination by expressing natural beauty. Although it is actually "man-made", it must look like a natural object. (S)

budō martial arts. *Budō* refers to the traditional arts of self-defense in Japan. There are several different kinds of martial arts. Among them *jūdō*, the art of throwing and grappling, is the most popular, and thus has been included in the Olympics since 1964. *Karate*, or "empty hand" as its name literally denotes, is the art of hitting and kicking with bare fists and feet. *Kendō* is Japanese fencing with a bamboo sword. *Aikidō* is the art of bending and twisting the joints without much power, and is very popular among men and women, young and old. In addition, *iaidō*, the art of quick drawing, wielding and shielding of a real sword, *kyūdo*, Japanese archery, and *naginata*, a kind of halberd fencing that is practiced exclusively by women, also draw, if without much fanfare, attention among the martial arts enthusiasts. Regardless of the different styles and forms of each art, the emphasis is always placed on the improvement of the learner's spirit and character. (Y)

言われています。盆栽の起源は平安時
代にさかのぼりますが，江戸時代後期
に南画の普及と共に流行しました。鉢
に植えた小型の植木は，枝を矯正した
り剪定したりして情趣のある形に仕立
てられ，美しい自然の風景を縮小した
もののように見えるように栽培されま
す。その栽培には細心の注意が払わ
れ，人工的な手が加えられますが，盆栽は見る人に自然美を想像
させるものです。実際には人工的なのですが，あくまでも自然の
ものに見えなければなりません。

　武　道　　武道は日本古来のマーシャル・アーツで，自己防衛
のための武術です。武道といってもいろいろありますが，柔道が
最もよく知られています。これは，主に投げと押え技の武道で，
1964年以来，オリンピックの競技種目にも加えられています。空
手は，その名が示す通り，素手や素足による打込みや蹴りを特徴
とします。剣道は竹刀による日本式フェンシングです。合気道
は，関節を曲げたりひねったりしますが，余計な力を必要としな
いので，性別・年齢を問わず人気があります。居合道は，本物の
刀を素早く抜き，振り，そして鞘に納める術です。弓道は日本式
アーチェリーであり，長刀は，槍と鎌をいっしょにしたような武
器を使った一種のフェンシングで，女性のみがします。これらも
武道愛好家の間で静かなブームを巻き起こしています。それぞれ
は型や技術の点で違いますが，目的は心身の鍛練ということで一
致します。

Bukkyō   Buddhism. The most influential religion of
eastern and central Asia, it was founded by Gautama Buddha
(or Sakyamuni Gautama) in India in the fifth century B. C. and
was introduced into Japan via China and Korea early in the
sixth century.   The Four Noble Truths (*shishō-tai*) and the
Eight-Fold Path (*hasshō-dō*) comprise the basic doctrines of
Buddhism, which holds that suffering, inherent in human
existence, can be evaded by means of mental and moral self-
purification.   The Four Noble Truths demonstrate first that
all life is subject to suffering, secondly that earthly desires are
the causes of sufferings, thirdly that the annihilation of desire
is the only way of attaining nirvana (*nehan*), which is the state
of eternal peace and freedom from karma, and fourthly that
one can eliminate selfishness by practicing the Eight-Fold
Path.   The Eight-Fold Path is rightness of belief, resolve,
speech, action, livelihood, effort, thought and meditation.
Thus the Buddhist ideal lies in the attainment of nirvana,
which may also be expressed in other words such as
Buddhahood (*jōbutsu*), supreme enlightenment (*satori*), and
salvation (*saido*).   Buddhism was established as the national
religion of Japan in the mid-seventh century, and during the
period of five centuries since, many differing sects arose with
the spread of Buddhism from the nobility to the common
people.   In addition to the Shingonshū and Tendaishū sects,
the two major sects in the Heian period (794-1185),
the Jōdoshū, Shinshū, Nichirenshū, and the Zen sects
such as Rinzaishū and Sōtōshū were founded in the
Kamakura period (1192-1333).   The Tokugawa Government,
banning Christianity, introduced the *danka* (Buddhist parish-

仏　教　　東アジア，中央アジアで最も有力な宗教であり，紀元前5世紀にインドで，仏陀（シャカムニ・ゴータマ）によって創始され，6世紀初めに中国，朝鮮を経て日本に伝えられました。四聖諦と八正道が仏教の根本教義をなします。仏教は，人間存在に本来的に伴う苦悩は精神的・道徳的自己純化によって避けられると教えます。四聖諦は，第1に，すべて生命は苦悩のあるものであること，第2に，世俗的欲望が苦悩の原因であること，第3に，欲望の滅却が，永遠の平安と業から解放された状態である涅槃に到達する唯一の方法であること，第4に，八正道を実行することによって人は利己心を排除できるということを説明します。八正道とは，正しい見解，決意，ことば，行為，生活，努力，思念，瞑想のことです。このように，仏教の理想は涅槃への到達ですが，これは成仏とか悟りとか済度とかいった概念で表わされることもあります。仏教は7世紀中頃に日本の国教となり，それから5世紀の間に，貴族から平民へと浸透するにつれて，多くの異なる宗派が生まれました。平安時代の2大宗派であった真言宗と天台宗に加えて，鎌倉時代には，浄土宗，真宗，日蓮宗，そして臨済宗や曹洞宗などの禅宗が開かれました。江戸時代に，キリスト教を禁じた徳川幕府は，檀家制度を導入し，寺院と僧侶を完全な支配下に置きました。明治時代に行われた信教の自由と神道と仏教の分離は，仏教の信仰を純化したといえます。今日では，仏教の信仰は衰退しているようですが，それでもなお日本では支配的な宗教です。

ioner) system during the Edo period (1603-1867) and brought Buddhist temples and priests under its complete control. Religious freedom and separation of Shintoism and Buddhism enforced in the Meiji period (1868-1912) can be said to have purified the Buddhist faith. Today people's faith in Buddhism appears to be somewhat declining, but it is still the dominant religion in Japan. (S)

Bunka-no-hi Culture Day. It is a national holiday on November 3, and is meant to celebrate the development of culture in Japan. This day was established in 1948 in commemoration of the post-war Japanese Constitution proclaimed on this day in 1946. The names of those who have contributed to the nation's cultural advancement are announced by the Government, and on this day, several of them are awarded a "Cultural Medal" by the Emperor at the Imperial Palace. In addition, many cultural festivals and events are held here and there throughout the nation. (Y)

butsudan the household Buddhist altar enshrining Buddhist images for worship. Household altars became popular during the Kamakura period (1192-1333) when priests and preachers delivered sermons at the houses of the common people. Later, in the Edo period (1603-1867), the Tokugawa Government banning Christianity virtually forced people to set up family altars in their houses. Today many people dispense with them owing both to a cramped housing situation and to loss of faith in Buddhism. Altars are generally box-like in structure and they have double-leafed hinged doors. They are

18

文化の日　11月3日で，国民の祝日の一つです。文化の発展を祝う日で，1946年のこの日に新憲法が公布されたことを記念して，1948年に制定されました。政府は文化の発展に貢献した人々の名前を発表し，そのうちの数名が当日皇居において，天皇より文化勲章を授与されます。また，各地では文化的な催し物が行われれます。

仏　壇　礼拝のための仏像を安置する家庭用の祭壇で，僧侶や説教師が庶民の家で説教を行った鎌倉時代に普及しました。江戸時代になって，キリスト教を禁止した徳川幕府は，各家庭に仏壇の設置を強制しました。今日では，悪い住宅事情や仏教に対する信仰心の喪失のために，多くの人々は仏壇  を置かずに済ませています。仏壇は一般に箱形の構造で，観音開きの扉がついています。大きさや様式は多種多様で，内装や付属

made in a variety of sizes and styles, and the manners in which they are furnished with fittings and articles differ among the various religious sects. An image of Buddha in picture, sculpture, or engraving is enshrined in the center, and on both sides are placed images of the founders of the sect or mortuary tablets (*ihai*) of the deceased. A candlestick, an incense burner, a flower vase, a bell, a mallet, and other articles used for religious service are also housed in the altar. Devout Buddhists make it a rule to sit at the altar in the morning and evening and chant a sutra, offering a candle and burning incense. (S)

cha　tea. The Japanese word for tea is *cha*, which is usually called *o-cha* with an honorific prefix *o-*. *O-cha* almost always refers to green tea, though it can sometimes include other types of tea. It may safely be said that green tea is to the Japanese what black tea is to the British. In spite of the increasing popularity of English tea and coffee, green tea has been a national drink for centuries. It was first brought to Japan from China as a kind of medicine in the eighth century. There are many kinds of green tea in Japan : *gyokuro*, *matcha*, *sencha*, etc., all drunk without sugar or milk. *Gyokuro* is the best tea. *Matcha* is finely powdered tea used for the traditional *sadō* (tea ceremony). Several other beverages have the suffix *cha* attached to their names, such as *mugi-cha*, *genmai-cha* and *kobu-cha*, which are infusions of roasted barley, roasted brown rice, and dried *konbu* (a kind of kelp), respectively. (T)

物は宗派によって異なります。中央には，絵画，彫塑または彫刻による仏像が安置され，その両側には宗派の開祖の像や故人の位牌が置かれます。燭台，香炉，花瓶，鈴，鈴棒その他礼拝に使われる道具も仏壇内に納められます。熱心な仏教徒は朝夕仏壇の前に座り，灯明をあげ線香を焚いて読経するのを日課としています。

茶　茶という日本語は，普通お茶と敬語の接頭辞をつけて用います。お茶といったら，たいていは緑茶を指しますが，他の種類の飲物を含めることもあります。緑茶と日本人との関係は，紅茶と英国人の関係と同じといってよいでしょう。紅茶とコーヒーの人気が高くなってはいますが，緑茶は何百年も昔から日本の国民的な飲物です。緑茶は8世紀に初めて薬用として中国から日本に伝わりました。日本の緑茶には，玉露，抹茶，煎茶，番茶などといろいろな種類があり，すべて砂糖もミルクも入れずに飲みます。玉露は最高級のお茶です。抹茶は細かい粉末状にしたお茶で，伝統的な茶道で使われるものです。麦茶，玄米茶，昆布茶など他にいくつか，語尾に茶がつく飲物がありますが，これらはそれぞれ炒った大麦・玄米・乾燥した昆布をせんじた飲物です。

chanoma a living room of a Japanese-style house. In this room, family members and their close friends sit around a tea table (*chabudai*), take their ease over a cup of tea, and have a relaxed conversation or enjoy watching TV. Occasionally meals are taken in this room. In winter the tea table may be replaced by a foot-warmer with a quilt over it (*kotatsu*). In the case of a farmhouse, a hearth made in the floor (*irori*) forms the center of the room. Among other things, a tea cabinet (*cha-dansu*) and a TV set are usually found in the room. (S)

chawan-mushi a steamed egg custard. *Chawan-mushi* is an egg custard dish which is popular in Japanese cooking. It is often used as a soup course in the Western concept and served hot. The basic ingredients consist of several eggs, soup stock (traditionally fish stock or broth), a little bit of meat, fish, and vegetables (mushrooms, carrots, spinach, etc.) for garnish. For single portions, the ingredients are ladled into teacup-type bowls, steam cooked, and served directly at the table. Since *chawan-mushi* is a quite economical and nutritious dish, it is often prepared in Japanese homes using their own unique recipe. (O)

chazuke a quick dish of boiled rice with hot tea poured on it. It is a dish that Japanese people are very fond of as a quick and easy home made "pick-me-up". Hot green tea is poured over a bowl of cold cooked rice into which some pickled vegetables are often added. Variations in preparing *chazuke* include combining vegetables, seaweed and/or dried

茶の間　　茶の間では家族や親しい友人が茶ぶ台を囲んで，お茶を飲みながらくつろいだり，談笑したり，テレビを見たりします。時には食事もこの部屋でとります。冬には，こたつが茶ぶ台の代わりになります。農家の場合には囲炉裏がこの部屋の中心となります。茶の間にはたいがい茶簞笥とテレビがつきものです。

茶碗蒸し　　茶碗蒸は日本料理の中で人気のある，蒸した卵料理です。西洋料理にたとえればスープコースに当たり，熱くして出します。基本材料は，数個の卵とだし汁で，それにつけ合わせとして，少々の肉，魚，野菜（しいたけ，にんじん，ほうれん草など）を使います。1人分ずつ，材料を湯呑茶碗型のカップに注ぎ，蒸し煮して，そのまま食卓に出します。茶碗蒸しはたいへん経済的で栄養価の高い料理なので，日本の家庭ではそれぞれ独特の作り方で，よく作ります。

茶漬け　　これは日本人がたいへん好む料理で，手早く簡単にできる家庭的な1品です。茶碗に冷御飯を盛り，漬物などをのせて，上から熱い緑茶を注ぐだけです。このやり方で，野菜，海藻，干した魚などをとり合わせることもあります。御飯も温かいものを使うことがあります。近頃では，茶漬け用のつけ合わせ材料が入った小袋が市販されています。

fish. The rice is sometimes served hot. Nowadays, special packages of garnish for *chazuke* are sold at stores. (O)

chikuwa a fish cake. *Chikuwa* (literally "bamboo rings") is a stick-shaped fish cake. The ingredients of *chikuwa* are: pureed white fish such as cod or shark, a binding agent such as potato starch or arrowroot (*kuzu*) to help mold the fish paste, and salt. The process of making *chikuwa* involves three steps. First, the pureed fish is blended with a binding agent and molded around a thin bamboo stalk (today a stainless steel rod). Second, the fish paste is steamed. The third step involves grilling the "fish stick" to color the outer layer brown. The fish product becomes firm when cooled, closely resembling bologna in texture. A fresh *chikuwa* is cut into slices and eaten as it is, or cooked with vegetables. (O)

chirigami-kōkan a swap of old newspapers for toilet rolls. If you have piled up a bunch of old newspapers or magazines, you can exchange it with a roll of toilet paper (*chirigami*). All you have to do is just wait for an exchange car (*kōkansha*) visiting your neighborhood. The visit is usually announced over a loud speaker. The exchange business has become very popular due to the current recycling fad. But the business pattern is that of traditional touring vendors: periodical sales visits with specially modulated calls for their commodities. The typical statement announced over a loud speaker runs like this: "Hello, folks. Sorry to be making a big noise again. This is your toilet paper exchange car. If you have old newspapers, old magazines, or old cloth

24

ちくわ　　ちくわは，魚肉の練り物を棒状にした食品です。材料は，たらやさめなどの白身の魚をこしてピューレ状にしたものと，それを型にはめやすくするために使う，くずか片栗粉のような凝固剤，それに塩です。ちくわの製造には3段階があります。第1に，こした魚に凝固剤を混ぜ，細い竹の棒（現在では，ステンレス製の棒）のまわりに形よく巻きつけます。次に，この魚の練り物を蒸します。3番目に，ちくわの外側を茶色の焦げ目をつけるために焼きます。冷えると，この魚製品は固くなり，きめがボロニアソーセージのようになります。新鮮なちくわは，薄く切ってそのまま食べるか，または野菜といっしょに調理します。

チリガミ交換　　古新聞や古雑誌がたまったら，トイレットペーパーと交換できます。交換車が近所にやってくるのを待っているだけでいいのです。交換車は一定の間隔をおいてやってきます。来たことはスピーカーで知らされます。交換業は今や資源再利用の流行で大変はやっています。しかし，仕事のやり方は昔の行商人と同じです。定期的にやってきて，独特の売り声を発します。スピーカーから流れる典型的な呼び声は次のようなものです。「ご町内の皆様，毎度おさわがせいたしております。こちらはチリガミ交換車でございます。古新聞，古雑誌，ボロきれなどがございましたら，多少にかかわらずお知らせください。トイレットペーパーと交換いたします。」

materials, however small your amount is, we will be glad to exchange them for our toilet rolls. Please let us know." (HO)

chōnaikai   a neighborhood association. It is basically a self-governing organization for the welfare of the members. It also helps local administration with public works. Some associations gave up the name *chōnaikai* in favor of *jichikai* (a self-governing community association), for the former reminds people of the conservative and totalitarian neighborhood organizations of the pre-war days. Prior to a general meeting, members of the executive committee meet periodically to discuss matters of public interest or to solve various kinds of problems occurring within the neighborhood. *Chōnaikai* is generally zealous for improvement or preservation of its living environment, and it can easily become a strong pressure group or counterforce against any threat to a quiet and healthy neighborhood. It also plays an important role in the social and cultural life of a community. It coordinates various recreational activities such as trips, sports and, Bon Festival dances, and provides informal social events among neighbors. In a community whose inhabitants are mostly parishioners (*ujiko*) of a shrine, the organization of local festivals is considered to be the most important function of *chōnaikai*. (HA)

chōnan   the oldest son. Under the old patriarchal family system, which lasted until the end of the war, the oldest son had the right of primogeniture. He inherited the largest portion, if not all, of the estate and succeeded his father as the

町内会　基本的には，地区の福利向上のために設けられた自治組織ですが，地方自治体の公共の活動に協力するという働きもしています。地区によっては町内会という呼称を嫌って，自治会という名称を使っています。町内会というと，戦前の保守的で全体主義的な隣組制度を想い起こさせるからです。多数の地区民が参加する総会に先立って，町内会役員は定期的に集まり，地区民の関心をさそう事柄を討議したり，その地区で起こっているさまざまな問題の解決に当たります。町内会は一般に生活環境の改善と保護に熱心で，閑静で健康的な街の環境が破壊されるおそれがあれば，すぐにでも強力な圧力団体か反対勢力になりえます。町内会は，地域社会の社会的・文化的生活においても重要な役割をはたしています。例えば，旅行，スポーツ，盆踊りといったリクリエーション活動の運営に当たり，普段着姿でできる近所づきあいの場を用意するのです。地区民の大半がそこの神社の氏子である場合には，お祭をすることが町内会の最も重要な仕事となります。

長　男　昔の家父長的家族制度は終戦まで続きましたが，その制度のもとでは長男は長子相続権を持ち，財産の全部ではなくても大半を相続し，家長として，また職業上も父親の跡を継ぎました。幼少時から引き立てられ特別扱いをされ，その結果甘やか

head of the family and in the family occupation. He was treated favorably and with distinction from early childhood, and consequently he could be often spoiled by excessive cares. There is an old proverb that goes, "*Sōryō no jinroku* (First born, least clever)." While the oldest son had these advantages over his brothers and sisters, he was also responsible for supporting the retired parents and other dependents of the family and for fulfilling social obligations on behalf of the family. Today the oldest son is no longer in such an advantageous position when inheriting his father's property, but he is still considered responsible for supporting the aged parents. A girl looking for a mate might ask her proposed husband if he is a *chōnan*, for to be the wife to the oldest son often means living together with the aged parents-in-law and looking after them. (S)

chūgen   a mid-summer gift. It is given as a mid-summer greeting to those whom one is indebted or obliged to, such as superiors, teachers, customers, etc. This custom of gift-giving is supposed to be done from July 1 through 15. During this period, housewives have to make a special budget and department stores enjoy stupendous profits. As with *seibo*, the other gift-giving custom practiced in the same fashion in December, the gratitude is expressed in the giving and not in the value of the gift. Nevertheless, the gifts have tended to become more flashy and expensive in recent times. Preceding both periods are the "bonus" months for the workers, which are said to ease their financial burden on one hand, and enhance the extravagance of gift-giving on the

されてしまうこともあります。「総領の甚六」という古い諺があります。長男は他の兄弟姉妹より優位にあった一方で，隠居した両親やその他の扶養家族を養い，家族を代表して社会的義務をはたす責任がありました。今日では，もはや長男は父親の財産相続時にそのような有利な立場にはありませんが，年老いた両親を養う責任はあると考えられています。配偶者を求めている女性は花婿候補に長男であるかどうかたずねることもあります。長男の妻になることは，老義父母と同居し，彼らの面倒を見ることにもなりがちだからです。

中 元　夏の挨拶をかねて，日頃お世話になっている人々（上司，先生，取引先など）に贈り物をすることです。贈答の期間は一般に７月１日頃から７月15日頃とされており，この時期になると，家庭の主婦は特別に予算を組みます。またデパートにとっては稼ぎ時となります。年末に行われる歳暮と同様に，感謝の気持ちは贈り物の価値よりも，贈るという行為そのものにあります。しかし今日，品物の高級化が目立ってきています。両贈答期間の前がボーナス支給の時期でもあるため，家計も助けられる半面，贈り物の高級化志向にも拍車がかかっているようです。

other.　(Y)

daibutsu　a huge statue of Buddha.　Buddha was said to be 16 feet tall, but Buddhists of ancient times throughout Asia erected even taller statues of Buddha to express his greatness as well as their own feeling of awe for him.　Big statues in Japan are usually seated figures in bronze.　Rushanabutsu at the Tōdaiji Temple in Nara, known as *Daibutsu* of Nara, is one of the most famous statues in Japan.　It was first built in 749, seriously damaged by wars in the late twelfth century, and finally rebuilt in 1692.　It is a sitting figure whose height is about 50 feet, and is enshrined in the Grand Buddah Hall (*Daibutsu-den*).　No less famous is Amidabutsu at the Kōtokuin Temple in Kamakura.　This statue, known as *Daibutsu* of Kamakura, was built in 1252.　It is also a sitting figure in bronze erected in the open air, and its sitting height is about 38 feet.　(S)

daikon-oroshi　grated white radish.　*Daikon-oroshi* is a giant white radish finely grated with an *oroshigane* (grater) with spikes on a flat surface.　It can be eaten for its own sake, but usually serves as a relish indispensable to many Japanese dishes.　For example, it is mixed in the dipping sauce for *tenpura* (deep-fried fish and vegetables), or eaten with grilled *sanma* (mackerel pike), which is a typical and inexpensive dish in autumn.　The Japanese favor *daikon-oroshi* all the more because it removes the fishy smell and helps digestion. (T)

大　仏　仏陀は16フィートの背丈
であるといわれていましたが，古代の
アジア各国の仏教徒たちは，仏陀の偉
大さと彼ら自身の畏怖の念を表わすた
めに，さらに巨大な仏像を建立しまし
た。日本の大仏は，たいてい青銅の座
像です。奈良県の東大寺にある盧遮那
仏は，奈良の大仏といわれ，日本の大
仏のうちで最も有名なものの一つです。これは749年に建立され
ましたが，12世紀後半に戦乱によってひどく破壊され，1692年に
ようやく再建されたものです。高さが約50フィートの座像で，大
仏殿に安置されています。これに劣らず有名なのは，神奈川県高
徳院の阿弥陀仏です。鎌倉の大仏として知られるこの仏像は1252
年に建立されました。これも青銅の座像で，屋外に造られたもの
ですが，その座高は約38フィートあります。

大根おろし　大根おろしは，平らな面に突起のあるおろしが
ねで白い大根をすりおろしたものです。大根おろしは独立した一
品として食べることもありますが，通常は，いろいろな日本料理
に欠かせない薬味として使います。例えば，天つゆに混ぜたり，
代表的な秋の味覚であるさんまの塩焼に添えて食べます。日本人
が大根おろしを好むのは，それが魚の臭みを除き，消化を助ける
からです。

danchi　a housing complex.　The dwelling shortage in urban areas has been one of the most difficult social problems in Japan since the end of World War II.　To cope with it, large blocks of apartments have been constructed in the suburbs of big cities, and sometimes a long way from them, because land prices are extremely high in cities.　Such housing complexes owned by the Japan Housing Corporation, local governments, or private companies are called *danchi*.　Families living in the *danchi* tend to have similar social backgrounds and ways of life.　Most of them are middle-class nuclear families.　A great majority of the husbands are wage earners who spend most of their waking hours in commuting and working away from home.　Generally speaking, apartment dwellers in the *danchi* do not want to live there for the rest of their lives, but hope to have a detached house of their own when they have a sufficient sum of money.　(T)

dango　a dumpling.　*Dango* is a simple confection made of rice flour.　Bite-sized balls of rice flour are boiled or steamed, and often served on *takegushi* (bamboo skewers).　They are flavored in various ways.　The most common are the dumplings dipped into sweetened soy sauce and grilled with charcoal, and those covered with sweetened red-bean paste or soybean flour.　*Dango* is popular all the year round.　Especially on the night of *tsukimi* (moon viewing), it is prepared as an offering to the moon.　It is also enjoyed at *hanami* (cherry blossom viewing).　Hence the Japanese saying : "Dumplings are better than cherry blossoms."　(T)

団　地　　都市の住宅不足は，第2次世界大戦後の日本の社会問題の中で，最も難しい問題の一つでした。これに対処するために，大規模なアパート群が建設されました。大都市の地価は非常に高いため，建設地は郊外や，時には都心から遠く離れたところになりました。日本住宅公団や地方自治体あるいは私企業が所有するこのような住宅群を団地と呼びます。団地に住む家族は，同じような社会的背景や生活様式を持つ傾向があります。その大部分は中流の核家族です。夫の大多数はサラリーマンで，起きている時間のほとんどを通勤と自宅から遠い職場での仕事に費しています。概していえば，団地居住者は一生を団地で送ることを望まず，十分な資金ができたときには一戸建ての持ち家を建てたいと思っています。

団　子　　団子は米の粉で作る素朴なお菓子です。こねて一口大に丸めた米の粉をゆでるか蒸すかして，しばしば竹ぐしにさして供します。味のつけ方はいろいろあります。最もよく見られるのは，しょう油のたれに浸して焼いた団子と，あんや黄な粉をつけた団子です。団子は一年中出まわっていますが，特にお月見の夜には月へのお供えとして用意します。また，花見のときにも好評です。それで，日本には「花より団子」という諺があります。

danson-johi   predominance of men over women, or the idea that men are superior to women.   While Amaterasu-ōmikami, the chief deity in Japanese mythology, is a goddess, Japan has been an androcentric country throughout recorded history.   The imported religions, having all been established in the ages of male chauvinism, justified male-dominated social institutions.   Women were regarded as inferior to men and their subjection to men was considered a matter of course. This notion prevailed among the middle and upper classes and set up the traditional family patterns of a husband-breadwinner and a wife-housekeeper.   Women were in a subordinate position even at home. As an old proverb implies, women could have no will of their own, for they had to obey their parents in their childhood, their husbands when married, and their sons in their old age.   The wife was expected to respect the husband and behave in a quiet and self-effacing manner in the presence of others.   Confucianism, which flourished in the seventeenth- and eighteenth-century Japan and attracted especially the warrior (*samurai*) class, condemned any mixed company in public places or any change in the roles of the two sexes in society.   The consequent lack of social interaction between young men and women seems to have prevented the Japanese males from a better understanding of the other sex.   The equality of the sexes was not actually established until after World War II, though there were occasional feminist movements during the early part of the twentieth century.   The Fourteenth Article of the Constitution of Japan, enacted in 1947, provides that sex discrimination must be abolished, but sexism still exists today especially in the business world.   The

男尊女卑　　日本の神話の主神である天照大神は女神ですが，有史以来日本は男性中心の社会でした。外来の宗教もすべて男性優位が信奉された時代に確立したものなので，男性支配の社会制度を正当なものとしました。女性は男性に劣るものとみなされ，男性に従属するのも当然と考えられました。この考え方は中流・上流階級に普及し，夫が働き，妻が家事をするという伝統的な家族形態を作りあげました。女性は家庭においてさえ従属的な立場に置かれていました。ある諺が暗示しているように，女性には自分自身の意志というものがありませんでした。というのは，子供時代には親に，結婚してからは夫に，老いては息子に従わなければならなかったからです。妻は夫を敬い，他人の前では静かに目立たないようにふるまうのがよいとされました。儒教は17, 18世紀の日本で盛んになり，特に武士階級の人気を集めましたが，公けの場所で男女が交際するのを良しとせず，また社会における両性の役割交換を非難しました。その結果，若い男女の社交が少なくなり，そのために日本の男性は異性を十分に理解することができなかったようです。20世紀の初頭には，女権拡張運動も起こりましたが，性の平等は実際には第2次大戦後になるまでは確立しませんでした。1947年に施行された日本国憲法の第14条は，性差別の廃止を規定していますが，今日でも，特に労働の分野では性差別が存在しています。例えば，不平等な雇用はまだ解決されていない問題です。しかし，社会における女性の位置は戦後大きく改善されました。もっとも，夫がオーバーを着たり脱いだりするのを手伝ったり，ドアを開けてやったりする妻は，必ずしも性差別の犠牲者というわけではありません。彼女は親切心から，あるいは習慣や風習からそうしているのかもしれないのです。

problem of unequal employment opportunities, for example, remains to be solved. However, women's position in society has been much improved since the end of the war. It should be remembered that a wife helping her husband on and off with his overcoat or opening a door for him is not necessarily a victim of sexism ; she may be doing so out of kindness, or just from habit and custom. (S)

daruma   Bodhidharma and a tumbler doll representing him.   Born of a royal family in a small country in the south of India, Bodhidharma founded Zen Buddhism in the sixth century and introduced it to China.   He is said to have sat in silent meditation for nine years, facing the wall of a room at the Shōrinji Temple in China and to have attained spiritual awakening or supreme enlightenment (*satori*).   A tumbler doll representing Bodhidharma sitting in meditation is papier-mâché, limbless and painted in red.   It is made in various sizes, but the *daruma* doll of standard size is as large as a watermelon.   Since this doll recovers its upright position when it is tumbled, it is also called *okiagari-koboshi*.   It is an embodiment of the proverb that says, "If you fall down seven times, get up eight (*nana-korobi-yaoki*)." *Daruma* is a popular mascot especially among shop-keepers.   *Daruma* fairs are held mostly at New Year's time, and *daruma* dolls sold at these fairs have no eyes painted on the face.   The eyes are put in by the possessor of the doll when he has had his wish realized. (S)

dashi   soup stock.   The success of traditional Japanese dishes depends largely on *dashi* (soup stock).   The ingredients

だるま　菩提達磨はインド南部の小国の王家に生まれ，6世紀に禅宗を起こし，それを中国にもたらしました。彼は中国の少林寺の一室の壁に向かって9年間座禅を組み，悟りを開いたといわれています。座禅を組んだ達磨大師の姿を表わした起上り人形は，張子製で，手足はなく，赤く塗ってあります。大小さまざまなものがありますが，標準的なものは西瓜ほどの大きさです。この人形は，倒してもすぐまっすぐな姿勢にもどるので，起上り小法師とも呼ばれ，「七転び八起き」という諺の具象化とみなされています。だるまは特に商店主に人気のあるマスコットです。たいてい新年にだるま市が立ちますが，この市で売られるだるまには目が描いてありません。目は，買った人が自分の願いのかなえられたときに描き入れます。

だし　伝統的な日本料理のできは主にだしによって決まるといわれていますが，その通りです。だしを取るために使う最も

most commonly used to make *dashi* are *konbu* (a kind of kelp), *katsuobushi* (dried bonito), *shiitake* (a kind of mushroom), and *niboshi* (dried young sardines). One or two of them are employed according to the menu. After their essence is drawn out into water, they are discarded, thus working behind the scenes. It is not easy to create the delicate flavor of *dashi*. Today many Japanese homes often use instant *dashi* mixes to save time and trouble. (T)

demae　food delivery service. *Demae* is the delivery of dishes from a restaurant to a customer's house upon request. The system is similar to that of pizza delivery in North America. Traditionally, a delivery man rode on a bicycle while skillfully balancing on one hand several layers of trays bearing dishes of *donburi-mono* (rice or noodles with meat or fish and vegetables for garnish). The most unique *demae* was seen on New Year's Eve with the delivery of buckwheat noodles, the eating of which at the year's end is said to bring a long, happy life. Usually on this occasion, the delivery man bore "towering stacks" of trays—no simple feat ! Nowadays, rather than balancing trays on the hand, he stacks them on a carrier mounted on the back of a motorcycle. (O)

donburi-mono　a big bowl meal. *Donburi-mono* is a general term which refers to one-dish meals served in large bowls. While Japanese-style meals traditionally require a large number of vessels, all you need for serving *donburi-mono*

普通の食品は，昆布，かつお節，椎茸，煮干です。献立に応じて，このうちの1種ないし2種を用い，うまみを引き出したあと捨てます。だしの材料は舞台の裏方役をはたしているのです。だしの微妙な味を作り出すのは容易なことではありません。今日では，即席のだしの素を利用して手間を省く家庭も多いようです。

出　前　　出前は，客の注文に応じて，飲食店から料理を客の自宅まで届けることです。このやり方は北米のピザの配達に似ています。一昔前，出前持ちは幾層にも重ねた丼物（肉または魚と野菜をつけ合わせとして，御飯またはうどんにかけた料理）の盆を片手でうまくバランスを保ちながら，自転

車に乗って配達しました。最もユニークなのは，大みそかに見られるそばの出前でした。大みそかにそばを食べると長寿をもたらすといわれています。このときには，出前持ちは塔のように重ねた盆を運んだものでした。これはそう簡単にできる芸当ではありません。今日では，片手でうまくバランスをとって盆を運ぶ代わりに，オートバイの後取りに付けた特別容器の中に盆を入れて運びます。

丼　物　　丼物は，大きな丼に盛った1食分の料理を指す一般的な名称です。日本料理は，伝統的には，多くの食器を使いますが，丼物はただ1つの丼を使うだけです。丼物には多くの種類がありますが，すべて基本的には，御飯かうどんやそばで，一品料

is one big bowl. There are many kinds of *donburi-mono*, but all basically consist of rice or noodles with a topping added to complete the dish. For example, *tendon* (short form of *tenpura-donburi*) is a dish of rice and *tenpura* with sauce. If noodles are used in place of rice, the dish is called *tenpura-udon*. *Oyako-donburi* is a rice dish with chicken and eggs cooked with some vegetables. Two other popular types of *donburi-mono* are *gyūdon* (rice and beef) and *katsudon* (rice and pork). At some restaurants, rather complicated types of *donburi-mono* are available. One such dish is *kama-meshi* (a mixture of vegetables, meat, seafood, and rice). It is served in a unique crockery pot in which it is cooked. (O)

ekiben　a station lunch. It is sold on train platforms by vendors calling out "Bento, bento, ...," while walking along the side of the train windows when a train stops at local stations. There are many kinds of *ekiben*. The *makunouchi* lunch is the best known of all and is sold at almost any station. It often contains a variety of local specialities. Some people prefer traveling by train simply to enjoy the taste of a particular locality, while some take the empty containers back home as travel mementos. This lunch is also sold by vendors coming down the aisles of super express trains. (Y)

ema　a votive picture tablet. *Ema* is dedicated to a Shinto shrine or a Buddhist temple, either in prayer for divine protection or as a token of gratitude for answered prayers. It is usually an oblong piece of wood with its upper side shaped like a roof. Originally horses were painted on the *ema*, since

理として十分なものにするためにその上に何かをのせます。例えば，天丼は御飯と天ぷらに汁をかけたものです。御飯の代わりにうどんを使えば，天ぷらうどんになります。親子丼は，数種の野菜と鶏肉と卵を煮たものを御飯の上にかけた料理です。もう2つの人気のある丼物は，牛丼（御飯と牛肉）とかつ丼（御飯と豚肉）です。料理店によっては，もっと手のこんだ丼物が食べられます。一つの例は，釜飯（野菜，肉，魚貝類と御飯を混ぜたもの）です。これは特別な陶器で料理され，そのまま出されます。

　駅　弁　　鉄道の駅のホームで，列車が駅に着くと，その窓のわきを駅弁売りが「弁当，弁当」と叫びながら売り歩きます。駅弁にはいろいろな種類があります。中でも幕の内弁当が最も有名で，ほとんどの駅で売られています。それには地方独特の味があります。地方の豊かな味覚を味わうために汽車旅行をする人もいますし，空の弁当箱を土産として持ち帰る人もいます。駅弁は特急列車の車中でも売り子が売りにきます。

　絵　馬　　絵馬は，神仏の加護を祈るとき，または願いごとがかなったお礼の印として，神社やお寺に奉納する額です。普通は長方形の木板で，上の辺が屋根の形をしています。もとは生

it was offered instead of live horses. However, many other things came to be depicted. Nowadays the most prevalent are the tablets which junior or senior high school students offer, praying for their success in the entrance examinations for prestigious high schools or universities. (T)

en　a relation. *En* is a term derived from the Buddhist belief that there is a cause to all things. The medium through which a cause brings about an effect is *en*. Any social relationship starts with and changes with *en*. It is *en* which realizes the relationship between man and woman, and that between neighbors or business partners. Thus *en* creates opportunities and occasions for forming relationships. It very often enables people to carry on things smoothly. For instance, if you want a project to be supported by a certain agency, it is almost always necessary to know some influential figure in the institution. Knowing the person is in itself *en*. There are many cases where people obtain their jobs quite unexpectedly. Here, too, *en* is operating. In daily life, people often talk about the relationship between man and woman in terms of *en*. Parents of a marriageable son or daughter receive *endan* (information about a prospective partner for marriage). If the proposal of marriage succeeds, it is said that the predestined relationship has been materialized ("*en ga atta*"), and if it does not, it is said that these persons have never been destined to get along ("*en ga nakatta*"). (HA)

engi　an omen. This idea originated from the funda-

きた馬の代わりに絵馬を奉納したので，馬の絵を描いたのですが，その後，他にいろいろなものを描くようになりました。文字だけ書くこともよくあります。現在最も流行している絵馬は，中学生や高校生が有名高校・大学への入学試験合格を願ってささげるものです。

縁　　縁とは，何事にも起因するものがあるという仏教思想からきています。因果の仲立ちをするのが縁で，社会的関係は何であれ縁で始まり，縁とともに変わります。男女の関係とか近所づきあいとかお得意さんとの取引きがうまくいくのは，縁があってのことなのです。だから，縁のおかげで，人との関係を築いていく機会が与えられるといえましょう。縁があってこそ，物事を順調にとり行うことができるのです。例えば，何らかの事業計画をある官庁に後援してもらおうとすれば，その役所の有力者と面識がなければなりません。面識があるということは，縁があるということなのです。思いがけなくもある所に就職したなどという話を聞きますが，そんな場合にも縁が働いているのです。ところで，日常生活で縁というと，しばしば男女の関係についていいます。適齢期の息子か娘がいる親は，縁談を受けます。結婚へと話がうまく進めば，縁があったといい，うまくいかないと，縁がなかったというものです。

縁　起　　本来は仏教の根本思想から生じたもので，この世の

43

mental Buddhist thought that all phenomena in this world result from *karma* or relations among various causes and occasions. In the Buddhist philosophy *engi* is the definite law that governs the mutation of the phenomenal world where all living things must die and nothing is permanent. In secular use, *engi* means an omen or luck, which is also called *kikkyō*. Folk beliefs about omens are numerous and vary with locality. Some superstitious people have pet superstitions of their own. To cite a few examples of common folk beliefs, a tea stalk floating erect in one's tea is believed to be a sign of good luck and a chopstick snapping off an ill omen. A dream about a snake is said to be a good omen and that about a fish a bad one. Good luck charms sold at fairs are called *engi-mono* and they are popular among shop-keepers. Some of the popular charms are the exorcising arrows (*hamaya*), the decorated bamboo rake (*kumade*), the figure of a beckoning cat (*maneki-neko*), the figure of a big-headed dwarf (*Fukusuke*), the tumbler doll representing Bodhidharma (*daruma*) and the treasure ship (*takara-bune*) with *shichifuku-jin* (the Seven Deities of Good Luck) on board. The word also refers to the history and legend of a temple or of a shrine. *Shigisan Engi Emaki*, completed in the twelfth century, is one of the most famous *engi* documents. It is made up of three picture scrolls illustrating the history of Myōren the Sage, and the Chōgoson-shi Temple in Nara. (S)

ennichi　a day consecrated to a certain Shinto or Buddhist god and deity. Old people believe that if they visit a shrine or a temple for religious services on such a holy day,

あらゆる現象は業，つまりさまざまな因果関係に由来するという考えを指します。仏教的な意味では，生あるものは必ず死ななければならず，何事も不変ということのない現象世界の転変を支配する確固とした法則のことです。世俗的な用法では，縁起は禍福の前兆や吉事を意味し，吉凶ともいわれます。吉凶についての俗信は数多くあり，地方によっても異なります。迷信深い人のなかには自分だけの縁起をかつぐ人もあります。一般的な俗信の例を少しあげますと，茶柱が立つのは縁起が良く，箸が折れるのは縁起が悪いといわれています。蛇の夢は吉，魚の夢は凶ともされています。縁日の市で売っている呪物は縁起物と呼ばれ，商店主に人気があります。その例をいくつかあげますと，破魔矢，飾りをつけた竹製の熊手，招き猫，福助，達磨大師を表わす起上り小法師（だるま），七福神を乗せた宝船などがあります。縁起という語はまた，神社や寺院の歴史や由来をも指します。12世紀に完成された『信貴山縁起絵巻』は，その最も有名なものの一つです。これは，命蓮聖人と奈良県の朝護孫子寺の歴史を描いた3巻からなる絵巻物です。

縁 日　　年をとった人のなかには，このようなありがたい日に宗教的な奉仕のために神社や仏閣を訪れる

they will receive special divine favors. Less religious towns-people also enjoy these days, as street peddlers (*yashi*) set up fair stalls (*roten*) on the grounds of shrines or temples and cry their wares. For example, the 8th of each month is observed as the *ennichi* of *Yakushi Nyorai* (god of medicine), the 18th as that of *Kannon* (goddess of mercy), the 24th as that of *Jizō* (guardian deity of children), and the 28th as that of *Fudō* (god of non-movement). (HO)

fugu　a globefish. It is also called swellfish, blowfish or puffer. It puffs up to several times its normal size when caught. Its flesh is quite a delicacy and is usually eaten raw in thin slices. However, this fish is also known to be deadly poisonous. Thus, the cook who prepares a *fugu* dish must be well skilled and licensed. There is a Japanese saying that goes : "I would like to taste a puffer, but I would not like to lose my life." The skin of *fugu* is made into *fugu-chōchin* or a globefish lantern. It is sold as a souvenir at some sea resorts. (Y)

Fujisan　Mt. Fuji or Fujiyama. It is the highest mountain (3, 776 m or 12, 285 ft) in Japan and is world-famous for its superb conical form. This symbol of the beautiful land is located on the border of Shizuoka and Yamanashi Prefec-tures. Although it has been dormant, it is classified by geologists as an active volcano. To the Japanese mind, *Fujisan* is much more than a single volcano. It is regarded as a sacred object, and the climbing of Mt. Fuji has long been a

と，特別の御利益が得られると信じている人がいます。それほど信仰心のない普通の人々もこれらの縁日を楽しみにしています。香具師とよばれる行商人が露店をひろげ，呼び売りするからです。例えば，毎月8日は薬師如来（薬の神），18日は観世音（慈悲の女神），24日は地蔵（子どもの守護神），そして28日は不動尊の縁日となっています。

ふ　ぐ　英語ではいろいろな呼び名があります。この魚は捕えられるとすぐ数倍の大きさにふくれあがります。ふぐの身はなかなかの珍味で，薄く切ったさしみで食べるのが一般的です。ふぐは猛毒のある魚としても知られており，その料理には資格を得た高度な技術が必要となります。有名な諺に，「ふぐは食べたし，死にたくはなし」というのがあります。ふぐの皮は，ふぐ提灯として観光地の土産物売り場で売られています。

富士山　海外でフジヤマと呼ばれるこの山は日本一高い山（標高3,776m）で，整った円錐形の山容で広く世界に知れわたっています。静岡県と山梨県の県境にそびえるこの秀峰は，長い間火山活動を休止しているものの，地質学上の分類では活火山です。日本人にとっては，単なる火山に終わりません。聖なる山として崇められていますから，富士登山には宗教的意味合いすらあります。富士山は日本の文化に多大な影響を及ぼしています。日本の美術と文芸の歴史をみると，この霊峰富士が無数の絵や詩に

religious practice. It has exerted a great influence upon Japanese culture. Throughout the history of Japanese art and literature, this holy mountain has been the subject of uncountable poems and pictures. The yearning for greatness and beauty symbolized by *Fujisan* led the ancients to name many local mountains and towns after this beautiful mountain. Some *sumō* wrestlers and popular stars also have ring names or stage names associated with *Fujisan*. (HA)

furo   a bath. A Japanese bath is taken not only for cleansing but also for getting warmed, refreshed and relaxed. People wash themselves outside the bathtub, not inside, by bailing some water out onto themselves from the deep tub with a bucket. When they become clean, they soak slowly and sit in the tub full of moderately hot water. Baths can be reheated when the water gets cold or when the level of water in the tub drops so that it has to be topped with cold water again. Several people use the same bath in turn, and therefore, the water is expected to be kept clean. This is why people do not wash themselves in the tub nor take a wash cloth with them into it. Before they leave the bathroom, they dry themselves with a towel. Modern baths are equipped with a shower. In fact, young people seem to prefer a shower to a bath. (Y)

furoshiki   a cloth wrapper. *Furoshiki* is a cloth, measuring about two square feet, which is used for wrapping, storing, and carrying things. Fabrics for *furoshiki* are cotton and silk, and they are dyed in various colors. Although *furoshiki* are gradually being replaced by handbags and shop-

とり上げられてきたことがわかります。この山のもつ偉大さと美しさに引かれて，昔の人は各地の山や町の名を富士になぞらえたものでした。相撲取りや芸能人の中にも富士の付くしこなや芸名を持つ人がいます。

風呂　日本の風呂は，単に汚れを落とすために入るのではなく，温まり，くつろぎ，そして疲労回復のために入るものでもあります。まず，湯槽の外で桶で湯をくみだし，からだの汚れを洗い流します。それから，適温の湯がいっぱい入った湯槽にゆっくりとつかります。湯槽の湯がさめたり，水を追加したときには，温めることができます。数人が順次同じ湯につかるので，湯は常にきれいに保たなければなりません。だから，湯槽の中で身体を洗ったり，タオルを持ち込んだりはしません。湯から出ると，タオルで体を拭いて乾かします。最近の風呂はシャワー設備が施されており，若者はシャワーのほうが好きなようです。

風呂敷　真四角な布で，ものを包んだり，しまったり，運んだりするために使います。綿か絹でできていて，さまざまな色に染めてあります。しだいに手さげと紙袋が替わりをするよう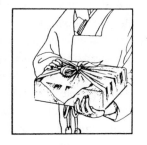

ping bags, their compactness and flexibility still attract many people. A colloquial phrase *ōburoshiki o hirogeru* (literally, "to spread out a big wrapper") is applied to an overly confident man who exaggerates, boasting that he can carry more in his *furoshiki* than is actually possible. (HA)

futon   bedding.   In the traditional Japanese household, a set of *futon* are spread on *tatami* mats at night, and are folded and stored out of sight during the day.   Thus a room can be used for various purposes such as a living room and a study as well as a bedroom.   Japanese bedding consists of *shikibuton* (a mattress), *shikifu* (a sheet), *kakebuton* (a quilt), and *makura* (a pillow).   *Kakebuton* and *makura* have seasonal variations due to the vast differences in temperature between summer and winter.   In the severely cold climate, *kaimaki* (sleeved quilts) are used.   Recently, however, younger people tend to give up sleeping on *futon* on *tatami* in favor of Western beds and bedclothes.   (HA)

gagaku   ancient ceremonial court music and dancing. *Gagaku*, which is a general term for such music and dancing, is one of the five major forms of traditional Japanese theater, along with *nō* (noh drama), *kyōgen* (noh farce), *bunraku* (traditional puppetry), and *kabuki* (classical theater).   It has preserved by the Imperial Court and several groups of civilians down to this day.   It flourished and was loved during the Heian period (794–1185).   It contains (a) music and dances native to Japan, (b) those introduced from China through Korea, and (c) the new repertoire created in the Imperial

になってきてはいますが，小さくていろいろと便利なので，まだまだ多くの人々が愛用しています。「大風呂敷を広げる」という慣用句は，実際は無理なのに「自分は風呂敷にもっとものを入れて運べる」と大げさなことをいってのける自信家を形容しています。

布　団　布団は夜に敷き，昼間はたたんで片づけておきます。このため，部屋は寝室の他に居間にも勉強部屋にもなります。寝具には，敷布団，掛布団，敷布，枕があります。掛布団と枕は，夏と冬の温度差が激しいので季節によって別のものを用います。寒さの厳しい地方では，掻巻という袖の

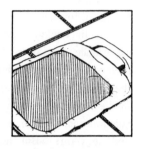

付いた夜着を使います。しかし，このごろの若い人は，畳の上に布団を敷くのを嫌い，西洋風のベッドとか寝具を好む傾向にあります。

雅　楽　古くからある宮廷音楽で，能，狂言，文楽，歌舞伎と共に日本の五大芸能の一つといわれています。現在まで，宮内庁をはじめ，いくつかの民間団体で保存されています。平安時代に始まり栄えた音楽で，(a)日本古来のもの，(b)中国から朝鮮を経て伝えられたもの，そして(c)宮中で生まれ演奏されていたものの3つに大別されます。今日ではお正月に，名高い神社やテレビやラジオなどでも演奏されます。「越天楽」，「大平楽」，「久米舞」などが中でも有名です。

Palace. Today these pieces are performed at some of the celebrated Shinto shrines and also on TV and radio on New Year's Day. Some of the best known selections are *Etenraku*, *Taiheiraku*, and *Kumemai*. (Y)

gaijin   a foreigner in Japan. The term *gaijin* literally means all foreigners in Japan, but it actually refers to those of Caucasian backgrounds. The *gaijin* say that they often experience special treatment in Japan. They never fail to receive kind guidance and devoted assistance from people on the street. Their Japanese friends will invite them to the fanciest restaurants. When they visit a business office or an acquaintance's house, they may be flooded with expensive gifts and souvenirs. But many *gaijin* who are with Japanese companies deplore and protest that they are treated as permanent guests in their offices, excluded from important decision-making procedures. Their original proposals are likely to be politely rejected or silently ignored simply on the ground that they are not in accordance with Japanese customs. One of the reasons for these apparently contradictory attitudes seems to lie in the self-image that Japanese people have traditionally fostered. They are inclined to believe that they are culturally so unique that it is almost impossible for them to explain themselves or for other people to adapt themselves to Japanese ways of life. This psychological orientation, reinforced by their traditional *uchi-soto* (insider–outsider) mentality, has resulted in Japanese people's hesitation at cross-cultural communication at deep levels. They have formed an extremely exclusive society of their own. They

ガイジン　　ガイジンとは，文字通りには日本にいる外国人すべてを指すはずですが，実際は白人系の人々を指します。ガイジンは日本で特別なあつかいをうけていると感じているようです。道がわからなければ必ずだれかが親切に教えてくれるし，こまったことがあればだれかが面倒がらずに助けてくれます。日本人の友人は高級レストランに招待してくれます。会社や知合い宅をたずねると，高価な贈り物やおみやげをもらいます。しかし，日本の会社に勤めているガイジンは，永久にお客さんあつかいをされていると不満をもらしています。重要な意思決定過程からはずされているというのです。彼らのだす独創的な提案はていねいに拒否されるか，無言で無視されるかどちらかです。提案の内容が日本の習慣に合っていないというだけの理由です。このような一見矛盾したように見える態度を日本人がとる理由は，一つには，日本人の伝統的文化観にあります。日本文化はきわめて独特なので，他国の者にはとても説明できないし，また他国の人が日本の生活様式にあわせることは困難であると日本人は考えています。このような考えが伝統的なう・ち・・そ・と・の感覚と結びついたため，日本人は深いレベルでの異文化間理解を躊躇するようになったのです。日本人は自分たちだけのきわめて排他的な社会をつくりました。他の文化の人々に対しては，外にいる限り親切にあつかいます。しかし，内に入れようとはしません。なぜならば，その人たちをどうあつかってよいかわからないのです。しかし，今日では異文化間コミュニケーションの必要性が理解されており，日本文化は日本人の力になると同時に日本人を束縛するという認識が生

treat other people kindly as long as they stay out.   But they do not allow other people to get in, because Japanese people do not know how to deal with them.   In the age of intercultural communication, however, they are now recognizing that their traditional culture is their force as well as their limitation. They are beginning to make a soul-searching effort to learn how to participate in a wider multicultural community. (HO)

gakusei-fuku   a student uniform.   For boys, the student uniform is usually a black jacket with a stand-up collar and black trousers.   This uniform, which originated from a European military uniform, was first introduced to Tokyo Imperial University in 1885.   It has gradually spread not only to other universities but also to lower educational institutions. High school boys today attend classes in this uniform. University students now rarely wear it except on ceremonial occasions such as matriculation.   But cheer leaders or members of some martial arts clubs tend to wear it, because it symbolizes vigor and self-discipline.   A high-school girl's uniform called *sērā-fuku* also came from Europe, probably from the traditional English sailor suit.   It consists of a jacket with a sailor-type collar and a pleated skirt usually of navy blue.   (HA)

gaman-taikai   an endurance contest.   Though the word *gaman* originally meant foolish pride or obstinacy, its modern meaning is perseverance, which is considered one of the masculine virtues.   The endurance contest is a contest in

まれています。日本人は，今，より大きな多文化的社会に参加する方法を新たな努力によって学ぼうとしているのです。

学生服　男子生徒の制服はたいてい詰め襟の黒い上着と黒のズボンです。男子用学生服はヨーロッパの軍服に由来し，1885年に東京帝国大学で初めて着用されました。それがしだいに他の大学や中学，高校にも広がっていったのです。今日，中高生はこの種の制服を着て通学しています。大学生

は，入学式などの行事があるとき以外は，学生服をめったに着ません。しかし，応援団とか武道関係の部員は学生服を着る傾向にあります。学生服は覇気と自己鍛練を象徴しています。セーラー服と呼ばれる女生徒の制服も，ヨーロッパ（おそらくイギリス水兵の服）に起源を求めることができます。この女生徒用制服は，セーラーカラーの付いた上着と紺のひだスカートを組み合わせたものです。

我慢大会　我慢という語は，もとは愚かな慢心や頑固さを意味していましたが，現在では忍耐という意味で使われます。忍耐は男らしい美徳の一つとみなされています。我慢大会は，参加者が忍耐力を競い合う会です。年のうちの最も暑い季節か，または

which the participants compete with each other in perseverance. It is typically held either in the hottest season or in the coldest season of the year to decide who among the contestants can best stand the heat or the cold. In the summer contest, the participants wearing thick clothes (or padded dressing gowns called *dotera* in old times) sit at a *kotatsu* (a foot warmer with a quilt over it) in a heated room and take heated foods. The person who utters the word *atsui* (hot) or who tries to take off his clothes is eliminated from the contest. The winner is the one who holds out to the last, pretending that he is, in this case, really cold. The endurance contest is considered to be a fun game rather than a serious competition. (S)

gasshō-zukuri　　a house with a steep rafter roof. *Gassho-zukuri* derives its name from the shape of the steep rafter roof, which looks like hands clasped in prayer (*gasshō*). Examples of such a structure are to be found among the old houses preserved in Shirakawa-go, a village surrounded by mountains in the countryside of Gifu. These houses with thatched and gabled roofs are three- or four-storied and big enough for a large family to live in. They were primarily designed for the residence of extended families sharing work and domestic life. Some of the houses are said to have been inhabited by a family of over thirty people. The extended family system developed in this region, because it helped prevent fractionalization of scanty farm lands. (S)

最も寒い季節に行われ，参加者のうちのだれが最もよく暑さまた
は寒さに耐えられるかを競います。夏の我慢大会なら，参加者は
厚い衣服（昔はどてら）を着て，暖房をした部屋で炬燵にあたり
熱い食物をとります。「暑い」といったり，衣服を脱ごうとした
りした人は競争から脱落します。本当に寒いというふりをして最
後まで耐え抜いた人が優勝者となります。我慢大会は，真剣な競
技というよりも娯楽と考えられています。

合掌造　　合掌造という名称は，急勾配の屋根の形に由来する
もので，その形が合掌した手に似ていることからそう呼ばれてい
ます。合掌造は，岐阜県の山村，白川郷に保存されている古い家
の構造を指すことがよくあります。茅葺きで切妻屋根のこれらの
家は，3，4階建で，大家族が住むのに十分の大きさがあります。
これらの家はもともと労働と家庭生活を共同して行う大家族用の
住居として設計されたものです。いくつかの家には30人を超える
家族が住んでいたこともあったといわれています。大家族制がこ
の地域で発達したのは，乏しい農地の細分化を防ぐのに役立った
からです。

geisha   a lady who professionally provides entertainment and lighthearted company at a feast.   Around the end of the seventeenth century, *geisha* girls came on the scene, replacing an erlier class of "courtesans" who were skillful in such arts as music and dancing.   *Geisha* no longer carries the sexual implication which is often suggested by the English use of the word.   Some *geisha* girls live in *okiya* (a *geisha* boarding-house) whose landlady acts as manager and sends them around to Japanese-style hotels and restaurants where drinking feasts are held.   Others live in their own houses and practice their business independently.   Dressed in *kimono* and often with their hair done in the old Japanese style, they entertain a group of men by playing the *shamisen* (traditional musical instrument), singing traditional songs, dancing a classical dance, serving food and drinks, or through lighthearted talk with a sympathetic smile.   Some of them, especially in urban areas, are highly educated and are intellectually stimulating enough to entertain elite businessmen.   (K)

gengō   the traditional Japanese era system.   The Japanese have a few methods of referring to a given year. While the Christian era is widely used, *gengō*, the Japanese era system determined by the reigns of the emperors, is more common in daily life, and compulsory for official documents. The use of *gengō*, introduced from ancient China, dates back to the seventh century.   Since then each emperor's accession to the throne has initiated a new era with its own name. However, it has not always lasted till his death, but has often been replaced by another on such occasions as a celebration or

芸　者　酒宴の席に興を添えることを職業とする女性のことです。17世紀末頃に生まれ，唄や踊りなどの芸事に熟達した高級娼婦の代わりをつとめるようになりました。現在の芸者には，ともすると英語につきものの性的意味合いはありません。芸者の中には，置屋に住み，そこの女主人の手配

によって旅館や料亭の酒宴に出る者もいますし，自分の家に住み，独自に商売する者もいます。芸者は普通，日本髪に和服姿で三味線を弾き，歌い，踊り，お酌をし，また持ち前のおしゃべりや愛想で男性客の接待をするのです。都会の芸者の中には，エリート社員を接待するに十分な教養や学歴を備えている者もいます。

元　号　日本人には，ある年を言い表わす方法が幾通りもあります。西暦もよく使いますが，日常生活においては，天皇の治世によって定まる元号の方をよく用います。公文書には元号の使用が義務づけられています。元号の使用は古く中国にならい7世紀に始まりました。天皇が即位すると，新しい呼び方の元号になります。しかし，以前は必ずしも一世一元ではなく，慶事とか異変などの際に改元することもありました。明治時代になって，一世一元と決まりました。元号によれば，西暦1986年は昭和61年です。昭和は，日本の長い皇室の歴史のうえで124代目に当たる現在の天皇裕仁の即位によって始まった元号です。

a disaster. In the Meiji era (1868-1912), the *gengō* system in which an emperor's reign constitutes an era was formally established. According to the *gengō*, the year 1986 is the sixty first year of Showa, the era which was started by the present emperor, Hirohito, the 124th in Japan's unbroken imperial line. (T)

genmai brown rice. *Genmai* is rice threshed and hulled but not yet polished. It still retains *haiga* (germ) and is covered with a brownish outer skin (bran). The germ and the bran contain most of the vitamins and minerals of the rice grain. Therefore, this brown unpolished rice is said to be more healthful than polished rice called *hakumai* (white rice). In recent years, as more people are interested in health foods, *genmai* is often recommended by those who believe in a health food diet. Despite its high nutritive value, however, *genmai* is felt to be inferior to white rice in regard to taste and to the body's ability to digest and absorb its nutrients. In fact, very few people prefer brown rice to white rice. (T)

gētobōru gate-ball. Gate-ball, which is modeled after English croquet, is an outdoor sport for elderly people. It is played in a court 20 meters wide and 25 meters long by two teams of five players each. With T-shaped wooden mallets, they knock wooden balls through small metal arches to a goal post. The game lasts 30 minutes. Since it is a new creation, its rules vary from place to place. It has become very popular now with senior citizens throughout Japan. The moderate body movement and the feeling of togetherness are believed to

玄　米　　玄米は，もみがらをとり除いただけで，まだ精白していない米です。胚芽を残しており，表皮（ぬか層）に覆われています。胚芽とぬか層は，米粒中のビタミンやミネラルのほとんどを含んでいます。したがって，玄米は白米よりも健康によいとされています。近年，健康食品に関心を示す人が多くなるにつれて，そのよさを信じる人たちがしきりと玄米食を勧めます。しかし，玄米は栄養価が高いとはいっても，味や消化吸収の点で白米に劣ります。実際，白米より玄米の方が好きだという人は少ないようです。

ゲートボール　　高齢者向けの屋外スポーツで，英国のクロッケーをモデルにして作られたものです。縦25m，横20mのコートで，5人編成の2チームがプレーします。木製のT字型をしたスティックで木製のボールを打ってころがし，3つのゲートを順次くぐらせ，ゴールボールに当てます。試合時間は30分ですが，まだ新しいスポーツとあってルールは地域によってまちまちです。ゲートボールは今日，全国の高齢愛好家の間で大変に好評です。適度な身体の動きと他の仲間との一体感が若返りの秘訣といわれています。

keep them alert and in good health condition. (Y)

Ginza   the most fabulous shopping (and window-shopping) quarter in Tokyo. With many famous fancy stores, restaurants, and nightclubs lining its beautiful and busy boulevards, the Ginza has always been one of the most sophisticated places in Japan. Most businesses there have a long history of operation and enjoy an established reputation. Their prices are usually a little higher, but many people are willing to pay for the reputed quality of their commodities. On the side streets are found various kinds of small shops and stalls. Although there are now some other fashionable places in Tokyo (such as Shinjuku, Roppongi, Harajuku, etc.), the Ginza still represents prosperity and superiority. Hence the name Ginza is applied to many shopping quarters of local towns and cities throughout the nation. (HO)

giri   mutual obligations. *Giri* is a deep-rooted concept of Japanese ethics which implies the give-and-take principle in social interaction. It is a concept which drives a person to fulfill one of life's duties as a Japanese. One feels obligated to do a favor of those who have been thoughtful or helpful in some way. If A treats B, B must host the next party for A. Thus, restaurants flourish as meeting places to fulfill host-guest roles. Gifts should be periodically given to such people as one's boss, parents-in-law, go-between, or chidren's tutor, so year-round, department stores are crowded with people concerned with gift-giving. Furthermore, *giri* applies in times of crisis, as well. Neighbors feel obligated to help each

銀　座　　有名な一流店，レストラン，ナイトクラブなどが，美しくてにぎやかな大通りに並ぶ銀座は，常に日本の最も洗練されたショッピングセンターの一つです。そこにある店は長い歴史をもち，確固たる名声をきずいています。多少値段が高いということもありますが，お客は品物の品質が高級であることにお金をはらうのです。裏通りにはいろいろな種類の小さな店や屋台が見られます。東京には他にもいくつか流行の中心地（新宿，六本木，原宿など）がありますが，銀座は今なお繁栄と優秀の代名詞となっています。このため地方都市のショッピング街でも銀座という名前をつけるものが多いのです。

義　理　　義理は，社会関係において相互扶助の原理を強調する日本的倫理と深くかかわっています。この観念ゆえに，日本人は日本人としての責務をはたすのです。いろいろな面で助けてくれた人がいると，その人のために尽くさなければならないと思うわけです。AさんがBさんにおごると，次に飲み食いするときには，Bさんが代わってAさんにふるまいます。レストランはこういった関係の人々でもっているともいえます。上司とか義理の親とか仲人とか子供の先生のような特別な関係にある人には，お中元やお歳暮を贈るので，デパートは贈り物を探す人々でいつもいっぱいです。近所づきあいの仲でも，火事とか浸水とか葬式の様なときには，おたがいに助け合わなければならないのです。こうして人々は，自分の体面を守り，将来得られる好意に期待を寄せ

other in the event of a crisis such as a fire, flood, or funeral. Consequently, people may act in such a way with the hope of not only of maintaining their respectability but also of benefiting from reciprocity on the other's part. Today young people tend to undervalue social obligations. However, they learn to conform to the traditional *giri* as they mature. People are bound by various social principles of mutual obligations. In short, *giri* is a key social force which holds Japanese society together. (HA)

go   the game of *go*. Having been introduced from China in the eighth century, it soon gained great popularity among the Japanese. It is now regarded as the national board game of Japan. Two players play at a *go* board (*go-ban*), each using either 181 black stones (*go-ishi*) or 180 white ones. The better player of the two usually has white stones. The board is divided by mutually intersecting lines with 361 intersections, on which the black and white stones are placed by turns. The players compete with each other in gaining the greater number of intersections by enclosing them with rows of their stones placed on the board. Stones surrounded by the opponent's are captured and removed from the board, the cleaned area passing into the possession of the opponent. The game ends when there is no room for stones left on the board or when one of the players gives up. (S)

gojū-no-tō   a five-storied pagoda. *Gojū-no-tō* is a five-storied wooden pagoda with a roof at each level, original-ly founded to enshrine Buddha's ashes. In the compound of a

て，いろいろとふるまいに気づかっているのです。今日，若い人は社会的義務を軽視しがちですが，年をとるにつれて義理堅くなります。おとなにはいろいろと付合いや務めがあり，そのような社会的ふるまいを無視しては，満足に生活が営めないのです。結局，義理とは，日本人どうしをしっかりと結び付けている社会的粘着剤といえるでしょう。

碁　碁は8世紀に中国から伝えられるとすぐに，日本人の間に広まりました。今日では碁は日本のゲームとみなされています。碁盤の上で2人がそれぞれ181個の黒石かまたは180個の白石を用いて行います。たいていは，2人のうち強い方が白石を取ります。碁盤には縦横の線の交わった361の交点があり，その上に白と黒の石を交互に置きます。対局者は自分の石で連続して交点をとり囲むことによって，その交点の数を競い合います。相手にとり囲まれた石は取られて，盤からとり除かれ，空いた部分は相手のものとなります。盤上に石を置く余地がなくなった時，または対局者の1人が負けを認めたときに，ゲームは終わります。

五重の塔　五重の塔は，各階に屋根を持つ5階建の木造の塔です。本来，仏舎利を安置するために建てたも

Buddhist monastery the most prominent building is a *gojū-no-tō*, or a *sanjū-no-tō* (three-storied pagoda). Since Buddhism first came into Japan in the sixth century, numerous pagodas have been constructed throughout the country. While many of them were destroyed by lightning, fire, or war, some are still in existence, attracting an enormous number of visitors each year. The sublime beauty and architectural perfection of these ancient towers invariably make a deep impression. The five-storied pagoda of the Hōryuji Temple near Nara is the oldest wooden building in the world. That of the Tōji Temple in Kyoto is the tallest *gojū-no-tō* (55m) in Japan. The highly developed construction techniques that enabled lofty temples to survive severe earthquakes have been applied to recent skyscraper construction in Japan, a country with frequent quakes. (T)

goma-ae   a dish mixed with a sesame seed dressing. It is basically equivalent to salads or hors d'oeuvres as served in Western cuisine. Literally, *goma* means sesame seeds and *ae* is a short form of *aemono*, or a dish mixed with dressing. Fresh vegetables such as cucumbers, spinach, Chinese cabbage, bean sprouts, etc. are mixed with one or two kinds of shellfish (such as abalone, scallops, clams, oysters, etc.) or other seafood (such as squid, octopus, white fish, etc.) along with a dressing. The dressing for *goma-ae* is a mixture of sesame seeds, often roasted and ground or pulverized, a little bit of sugar, *sake* (rice wine), and soy sauce. (O)

gōruden-uīku   "Golden Week". It refers to the period

のです。お寺の境内において最も目立つ建物が五重の塔または三重の塔です。仏教が6世紀に日本に伝わってから，国内各地に数多くの塔が建立されました。その多くは雷や火災や戦火により焼失しました。しかし，まだ多くが残っており，毎年大勢の人々が訪れています。これら古代の塔が持つ崇高な美しさと建築上の完成度はいつも深い感銘を与えます。奈良市外にある法隆寺の五重の塔は世界最古の木造建築です。京都にある東寺の五重の塔は日本で一番高い五重の塔（55m）です。強い地震にも倒れない高い塔を作り出した高度の建築技術は，地震国日本の最近の超高層ビルに生かされています。

　　胡麻和え　　胡麻和えは基本的には，西洋料理でサラダかオードブルに相当する日本料理です。文字通りゴマは胡麻のことで，アエは，ドレッシングソースで混ぜ合わせた料理を意味する和え物の短縮形です。きゅうり，ほうれん草，白菜，もやしなどの生野菜と，あわび，帆立貝，はまぐり，かきなどの貝類，または，いか，たこ，白身の魚などの海産物を，ドレッシングを使って混ぜ合わせます。胡麻和えのドレッシングは，炒ってすったり砕いたりして粉状にした胡麻，砂糖，酒，そしてしょう油で作ります。

　　ゴールデン・ウィーク　　4月29日から5月5日までの連休のこ

from April 29 to May 5, which is full of national holidays. April 29 is the Emperor's Birthday, May 3 Constitution Day, and May 5 Children's Day. Though May 1 is not a national holiday, workers celebrate it also as May Day. Sunday may come between these national holidays. If one of them should fall on Sunday, the following Monday becomes another holiday. This period is the longest continuous holiday week that everyone can look forward to. Some offices tend to close during this whole week. （K）

hachimaki a headband. People wear this kind of headband, usually a Japanese towel, for festivals and sports events. They also wear it when they are engaged in strenuous work (such as a walk-out for a wage-hike or a political demonstration in the streets). It is regarded as a symbol of mental concentration and hard work. Some students wear it as a mark of their strong wish for success in an entrance examination. In this sense, *hachimaki* can convey a differing signal from the headband which sports players wear in the West. （K）

hade brightness or showiness. The Japanese word *hade* has no precise English equivalent. It corresponds partly to brightness, gaiety, showiness, lavishness, etc., according to the context, and can be used in describing various things such as color, design, character, and behavior. Representing the opposite of *hade* is *jimi*, which is also extensively employed to depict people or things plain, quiet, subdued, or modest. There

とです。4月29日が天皇誕生日，5月3日が憲法記念日，そして5月5日が子供の日というわけです。5月1日は別に国民の祝日ではありませんが，労働者はメーデーとして祝います。祝日が日曜日と重なると，月曜日が振替え休日になります。1年のうちで，国民が最も楽しみにしている期間でもあり，中にはこの期間中ずっと休業する会社もあります。

はちまき　祭りや運動会では，はちまきといって，手ぬぐいなどを頭に巻きます。また，一生懸命に仕事をしているときもします。例えば，賃上げのストライキや政治デモなどをするときです。はちまきは，精神を集中させていること，真剣に仕事に取り組んでいることを象徴するものとされています。受験生の中にも，合格を祈願してはちまきをする者がいます。この意味で，外国のスポーツ選手が頭に巻いているヘアバンドとは違います。

派　手　日本語の派手に厳密に対応する英語はなく，前後関係によって部分的に華美，けばけばしさ，ぜいたくなどの語が当てはまります。派手ということばは，色，デザイン，性格，行動などさまざまなものを描写するのに用いることができます。派手の反対は地味で，質素で目立たず，控え目な人々や事物を描くのに広く使います。日本には「出る杭は打たれる」という諺があります。これは，日本人には，人並みであることを欲し，目立つこ

69

is in Japan an old saying, "The nail that sticks out gets hammered down." This explains the tendency of the Japanese to avoid standing out from others in favor of conformity. It is closely associated with the concepts of *hade* and *jimi* : the former usually has more or less reproachful connotations, while the latter does not. General preference for *jimi* rather than *hade*, combined with the traditional stress on age difference, is reflected in diverse areas of Japanese life—most typically in women's dress. Elderly women take care to look their years. (T)

haiku　a short poem of seventeen syllables written in 5-7-5 meter. It is shorter than a *tanka*, which is composed of thirty-one syllables in 5-7-5-7-7 meter. *Haiku* originated from the medieval *haikai* or *haikai-no-renga*, the improvised short poems in which wit and humour were emphasized. Matsuo Bashō (1644-1694), a great poet and essayist of the Edo period (1603-1867), established *haikai* as a literary art. The two basic rules are to regulate the poem metrically and to include in it a word expressing one of the four seasons (*kigo*). *Haikai* poetry won general popularity in the late Edo period. However, it later became so conventionalized that in the Meiji period (1868-1912) an innovation had to be brought about by Masaoka Shiki (1867-1902) and others, who advocated a realistic representation of nature. The term *haiku*, a new name for *haikai*, very often refers to this modernized short poem. *Senryū*, another kind of short poem written in the same meter, aims chiefly at comical satire. (S)

とを避ける傾向があることを示しています。それは，派手と地味に対する考え方と密接な関係があります。前者には多少非難の意味合いがこめられていますが，後者にはそのような含みはありません。一般に派手より地味である方が好まれ，これが年齢差を重視する伝統と結びついて，日本人の生活のいろいろの面に反映しています。その典型的な例は，女性の服装です。年輩の女性は年齢相応に装うよう気を配ります。

俳　句　　短歌は5・7・5・7・7調の31音節で作られますが，俳句はそれよりも短く，5・7・5調の17音節からなる詩です。俳句の起源は，中世の俳諧，つまり俳諧の連歌にあります。これはユーモアや機知を中心とした即興的な短詩です。俳諧を文芸として確立したのは，江戸時代の偉大な俳諧詩人で随筆家の松尾芭蕉です。2つの基本的な原則は，韻律を定型にすることと，四季の一つを表わす語（季語）を入れることです。俳句は江戸時代後期に一般の人気を得ましたが，その後あまりに因襲化してしまったので，明治時代になって正岡子規などによって改革がなされるようになりました。子規たちは自然の写実的な描写を唱道したのです。俳句という語は，俳諧の新しい名称ですが，現代化されたこの短詩を指すことが多いようです。同じ型の調子で作られる川柳は，主に滑稽な風刺をねらいとしています。

haji   shame. Ruth Benedict says in her famous book *The Chrysanthemum and the Sword* that the Japanese live in a typical shame culture, which demands external sanctions for an individual's good behavior. Some people stress, however, that the Japanese have internal behavioral standards and a deep sense of conscience regarding personal conduct whether or not exposed to public scrutiny. They say that Japanese people feel ashamed of themselves when they fail to live up to an internalized ideal image of themselves. Whether it is an individual's conscience or sense of shame that governs his behavior is a controversial question, but it is a fact that Japanese people take much account of the public eye. For example, a wife would feel ashamed to learn that her husband has gone out in a soiled shirt. She would suspect that people might blame her for negligence of her household duties. If a scandal occurring within an institution is publicly disclosed, the members of the institution would all feel ashamed, for a person's group is the extension of one's ego. However, the same person can lose his sense of shame and become ill-mannered and rude when he leaves his community and travels to other places. An old saying well illustrates this point : *Tabi no haji wa kakisute* ("While on a trip shame can be thrown away"). (HA)

hakoniwa   a miniature garden. It is a miniature representation of a landscape garden arranged in a shallow box with natural materials—mud, sand, stones, plants, trees —combined with man-made materials. It was originally started during the Edo period (1603-1867) as a miniature

恥　ルース・ベネディクトは，名著『菊と刀』の中で，日本の文化は典型的な恥の文化で，個人の行いの良し悪しは世間の目に委ねられているといいました。しかし，日本人には内的な価値基準があって，他人に見られていようがいまいが自分の振舞いについて深い道義心があると主張する立場もあります。そのような考え方では，日本人は心に描いた自己の理想像に従って行動することができなくなったとき自ら恥ずかしく思うというのです。人々の行動を支配するものが，個人の道義心であるかそれとも恥の感覚であるかは，議論をよぶところですが，日本人が世間の目をたいそう気にすることは事実です。例えば，夫が汚れたワイシャツを着たまま外出すると，妻は恥ずかしい思いをするでしょう。というのも，自分が家事をおろそかにしていると責められるのではないかと気づかうからです。会社などの醜聞が世間に暴露されると，そこに勤めている人はみんな恥ずかしい思いをするのです。自分の属する集団は，自我の延長線上にあるからです。ところが，他人の目を気にする同じ日本人が自分の土地を離れて他郷に入ると，無作法で粗野なふるまいをしがちになります。「旅の恥はかき捨て」という諺は，このことをうまく言い当てています。

箱　庭　浅い箱の中に土砂や石を入れ，草木を植え，添景物をも使って庭園を小さく模したものです。江戸時代に，実際に造園するにあたり，模型を修正しながら構想が練られるように

model for the purpose of drawing up plans for a real garden. Any arrangements or corrections could be made at this blueprint stage. Later it was further developed and refined into *bonkei*, or the art of making a miniature landscape on a tray. The *hakoniwa* has now been popular for those who cannot afford to have big gardens on their housing properties. (Y)

hamaya　an exorcising arrow. It is a sacred arrow with a white feather used as a special charm for good fortune. It is sold at Shinto shrines during the New Year season. Many people make the first-of-the-year visit to shrines to pray for a happy new year and a long life. They purchase the *hamaya* along with other talismans. The *hamaya* is also placed atop the roof of a house under construction. *Ha-ma* in Chinese characters means "to destroy the evil". (Y)

hanafuda　flower cards. It is a game using 48 flower-cards, four for each month of the year, each month of which is represented by one of twelve flowers and plants. These flower- and plant-cards describe pictorially pine, plum blossom, cherry blossom, wisteria, iris, tree peony, lespedeza, pampas grass under the moon, chrysanthemum, maple, willow, and paulownia, designating each month of the year. Each card has a different number of points in accordance with the picture. Thus, the game is played by several people matching the various kinds of pictures of flowers in order to make some combination with higher points. More frequently, this game is played to gamble for money rather than for fun. (Y)

と生まれました。後にさらに洗練されて，盆の上に庭園を模す盆景が発達しました。箱庭は今は，大きな庭を持てない庶民の間で流行しています。

破魔矢　　白い羽根のついた神聖な矢で，正月になると縁起物として神社で売られます。人々は来る年の無事を祈って初詣をする際に，他のお守りとともに破魔矢を買い求めます。また，破魔矢は新築中の家の屋根に取り付けたりします。「破魔」とは悪霊を滅すことを意味します。

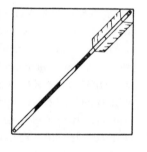

花札　　48枚の絵模様の札を用いたゲームです。1年の各月を表わす札が4枚ずつあり，花や草木などが描かれています。松，梅，桜，藤，あやめ，ぼたん，やはず草，月にしろがね，菊，かえで，柳，桐，とそれぞれが各月に対応し，その絵模様によって点数が決まっています。花札は，何人

かが花合せをすることにより勝負を競うゲームですが，どちらかといえば，娯楽というよりも賭事としての色合いが強いようです。

hanami   cherry-blossom viewing. *Hanami* is literally "flower viewing". Japanese people appreciate cherry blossoms greatly. Since cherry blossoms remain in bloom only for a few days, they were formerly considered a reminder that this world is mutable and impermanent. They also symbolized the Japanese military spirit during the war. Death in battle was glorified and likened to falling cherry blossoms. During the cherry blossom season, newspapers provide *sakuradayori* (cherry blossom reports), which can be a handy guide for the viewers in deciding when and where to enjoy beautiful cherry blossoms. When they bloom, usually early in April, people go on a picnic. Sitting under the cherry trees, they enjoy the beauty of the blossoms. This annual custom started as a Buddhist ceremony among court nobles of the twelfth century. It gained widespread popularity by the seventeenth century. It still remains popular, though the religious implication has died out. The customs and traditions of *hanami* vary from one locality to another. For example, azaleas and rhododendrons rather than cherry blossoms are the kinds of flowers enjoyed in certain regions. (O)

hanko also **inkan**   a personal seal. People are required to imprint their personal *hanko* seal below their signature on a formal or legal document. Without this seal, business in Japan would immediately stop, for only the *hanko* has legal force. For instance, an imprint of your seal is necessary when you write a curriculum vitae, when you fill in an application form or a banking slip, or when you receive registered mail. *Hanko* is abbreviated to *han* and is often

花　見　　花見とは文字通り花を見
ることです。日本人は特に桜の花をめ
でます。この花はわずか数日間咲いて
散ってしまうので，この世の中は移ろ
いやすく，はかないものであることを
気づかせるものと考えられていまし
た。桜はまた戦時中に日本人の軍国精
神を象徴するものでした。戦死が美化
され，散っていく桜の花になぞらえられました。桜の開花期に
は，桜便りが新聞にのります。これは，花見客が美しい桜の花を
観賞しに行く時期と場所を決めるときの案内として便利なもの
です。4月の初旬に開花すると，人々は花見に出かけます。桜の
木の下に座り，花の美しさを楽しみます。年1度のこの慣習は，12
世紀の宮中貴族の間で，仏教の儀式として始まり，17世紀までに
は庶民の間にすっかり広まりました。今日までずっと続いていま
すが，宗教的な意味はなくなりました。花見の風習，習慣は地方
によって異なります。例えば，ある地方では，桜の花よりも，つ
つじやしゃくなげの花を見に出かけます。

判子・印鑑　　公の書式では署名の後に本人の捺印が必要です。
判子だけが法的効力を持っているので，これがないと日本のビジ
ネスは一度に止まってしまうでしょう。例えば，履歴書を書いた
り，申込書や預金払戻請求書を出したり，書留郵便を受け取った
りするときには，押印が必要です。判子は，略して判ということ
もあり，三文判のように接尾辞に使うとバンと読みます。印鑑
は，実印とか銀行印のように，縮めて印と呼ぶことがあります。
三文判は安価な既製品で，文房具屋で売っています。実印は公に

pronounced *ban* when used as a suffix as in *sanmon-ban*. *Inkan* is shortened to *in* as in *jitsu-in* and *ginkō-in*. *Sanmon-ban* is a cheap ready-made seal, which is available at stationary stores. *Jitsu-in* is an officially registered seal, while *ginkō-in* is used mainly for a bank account. Specialized *hanko* shops make and sell various seals. Their cost depends not only on the size but also on the material. A *hanko* made of ivory is the most expensive and is believed to bring good luck. (HA)

haragei　　a traditional technique of problem-solving. *Haragei* is a compound of *hara* (belly) and *gei* (art). Literally it means "beliy art". Most dictionaries define it as the verbal or nonverbal act one utilizes to influence others by drawing upon one's power of accumulated experience in an attempt to solve a mutual problem. In using *haragei* tactics, one must, first, understand one's opponent's interests, desires or experiences and possess any other background information necessary concerning the circumstances. Secondly, the *haragei*-strategist has to be trusted and respected by the person with whom he is negotiating. Thirdly, this political technique must be used at the right time of discourse. With these requirements combined, *haragei* will enable people to reach mutual understanding without confrontation. As a traditional problem-solving technique it is often appropriately used by those in higher positions as is illustrated in the following example. The managers and union leaders spent much time attempting to negotiate an agreement of a wage increase. At a deadlock, one of the managers suddenly cried

登録した印で，銀行印は主に銀行預金勘定に使うものです。判子屋はさまざまな印鑑を作って売っています。値段は大きさとか材料によって異なります。象牙製の判子はたいへん高価ですが，開運の印として尊ばれています。

腹芸　腹芸ということばは，字義どおりに解釈すれば，腹の芸ということになりましょう。辞書にはたいてい，「豊富な経験にまかせて，ことばとかその他の方法で巧みに人を動かし，問題解決をはかる術」と書いてあります。腹芸をうまく使うにはまず第1に，駆引きの相手の興味とか願望とか経験などを十分に知っていなければなりません。第2に，駆引きの相手に信用され，一目置かれていなければなりません。第3に，好機を選ばなければなりません。これらの要件を揃えた上で腹芸を使うと，相手との対立をさけ合意に達することが可能となります。腹芸は伝統的な問題解決の方法で，以下の例に示すように，高い地位にある者が巧みに用いる手なのです。経営者と組合側代表が賃上げをめぐる交渉を延々と続け，双方が譲れない壁にぶつかった時に，重役の一人が突然奇妙なうわずった声でこう叫びました。「お願いだから，これで勘弁してくれ。」そして土下座をしたものですから，組合側はあっけにとられました。この重役の声は哀れを催すものでありながら，同時に愛すべきものに聞こえました。またその姿は低姿勢そのものでした。組合代表は，このような行為を敢えてした重役にあわれみを覚え，妥協してもよいという気持になりました。そこで，急転直下歩みよりが始まったというわけです。労

in a strange high pitch, "I beg you to agree to this figure as the average increase of your salary." To the union leaders' surprise, he solemnly kneeled down and bowed politely, forehead to the floor. The union leaders were immediately touched by the warm appealing tone of the manager's voice and by his humble posture. His unpretentious act aroused their sympathy, as well as their desire to reach an accord. As a result, a compromise, acceptable to both sides, was achieved without further delay. Indeed, this clever manager showed great insight and understanding in the art of *haragei*. (HA)

haramaki   a stomach band. It is usually made of wool, and is worn to keep the abdomen warm. Many people use one for different purposes : small children wear one in bed to keep their tummy warm when they roll out of the blanket ; some tradesmen and travelers wear one as a wallet to keep their money in ; truck drivers wear one tight to keep their stomach from hanging down and to prevent gastroptosis. It is also customary for pregnant women to put a long cotton sash (*sarashi*), called *iwata-obi*, around their abdomen starting during the "dogs' days" of the fifth month of pregnancy according to the Oriental zodiac cycle, with a hope of ensuring themselves an easy delivery. The idea came from the easy birth of dogs. This sash is also kept on even after the delivery just as a girdle. Warriors in the old days, gangsters and gamblers even today are also known to wear one as protection against an enemy's swords and knives in battle. (Y)

使双方とも満足した妥結であったことはいうまでもありません。この重役は，腹芸という術を十分に心得た知恵者であると評すべきでしょう。

腹　巻　綿布などで作られた腹に巻く帯で，通常，冷えを防ぐために着用します。用途は広く，例えば，子供は夜中に布団をはいでも寝冷えをしないようにこれを着用します。商売人や旅行者の中には，財布の代わりに腹巻を着用する者もいます。トラックの運転手は胃下垂を防ぐために腹巻をしま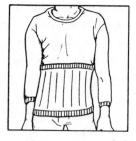す。また，妊婦が妊娠5ヵ月の戌の日に，岩田帯と呼ばれるさらしの腹巻を巻いて安産を願うことも，よく知られています。これは犬の安産からヒントを得たようです。この帯はまた出産後もガードルの代わりに使われます。昔の武士や博徒，そして現在のやくざが，戦場や出入りで刃物から身を守るためにさらしを着けることも知られています。

hari-kuyō   a memorial service for needles.   In Japan memorial services have been held on various occasions to console the spirits not only of dead people but also of other animate things and even of man-made objects such as dolls or knives.   One such service is *hari-kuyō*, which is observed annually on February 8 and/or December 8.   In old times, when women, in general, made *kimono* themselves, this custom was seen in many homes.   Nowadays it is confined chiefly to those who always do needlework, such as professional *kimono*-makers and sewing school students.   On the day of *hari-kuyō* they take old, broken, or blunted needles to temples or shrines, and stick them into a cake of *tōfu* (soybean curd) or *konnyaku* (devil's tongue jelly) placed on the altar.   They thank the worn-out needles for their faithful work during the past year, and comfort their spirits, often with a priest reciting *o-kyō* (a Buddhist sutra).   (T)

hashi   chopsticks.   Chopsticks are the most important tool in the daily life of the Japanese.   They serve not only as knife, fork, and spoon at the table, but also as utensils in the kitchen.   They usually are about 8 inches long and pointed at one end.   They are made of a variety of materials including plastic, ivory, and wood.   Cedar, bamboo, pine, and willow are commonly used for wooden chopsticks.   In Japanese cuisine, the same pair of chopsticks is used throughout the meal. Disposable *hashi* are very common in restaurants, take-out shops, and inns.   Each set of *hashi* used at such an institution is enclosed in a long, white, open-ended envelope on which the institution's name and address is printed.   The Japanese have

針供養　　日本では，人間だけでなく，他の生き物や，そればかりか人形とかナイフのように人間が作った物にさえ霊があるとされ，それを慰めるために昔からさまざまな供養が行われています。そのような供養の中で最も広く知られているのは針供養です。毎年2月8日か12月8日のいずれか，または両日に行われます。かつて一般の女性が自分で着物を縫っていた頃は，針供養は多くの家庭で見られました。しかし今日では主に和裁師とか裁縫学校の生徒のように，いつも針仕事をする人に限られています。針供養の日には，古くなったり折れたりした縫針をお寺や神社に持って行き，祭壇に供えた豆腐かこんにゃくに突き刺します。使い古した針に，それまで忠実に仕事をしてくれたことを感謝し，お経を唱えて針の霊をとむらいます。

箸　　箸は日本人の日常生活の中で最も大切な道具です。食卓では，ナイフ，フォーク，スプーンとして，また台所では料理道具として役立ちます。箸は通常約 20 cm の長さで，一方の端がとがっています。材料はいろいろで，プラスチック，象牙，木などです。木製の箸としては，杉，竹，松，柳をよく使います。日本食の場合，同じ一対の箸を食事の全コースを通じて用います。料理店，持帰りの店，旅館などでは，使い捨ての箸を出すのが普通です。このような場所で使う箸は，一対ずつ，細長くて白く，片端が開いた袋に入れてあり，その箸袋には

been using chopsticks for hundreds of years, and over the centuries many taboos and superstitions have developed around *hashi*. *Aibasami*, an absolute taboo, refers to using one's *hashi* to take some food from someone else's *hashi*. Sticking *hashi* upright in a bowl of rice is equally unacceptable. Both relate to Japanese funeral customs. (O)

hesokuri   secret savings. Generally, Japanese housewives take the responsibility of looking after most household affairs including financial management. Besides well planned and budgeted savings, they may attempt to save small amounts of money from various household allowances or accounts and hide them away. These "secret savings" are called *hesokuri*. They are not usually put into a bank account. The word *hesokuri* sounds rather comical to the Japanese, since *heso* means a belly button—a tiny, personal hiding place! The *hesokuri* savings are often hidden where other members of the family will not be able to find them. After a while, it is not uncommon for the women themselves to forget where they put their savings. The act of saving *hesokuri* money is, therefore, a favorite subject of comic strips and cartoons. Though the secret savings are usually kept by the housewives, they are sometimes kept by the husbands, too. (O)

hibachi   a brazier. In old days this was used as a heating appliance in the Japanese household. In the traditional extended family, people used to gather around it to enjoy conversation. Charcoal was used as fuel. As Japanese life style has undergone tremendous changes, it is very difficult to

店名と住所が印刷してあります。日本人は数百年も前から箸を使っています。この間に，箸に関して，多くのタブーや迷信が生まれました。相ばさみは絶対的タブーで，他の人が箸ではさんでいる食物を自分の箸で受け取ることを指します。茶碗に盛ってある御飯に箸を突き立てることも，同様に認められません。両者とも，日本の葬儀の習慣に関連しています。

へそ繰り　一般に，日本の主婦は，家計を含めて，ほとんどの家事をとりしきります。うまく計画し予算に組んだ貯金の他に，主婦はさまざまな家計費や口座から少額のお金を貯え，隠そうとします。この秘密のお金がへそ繰りと呼ばれるものです。へそ繰りはふつう銀行の口座には入れません。へそ繰りということばは，日本人には滑稽に聞こえます。へそはお腹のおへそのことで，小さな私的隠し場所とはよくいったものです。へそ繰りは，家族の者が見つけられないような所に隠します。しばらくすると，隠した当人がどこにそのお金を隠したか忘れてしまうこともよくあります。したがって，へそ繰りは漫画の題材によく使われます。へそ繰りは普通は主婦がするものですが，時には夫がすることもあります。

火　鉢　昔，日本の家庭で暖房器具として使われました。伝統的な大家族では，皆が集まり火鉢を囲んで会話を楽しんだのです。燃料には炭が使われました。現在では，日本人の生活様式もすっかり変わり，火鉢はほとんど

find a traditional *hibachi* these days.　But some people seem to enjoy an electric one.　(K)

higan　the equinoctial week.　In Buddhist terms, it is the time when people can meet their ancestors.　During these weeks in spring and fall, people pay a respectful visit to their ancestors at their family graves.　They tidy up the graves and offer flowers, incense, and food there.　*Ohagi* (rice balls covered with sweet bean paste) are the most common food to be eaten on these occasions.　This ceremony is said to have been initiated by Prince Shotoku (574-622) during the seventh century, and it seems to have been practiced by all Japanese families, regardless of their religion.　As an old saying goes that no heat or cold lasts over the equinox, *higan* also suggests a change of seasons.　The warm season or cold season will begin right after the equinox days.　(Y)

himono　dried fish.　As Japan is an island country blessed with good fishing places, people have long been enjoying a rich harvest from the sea—fish, seashells, and seaweed.　They have developed various ways of cooking and preserving them.　*Himono* is one of the most commonly preserved foods.　Many kinds of fish, some of them cut open, are generally salted, and in some cases seasoned with *mirin* (sweetened cooking *sake*), and dried in the sun or by electric heat.　*Himono*, broiled just before it is eaten, is served as a side dish at a homely Japanese-style meal, or as a relish taken with *sake*.　(T)

見られなくなっていますが，中には電気火鉢などというものを愛好する人もいるようです。

　　彼　岸　　仏教信仰で先祖に会えるといわれる春分と秋分を中心とした期間を指します。春秋のこの時期には，人々は先祖の墓参りに行き，墓の掃除をし，花，線香，食物などを墓前に供えます。特に，御飯をあんでくるんだお·は·ぎ·がよく供えられます。彼岸の習慣は，7世紀に聖徳太子によって始められたといわれ，今日まで宗派を問わずほとんどの国民によって受け継がれているようです。「暑さ寒さも彼岸まで」という決まり文句がありますが，彼岸は季節の変り目をも意味します。春分・秋分を境に急に暖かくなったり寒くなったりするからです。

　　干　物　　日本は漁場に恵まれた島国で，人々は昔から魚，貝，海藻など豊かな海の幸を味わってきました。魚貝類の料理法や保存法もいろいろと発達しました。中でも干物は最もなじみの深い保存食です。各種の魚を，あるものは開きにして，普通は塩で，時にはみ·り·ん·で味つけをします。そして天日または電気で乾かします。干物は食べる直前に火にあぶり，和風の家庭料理のおかずとして，あるいは酒のさかなとして供します。

hinamatsuri   the Doll Festival. It is the Girls' Festival celebrated on March 3. It is also a seasonal festival called *momo-no-sekku* featuring peach blossoms. A group of beautifully dressed dolls are displayed on tiers of shelves in the home of the family that has a young girl. The dolls represent members of the ancient imperial court. The Emperor and the Empress (*dairi-bina*) are displayed on the top shelf, and their two eminent lords (*udaijin* and *sadaijin*), three ladies(*sannin-kanjo*), five musicians(*gonin-bayashi*), and three servants are arrayed below them. Even small representations of furniture and foods are displayed on the lower shelves. *Hinamatsuri* dates from the medieval times, but the custom of displaying dolls in this fashion started in the eighteenth century. Whereas originally the hand-made dolls were thrown into the river along with offerings on March 3, today the commercially made and expensive dolls are stored away for the next year. They are often passed from generation to generation. Sweet rice wine called *shirozake* is prepared as well as special dishes on this girls' day. (O)

hinomaru   the symbol designating the rising sun. A red circle against a white background symbolizing the rising sun, also represents the Japanese national flag. It was officially selected as the Japanese national emblem by the Meiji Government in 1870, because it had been one of the symbols of authority granted by the preceding Tokugawa Shogunate. For example, the ships carrying rice to be paid in lieu of tax had flown a *hinomaru* flag in the Edo period (1603-1867). This symbol is very popular in Japan. *Hinomaru-*

ひな祭　ひな祭は女の子のための祭で，3月3日に行われます。この祭はまた，桃の花が主要な飾りとなる季節の祭で，桃の節句とも呼ばれます。女の子がいる家庭では，美しい着物を着た一群の人形を数段の棚に並べます。人形は昔の宮廷人を模したものです。最上段に天皇・皇后ひな（内裏びな），その下の段には順に，2人の高位の貴族（右大臣と左大臣），3人官女，5人ばやし，3人の召使が並びます。さらに下段には，小さな家具や食物の模型まで飾ります。ひな祭の歴史は中世にさかのぼりますが，このようなやり方で人形を飾る習慣は18世紀に始まりました。元来は，手作りの人形を供え物といっしょに，3月3日に川に流したものです。しかし今日では，商品として作られた高価な人形なので，翌年のためにしまっておきます。多くの場合，人形は代々受け継がれます。ひな祭の日には，特別の料理の他に，白酒という甘い酒が出されます。

日の丸　白地に赤い丸を描き日の出を象徴するこのシンボルは日本の国旗になっています。1870年，明治政府により正式に日本の国旗として選定されました。これは徳川幕府が定めた上意の象徴のうちの一つでした。例えば，江戸時代に，税となる米を運ぶ船は日の丸を掲げていました。このシンボルは広く使われています。例えば，日の丸弁当といえば，弁当箱のごはんの真ん中に梅干しを置いたものですし，日の丸扇といえば，中心に赤い丸を描いた扇子のことです。

bentō is a packed lunch of white rice with a red pickled Japanese apricot in the middle. *Hinomaru-ōgi* is a folding fan with the symbol of a rising sun at the center. (K)

hitodama the spirit of a dead person, or a jack-o'-lantern. According to a folk belief, if the spirit of a dead person is not satisfied with the way it is treated by the bereaved family, it hovers around in graveyards at night in an effort to locate the right place for a peaceful settlement. The form it supposedly takes when traveling is a reddish-, yellowy-, or bluish-white ball of fire with a tail. (HO)

hōgaku traditional Japanese music. It is a generic term for traditional Japanese music in its broadest sense. However, it usually refers to those types developed during and after the Edo period (1603-1867) when the *shamisen*, a traditional Japanese three-stringed banjo-like instrument, increased in popularity. Subsumed under the heading *hōgaku*, there are, namely, *nagauta*, *kouta*, *kiyomoto*, *hauta*, *shinnai*, and *gidayū*. *Nagauta* is a long epic or ballad sung for *kabuki* dancing. *Kouta* is a short song and is accompanied by a *shamisen* plucked with the fingers instead of a *bachi*, a plectrum. *Kiyomoto* is a traditional singing style in falsetto. *Hauta* is a short song, sung without delicate techniques. Its rhythm is clear and the melody is simple. One offshoot of *hauta* is *kouta*. Finally, *shinnai* is a plaintive narrative-style song. Finally, *gidayū* is a school of *jōruri*, a story-song sung for *bunraku* (the traditional puppet drama show). (Y)

人　魂　　民間信仰によれば，死者
の魂は，遺族のあつかい方に満足しな
いと，夜，墓地のまわりをさまよい，
平和な安住の場所を探し求めます。そ
れがさまよう時にとるとされる形は，
赤っぽい，あるいは黄色っぽい，また
は青白い火の玉で，尾がついていま
す。

邦　楽　　広義には，日本古来の音楽の総称です。狭義には，
江戸時代からの日本音楽，主として三味線を使った曲を指し，長
唄，小唄，清元，端唄，新内，義太夫などがあります。長唄は，
歌舞伎の伴奏音楽として発達した長い叙事詩や物語詩の三味線音
楽です。小唄は，短い三味線音楽で，ばちを使わず爪弾きをしま
す。清元は裏声を取り入れています。端唄は，細かい技術の必要
もない短い歌で，リズムもメロディもわかりやすく，小唄の産み
の親ともいわれています。新内は語り調子の歌です。最後に，義
太夫は浄瑠璃の一派で，日本固有の人形劇である文楽に欠かせな
い音曲語り物です。

hōi   a folk belief in a direction being characterized by good luck or bad luck.   According to the Chinese-originated fortune-telling system of *onmyōdo*, every direction is marked by a certain set of taboos.   In an "unlucky" direction, a tragic accident is believed to occur.   A fortune teller usually determines what direction is doomed with what evil.   If a person believes in what his fortune teller says and if he is traveling in a direction which his fortune teller regards as disastrous, he often makes a detour in a different direction before he reaches his final destination.   In the physiognomy of a house (*kasō*), the northeastern direction, often referred to as the devil's gate (*kimon*), is believed to be an unlucky quarter.   Therefore, a house is supposed to be built so as not to face northeast.   In case this is impossible, a charm is provided against misfortunes arising from the tabooed exposure.   (HO)

hōji   the Buddhist memorial service held on the anniversary of a person's death.   Usually memorial services are performed on the first, second, seventh, thirteenth, and seventeenth anniversaries or thereabouts.   The first anniversary is called *isshūki* or *ikkaiki*, the second *sanshūki* or *sankaiki*, seventh *shichishūki* or *shichikaiki* and so on.   These services are more often held at home than at a temple.   The family and relatives of the deceased attend the service and pray for the repose of the dead, while the priest conducting the service reads a sutra (*okyō*).   It is customary for the members of the gathering to dine together after the service, cherishing the memory of the deceased.   The term also refers to services held on the 35th day (*goshichi-ki*) or on the 49th day (*shijūku-*

方　位　　中国発生の占いの体系である陰陽道によると，すべての方角には一定の吉凶があるとされています。凶の方角では悲しい出来事がおこると信じられています。占い師は，どの方角がどの悪霊にとりつかれているかを示します。占い師のいうことを信じている人が，災害が起きるといわれた方角に旅をする場合は，方違えといって，別の方向からまわり道をして目的地に着くことをします。家相では北東の方向が鬼門とみなされ，凶と信じられています。だから，家は北東に面しないよう建てるものとされています。これが不可能な場合には，凶事が起こるのを予防するためにまじないをします。

法　事　　一般に，故人をしのぶ法要は，1年目，2年目，7年目，13年目，17年目の命日，またはそれに近い日に行われます。1年目の命日は一周忌または一回忌，2年目は三周忌または三回忌，7年目は七周忌または七回忌といったように呼ばれます。これらの法要は寺院よりも自宅で行われることが多いようです。法事に出席するのは故人の家族や親類で，法要を勤める僧侶が読経している間に，故人の冥福を祈ります。法事の後に，出席者は故人の思い出を語り合いながら食事を共にするのが習慣となっています。法事はまた，故人の死後35日目（五七忌）または49日目（四十九日）に営まれる法要を指す場合もあります。

nichi) after a person's death.　(S)

honne-to-tatemae　　an opinion or an action motivated by one's true inner feelings and an opinion or an action influenced by social norms. These two words are often considered a dichotomy constrasting genuinely-held personal feelings and opinions from those that are socially controlled. *Honne* is one's deep motive or intention, while *tatemae* refers to motives or intentions that are socially-tuned, those that are shaped, encouraged, or suppressed by majority norms. For example, an accepted code of *tatemae,* "Be kind to everyone," may be broken in order to justify the *honne* that one's own children are not expected to make friends with slow learners. However, *honne* and *tatemae* are not actually opposites as these two values are relative to people and situations. For instance, when a liberalist is asked to tell his *tatemae*, he may say that armament is unnecessary and so is the state. When he is asked to tell his *honne*, however, he may say that he recognizes the necessity of a state. On the contrary, a conservastive's *tatemae* is that a state is good and so is armament. His *honne*, however, can be that the state is an evil because it can lead to the outbreak of war. In spite of these obvious discrepancies, Japanese people continue to use these two forms of communication and they switch from *tatemae* to *honne,* or vice versa, according to the context. Consequently, an inexperienced listener may find it difficult to distinguish, for instance, whether a host is really expressing a sincere invitation to dinner, or whether he is merely paying lip service. Socially-skilled guests, however, are expected to

ホンネとタテマエ　　この2つの語は，個人の本心と社会的に制限された意見という対立概念として日常よく使われています。ホンネは心底からの動機とか真意のことですが，タテマエは，社会的規範に合ったもの，あるいはそれに支えられたもの，または抑圧されたもののことです。例えば，「誰にでも親切にしなさい」というタテマエは，「自分の子供は勉強のできない子供と仲よくなってもらいたくない」という親のホンネによって破られることがあります。しかし，ホンネとタテマエは，実際には対立概念ではないのです。この2語の意味は，話し手と状況によって変化するのです。例えば，自由主義者がそのタテマエをいうときには「軍備も国家も不要」となりますが，ホンネを語るときには，軍備も国家も必要であることを認めるかもしれません。一方，保守主義のタテマエは「国家は善であるがゆえに軍備も善である」というものです。しかしそのホンネは，戦争勃発の引金を引くがゆえに国家を悪とみなすかもしれません。このように明白な矛盾はあるにもかかわらず，人びとは言語生活の上で2種の意見を使い分けます。つまり，場面によって，タテマエからホンネへ，ホンネからタテマエへと巧みに切り替えるのです。そのため世間知らずの者には，相手が本当に夕食に招いているのか，それとも口先だけの好意を示しているのかがわかりません。ところが，世慣れた者には，声の調子とか他のことば以外の手がかりなどから，相手の偽らざる感情を察知して，両者を区別するのが，当り前のこととされています。別の側面から言えば，ホンネは私的なやりとりの中で出ますが，タテマエは公の場で語られます。会議では形式的な議事進行に従い，外交辞令に徹するという人が，同僚と一杯傾けて談笑する段になると，先刻の会議で取り上げられたことがらについて自分のホンネを率直に表します。公の場では和を求

determine, by the tone of voice and other nonverbal clues, the depth of the host's intentions. Another dimension of this dichotomy is that *honne* is expressed privately while *tatemae* may be openly professed. Observing the formalities of a business meeting, a person tends to follow protocol. Later, while enjoying conversation with his colleagues over a glass of beer or *sake* (rice wine), the same person will frankly express his *honne* regarding the issues raised at the meeting. Aiming at peace and harmony, the public self avoids confrontation, whereas the private self tends toward sincere self-expression. (HA)

hotaru   a firefly. This insect shows up in early summer in Japan, around May in the southern, and in mid-July in the northern part of the country. Three kinds of *hotaru* exist in Japan. A larger variety called *genji-botaru* lives in bush areas near clean water. Two smaller varieties live in grassy areas by rather dirty water, or even in the dry bush. The glow of a firefly provided the basis for various superstitions among local people throughout Japan's history. It was once believed that fireflies were the transformed souls of ancient warriors slain in battles, and that they appeared each year on the anniversaries of their death. Hunting for fireflies was a popular pastime which originated in the Edo period (1603-1867). Now children in some rural areas enjoy catching fireflies. However, there exist today very few fireflies in or around urban areas. (O)

めて対立を避けますが，くつろいだ場では無礼講と相成るので
す。

ほたる　　　この昆虫は，日本の南の
地方では初夏の5月頃に，北の地方で
は7月の中頃に姿を見せます。日本に
は3種類のほたるが生息しています。
源氏ぼたると呼ばれる大きな種類のほ
たるは，きれいな水の近くの茂みに住
みます。他の2種類の小さなほたる

は，やや汚れた水の近くの草原や，乾いた茂みに住んでいます。
ほたるの光は日本の歴史を通じて人々の間にさまざまな迷信をも
たらしました。昔は，ほたるは戦争で殺された兵士の魂が姿を変
えたもので，毎年その命日に現われると信じられていました。ほ
たる狩りは人気のあった遊びで，江戸時代に始まりました。現
在，いなかの子供はほたる狩りを楽しむこともありますが，都市
部ではほたるの姿はほとんど見られません。

hyakunin-isshu   the card game of one hundred poems. *Hyakunin-isshu* is a collection of one hundred *tanka* poems by one hundred poets, dating from the seventh to the thirteenth century.   The term also refers to the card game using these poems, commonly played during the New Year's days not only in the home but also in regional or nationwide tournaments. The players compete in matching two cards : one is a reading card with a complete poem printed on it, while the other is a matching card with only the second half of the same poem. All the matching cards are spread out on the floor to be picked up by the players as the reader recites one poem after another. The winner is the one who matches the most poems.   Skilled players can locate the correct card on hearing only a syllable or two.   Through *hyakunin-isshu*, part of the tradition of Japanese poetry has been handed down for generations.   (T)

iki   high spirit. *Iki* is an aesthetic and moral ideal developed by urban commoners in the late Edo period (1603-1867).   This idealizes not only an urbane, chic, or bourgeois type of beauty but also the sophisticated life of a person who enjoys sensual pleasure.   *Iki* originally denoted "spirit" from which its secondary meaning "high spirit" was derived.   Its adjectival form refers to the way that a high-spirited person talks, behaves, or dresses.   *Iki* has a coquettish connotation represented by a high standard *geisha* woman with a feminine charm.   A lady possessing *iki* is highly-spirited in her manner, and is always willing to make sacrifices for her lover.   *Iki* had its best literary expression in the works of Tamenaga Shunsui (1790-1843).   His novel *Shunshoku Umegoyomi,* for instance,

百人一首　　百人一首は，7世紀から13世紀までの100人の歌人がよんだ100首からなる和歌集です。百人一首はまた，この和歌を使ったカードゲームのことでもあります。このゲームをするのは普通お正月で，家庭で楽しむばかりでなく，地方大会や全国大会も開かれます。競技者は2枚のカードを組み合わせることを競いますが，2枚のうち一方は読み札で，和歌が1首書いてあり，他方は取り札で，その和歌の後半しか書いてありません。取り札はすべて畳の上に並べられ，読み手が次々に歌を読みあげていくと，競技者が拾いあげるのです。一番多く歌を組み合わせた者が勝ちです。上手な人は，最初の1文字か2文字を聞いただけで正しい札を見つけることができます。日本の詩歌の伝統は，いくぶんかは百人一首のおかげで代々伝わってきたのです。

い　き　　いきは江戸時代後半に町民が求めた美的・道徳的理想です。この理想は，都会的で洗練された金持ちの美意識と，官能的快楽を求めた者の風雅な生活に根ざしたものでした。いきとはもともと意気のことでしたが，そこから意気地の意が派生しました。そして，この語の形容動詞形であるいきなということばは，意気地のある者の話しぶりやふるまいや着こなしぶりを形容したものです。いきには，評判の高い魅力的な芸者に見られる媚態もしくは色っぽさが必要です。いきな女は，意気地のあるふるまいをする一方，ほれた男にはとことん尽くすという日々を過ごしました。いきの世界は為永春水の人情本によく表現されています。とくに『春色梅児誉美』は，いきの理想を求めた人々を知る上でまさに好例といえるでしょう。

99

presents the fineset example of people who pursued the ideal of *iki*. (HA)

imi-kotoba a taboo word. The Japanese language has a certain group of words or expressions which are believed to be associated with bad luck. Their use is taboo, particularly on ceremonial occasions. When used, they are often pronounced differently or replaced by other words. For example, the number "four", when pronounced as *shi,* happens to be a homonym for "death". Thus, it is supposed to be pronounced as *yo(n)*. Similarly, a pear or *nashi* can mean "none", and is replaced by *ari-no-mi* (fruit that invites fortune). A ditch reed or *ashi* denotes "bad", and is substituted by *yoshi* ("good"). *Surume* (dried squid), when served at drinking places, is often called *atarime*, for *suru* means "to lose a bet" while *atari* means "to win a bet". Likewise, *owari* (end) sounds so unauspicious that it is replaced by *ohiraki* (development). At wedding receptions, words like *kaeru* (going home) and *kireru* (cutting or separation) are carefully avoided. (Y)

in'yō the cosmic dual forces of shade and light. The idea of *in'yō,*which evolved from the cosmology of the ancient Chinese, explains every phenomenon of the universe by dualism of shade (*in*) and light (*yō*). For example, day and night, heat and cold, and male and female all comprise *in'yō,* day, heat, and male being *yō.* In the first century B.C., this idea was combined with the *gogyō-setsu* theory, which holds that the universe is regulated by the law of cyclic alternation

忌みことば　　縁起や語呂がよくないとされている，ある特定の語や表現のことです。特に冠婚葬祭での使用は忌み嫌われています。こういったことばが使われる場合には，発音を変えたり，言い変えたりします。たとえば，4 という番号は死と同音なので，使用を避けるか，ヨ（ン）と読みます。同様に，果物のナシは無しと同音なので，有りの実といわれます。植物のアシは悪しと同音のためヨシに代わります。スルメが飲み屋でアタリメと呼ばれるのも，失うという意味の擦るを当たりに置き変えたものです。また，散会の時に，終りというのは縁起がよくないので，お開きということがあります。結婚式では，帰るや切れるといったことばの使用は慎むものとされています。

陰　陽　　陰陽という考え方は，古代中国の宇宙論から発展したものですが，宇宙のあらゆる現象を陰と陽の二元論で説明します。例えば，昼と夜，熱さと冷たさ，男性と女性は，すべて陰陽をなし，最初にあげたものがそれぞれ陽となります。紀元前1世紀に，この思想は五行説の理論と結びつきましたが，これは，5つの自然の要素，つまり，木，火，土，金属，水が順々に交替してゆくという法則によって宇宙が支配されていると考えるものです。陰陽五行説は，占いや天文学やその他中国人の哲学的思想の

of the five natural elements, i. e. wood, fire, earth, metal, and water. The *in'yō-gogyō-setsu* theory formed the basis of divination, astronomy, the calendar, and other philosophical ideas of the Chinese. It filtered into people's mind and became a deep-rooted belief to be carried into the practice of life. Confucianism, which was popular especially with the Japanese warrior (*samurai*) class of the seventeenth century, shares with it in some basic ideas. The traces of the *in'yō* theory can be seen even today in several kinds of divinations performed by fortune-tellers. (S)

iroha-karuta   the card game of the Japanese alphabet. The game of *iroha-karuta* is peculiar to Japan, and commonly enjoyed by children during the New Year's days. *Iroha* is the ABC's of the Japanese alphabet, and *karuta* is a general term for various card games. *Iroha-karuta* consists of two sets of cards : forty-eight reading cards which have proverbs printed on them, and as many picture cards which are paired with the reading cards. The proverbs are carefully chosen so that all their very first letters, if arranged in order, will complete the Japanese alphabet. Hence the name of *iroha-karuta*. To play the game, a number of people sit around with the picture cards all spread out on the floor, and as soon as the reader begins to read a proverb, they compete for the matching card. The winner is the one who picks up the most cards. This game is not only amusing but helpful in initiating children into practical wisdom. (T)

基礎となりました。それは民衆の心に浸透し，実生活で実行すべき信条として深く根づいたものになりました。儒教は，17世紀の日本の武士階級に人気がありましたが，基本的思想において陰陽五行説と共通したところがあります。今日でも，占い師の行う何種類かの占いに，陰陽のなごりを見ることができます。

いろはカルタ　いろはカルタは日本独特のゲームで，通例，正月に子供たちが楽しむものです。いろはは日本語の字母表の最初の3文字で，カルタとは種々のカードゲームに対する総称です。いろはカルタは2組の札からできています。1組は諺が書いてある48枚の読み札で，他の1組は読み札と組になる48枚の絵札です。48の諺は，その冒頭の文字を全部そろえて順に並べると日本語の全音節を構成するように選んであります。それでいろはカルタという名がついているのです。このゲームをするには，絵札をすべて床に並べ，そのまわりに何人かが座ります。1人が諺を読み上げるやいなや，競ってそれに合う絵札を探すのです。一番多くカードを拾った者が勝ちです。いろはカルタは，面白い遊びであるばかりでなく，子供たちに実用的な知恵を授けるのに役立っています。

irori   a hearth made in the floor of the living room of a farmhouse.   It normally measures four or five feet square and has, instead of a chimney, a pothook hanging over it. Firewood is burnt for heating and cooking purposes.   Family members may sit around it and enjoy a fireside chat.   The top seat facing the entrance of the room is called *yokoza*, which is taken by the head of the family.   Recently, modern heating systems have brought about its rapid disappearance.   (S)

itako   a female spiritualistic medium.   According to a folk belief in the northeastern region, these women are divinely inspired and supernaturally possessed.   Therefore, they are capable of spiritualistic communication.   They are specifically supposed to be able to bring forth messages of ancestors to their descendants, mediate between the spirits of dead and living persons, and divine the fate of a family or an individual.   There are now an increasing number of people visiting those women to ask for their spiritualistic services. Before these women become independent practitioners, they live with experienced masters of these magic acts to get special training in spiritualism, necromancy, and telepathy. They also have to pass a series of tests to prove that they are capable of divine inspiration.   There also are similar women in Okinawa, but there they have a different label.   (HO)

janken   a hand game, known as rock-paper-scissors. In this game two or more players make signs by the fingers of

囲炉裏　農家の居間の床に設ける囲炉裏は，たいていは4〜5フィート平方で，煙突ではなく自在鉤がその上に吊り下がっています。暖房や料理のために薪を燃やします。家族は囲炉裏を囲んで座り，団らんを楽しみます。部屋の入口に面した上座（かみ）は横座と呼ばれ，家族の長が座ります。最近は，現代的な暖房設備が普及したため，囲炉裏は急激に少なくなりました。

いたこ　東北地方の民間信仰によると，これらの女性は霊感と超自然的能力を働かせることができます。だから彼女たちは心霊交信が可能です。特に，先祖から子孫へメッセージをもたらし，死者と生者の意志を仲介し，そして家族または個人の運命を予言することができるとされています。これらの女性に心霊術をたのみに訪れる人々の数はふえています。彼女たちは，独立して術を行うようになるために，先輩の心霊術師につかえ，心霊術，降霊術，テレパシーの特別訓練を受けます。そして，神がかりであることを証明する一連のテストに合格しなければなりません。沖縄にも同じ仕事をする女性がいますが，呼び名が違います。

じゃんけん　2人以上の人が手指の形によってするゲームです。3種類の形があり，グウ，チョキ，パアと呼ばれています。

their hands.   Three kinds of signs are called *gū*, *choki*, and *pā*. *Gū* is a clenched fist signifying a rock or a stone, *choki* is a V-shape formation of the forefinger and middle finger representing a pair of scissors, and *pā* is an open hand signifying a sheet of paper.   Each player gives one of these signs simultaneously with the shout *"jan-ken-pon"*.   *Gū* defeats *choki*, and *choki* in turn defeats *pā*.   The meaning is that a rock can break scissors, which can, however, cut paper.   *Pā* defeats *gū*, because paper can stifle a rock by wrapping it in.   When the same sign is given by all the players, or when all the three signs are given by some of them, the round is called *aiko* or a draw. The players then try again with the shout '*aiko-de-sho*', until someone wins.   *Janken* is rarely played for its own sake.   It is usually played for the purpose of settling relatively small matters—for deciding order, turns, or who is "it" in a game of tag.   Thus, in most cases, it is followed by another kind of game.   (S)

jichin-sai   the ceremony of purifying a building site. It is usually held before the groundwork gets under way for a building or construction project.   Administering the ceremony is a Shinto priest (*kannushi*) who appeases revengeful spirits underground and prays to the gods of the territory for the safety of workers and the happiness of potential project utilizers.   (HO)

jinja   a Shinto shrine.   Sanctified by its parishioners and served by priests (*kannushi*), it enshrines a Shinto deity, who is often popularly called *ujigami*.   An *ujigami* is an

グウは石を表わす握りこぶし，チョキ
は人指し指と中指をＶ字形に開いたも
ので鋏を表わし，パアは全部の指を開
いて紙を表わしたものです。このゲー
ムをする人は，「じゃんけんぽん」と
いうかけ声と同時にこれらのうちの一
つを出します。グウはチョキに勝ち，
チョキはパアに勝ちます。そのわけ

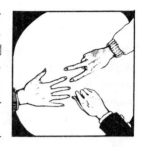

は，石は鋏をこわし鋏は紙を切るからです。紙は石を包み込んで
しまいますから，パアはグウに勝ちます。全員が同じ手のサイン
を出したとき，またはまったく別々のものを出したときには，そ
の回はあいこと呼ばれます。つまり引分けです。その場合には
「あいこでしょ」というかけ声とともにもう一度行い，だれかが
勝つまで続けます。じゃんけんのためにじゃんけんをするという
ことはめったにありません。たいていは，比較的些細なこと，た
とえば順序や順番や鬼ごっこの鬼などを決めるためにします。多
くの場合，別のゲームに先立って行われます。

地鎮祭　これは建築や工事の基礎作業が始まる前に行われる
儀式です。儀式をとりしきるのは神主で，地下の悪霊をしずめ，
そして労働者の安全とこれらの施設を利用することになる人々の
幸せを土地の神々に祈ります。

神　社　神社とは神道の神様を祭っているところで，地区の
人々によって神聖なものとされ，神主がつねに仕えています。そ
の神様は一般に氏神と呼ばれます。氏神とは，ある一族の先祖の

ancestral deity of a certain clan (*uji*). He is venerated because he is believed to look after its descendants called clan children (*ujiko*), who are actually all people living in the neighborhood of the shrine. The *jinja* typically has a gate (*torii*) at its entrance. The gateway leads to the hall of worship (*haiden*), behind which stands the main sanctuary (*honden*). Near the *haiden* a pair of stone lions (*komainu*) guard the shrine from evil spirits. In addition to these local shrines, there are some national shrines dedicated to the gods of "national foundation". The Grand Shrine of Izumo (Shimane Prefecture), the Grand Shrines of Ise (Mie Prefecture), and the Meiji Shrine (Tokyo) are some of the most famous ones visited by people from across the country. (HO)

jizō the guardian deity of children. It is customarily found in the form of a stone statue of a Buddhist saint with a gem in the left hand and a staff in the right. The *jizō* statues can usually be seen standing along country roads. *Jizō* is believed to be the guardian deity of children. When a child dies, stones are placed before a *jizō* statue, the idea being for the deity to take on the burden of the deceased. (Y)

juku a supplementary private lesson. It refers to small private classes where supplementary lessons are provided to pupils who tend to fall behind the average in formal education. These classes are usually taught by experienced retired teachers, or recent graduates from universities who failed to find more appropriate jobs. Recently many *juku* have

神様です。氏神は，氏子と呼ばれる子孫を見守ると信じられているので，尊敬されています。氏子とは，実際には神社のまわりに住んでいるすべての人々を指します。たいてい神社には入口のところに鳥居と呼ばれる門があります。門の道は拝殿（礼拝をする広間）につづき，そのうしろには本殿（神殿）があります。拝殿の近くには，一対の石の狛犬が悪霊から神社を守っています。これらの地区的な神社のほかに，全国的な神社もあり，建国の神様を祭っています。最も有名なものに出雲大社（島根県），伊勢神宮（三重県），そして明治神宮（東京都）などがあり，全国から参拝客が集まります。

地　蔵　　仏教の一菩薩の石像で，左手には宝珠を，右手には錫杖を持っています。一般に，田舎の道路添いに立っているのがみかけられます。地蔵は子供の守護神とされており，子供が死ぬと，死後の苦を地蔵にしょってもらうことを願って，石を地蔵の前に積みます。

塾　　学校教育で落ちこぼれた生徒に対して特別に補習をしている私的教室のことです。塾はたいてい，経験のある元教師や，希望の職業につけなかった大学出の人が教えています。最近では，有名校をねらう生徒のために集中コースを設けるところもあります。

started to offer cram courses for pupils and students who wish to enter prestigious high schools and colleges. (K)

Jukyō Confucianism. Confucianism is a philosophical, ethical, and political teaching with some of those religious aspects fathered by Confucius, the Chinese philosopher of the sixth century B.C. It is the moral architecture of Japanese society. Confucianism reached Japan by way of Korea in the early fifth century and had a great influence on the creation and development of Japanese society. It taught the importance of children's respect for parents and subordinates' obedience to superordinates. This inspired an ideology of kinship and clanship in the feudal age. This can still be seen in today's business and politics in the form of loyalty and paternalism. Probably the most important influence remains in the field of education, where Confucius taught that men should study and cultivate themselves to become the master of all, and that success in academic life is the measure of an individual. In recent years, however, the Confucian heritage seems to have begun diminishing from the minds and lives of Japanese people as social change proceeds. (Y)

jūnishi the twelve symbols of the Chinese zodiac. Based on the twelve years which Jupiter takes to circle the heavens, the ancient Chinese were able to indicate a season by the position of this mysterious star in the sky. After this system came to Japan, the Japanese used animal names to designate the twelve positions. They are *ne* (rat), *ushi* (cow), *tora* (tiger), *u* (rabbit), *tatsu* (dragon), *mi* (snake),

儒　教　　紀元前6世紀に，孔子を始祖として説かれ始めた中国古来の哲学的，倫理的，政治的な教えで，宗教色もあります。日本社会の道徳体系の基礎ともなっています。5世紀初頭に朝鮮半島を経て日本に伝わりました。両親に対する孝行，下位の者の上位の者に対する忠誠心などを強調し，日本社会の形成・発展に大きな影響を及ぼしました。さらに封建時代になると，庶民の家に対する，また武士の藩に対する帰属意識をも強めました。これは現在の財界や政界にも，忠誠心や温情主義という形でなごりをとどめています。今日，儒教の影響が最も強く残っているのは教育の場でしょう。儒教は，自己を知り鍛えることの徳を教え，学問に秀でることの大切さを説きました。しかし，社会の変化にともない，儒教の教えも人々の心と生活からだんだんと消え去りつつあります。

十二支　　木星が天空を12年間で一周するのを基に，古代中国人はこの神秘的な星の位置を観察することで季節を知ることができました。この方法が日本に入ってきたとき日本人は，これら12カ所の各々に動物の名前をあてました。子，丑，寅，卯，辰，巳，午，

uma (horse), *hitsuji* (sheep), *saru* (monkey), *tori* (rooster), *inu* (dog), and *i* (boar). This zodiac cycle was also used to tell the direction, the hour and the day as well as the year. Today it is mainly used in reference to the year. For example, the years 1950, 1962, 1974 and 1986 are all "tiger" years. As a matter of fact, instead of asking how old you are, people are likely to ask in what year of the zodiac you were born. Thus they are able to guess your age almost correctly. (K)

kabuki   a traditional Japanese theater. *Kabuki* is one form of classical dramatic arts of Japan. It has become far more popular than either *nō* or *bunraku*, the other two forms of the traditional Japanese theater. It is a colorful combination of acting, dancing, singing, and spectacle, representing scenes from three main kinds of plays : *jidai-mono* (histories) often with *aragoto* (scenes of exaggerated action), *sewamono* (domestic tragedies), and *shosagoto* (dances). As a rule, individual scenes from several different plays are acted in the course of one performance. One characteristic of the *kabuki* stage is the *hanamichi* (an elevated passageway), which runs from the stage to the rear of the theater through the audience. The characters make their entrances and exits along this passageway which also serves as an acting area. The scenery and props are elaborate, and the costumes are rich and bright especially in historical plays. Stage assistants called *kurogo* (hooded and dressed in black) and *kōken* (dressed in a traditional formal wear) are employed to help the actors. Though they do their job on the stage in open view, they are

未，申，酉，戌，亥です。この十二宮は，年，日，時刻の他に，方角を知るのにも使われました。今日では主に，年を表わすのに使われます。例えば，1950年，1962年，1974年，1986年はすべて寅年になります。実際，年齢の代わりに，生まれた年の干支をたずねることがよくあります。この方法で年齢がわかるのです。

歌舞伎　　日本の古典演劇の一つです。歌舞伎は他の2種の伝統演劇である能や文楽よりもずっと人気があります。歌舞伎は，演技，踊り，歌，スペクタクルなどから成る華やかな総合芸術です。さまざまな場面を上演しますが，それは3種に大別できます。つまり，しばしば荒事をともなう時代物と，世話物と，所作事です。通例，1回の公演中に，数編の芝居から取った特色のある場面が上演されます。歌舞伎の舞台の特徴の一つは花道です。これは，舞台から劇場の後部まで客席を貫いて設けてある通路です。登場人物はこの通路を通って登場したり退場したりします。また花道は演技をする場所にもなります。装置や小道具は精巧で，衣装は，とりわけ歴史劇において，けんらん豪華です。黒子と後見と呼ばれる人たちが，舞台の上で俳優の手助けをします。この助手たちが舞台の上でする仕事は，すっかり観客に見えるのですが，慣例として見えないことになっています。三味線による音楽や音響効果も用いられております。文楽を脚色した場面では，浄瑠璃が語られることもあります。俳優は，伝統的なやり方で濃いメーキャップをします。女形を専門とする男性俳優が女の役を演じます。歌舞伎俳優は幼少の頃から仕込まれ，通常，演技スタイルを世襲します。芝居そのものよりも俳優の方が重視され，各俳優独特の演技スタイルや演技力に合うように，上演場面が設定さ

113

conventionally supposed to be invisible. *Shamisen* music and sound effects are provided, and occasionally *jōruri* recitation accompanies the performance of scenes adapted from the *bunraku* theater. The performers are sometimes heavily made up in conventional style. Male actors specializing in female roles take the parts of female characters. The *kabuki* actors are trained from a very young age and they usually inherit the family tradition of performing styles. The actor is considered more important than the play itself, and the scenes are arranged to fit each actor's particular style and skills. (O)

kadō The art of flower arrangement. Flowers are arranged in a flower container and placed for display in *tokonoma* (the alcove made in a Japanese-style room) or elsewhere. Originating from ritual flower offerings by Buddhist priests, *kadō* (also called *ikebana*) became an established art around the sixteenth century. Many schools were founded in the course of its history by head masters (*iemoto*) advocating different styles of flower arrangement, such as *rikka* (standing flowers), *nageire* (flowers randomly arranged in a vase), and *shōka* (living flowers). The Ikenobō school, known as the oldest flower arrangement school, specialized in *rikka*-style. *Nageire*-style flourished in the late sixteenth century when tea-ceremony became a fashion. In traditional *shōka*-style *kadō*, three main branches or flower stems symbolizing "heaven", "earth", and "mankind" are arranged in such a way that the three may achieve natural harmony and represent the entire universe. During the 1920s, new schools such as Ohara and Sōgetsu were founded, and

れます。

　華　道　　花をアレンジする芸術で，花を花器に生け，床の間やその他の場所に飾ります。華道は生け花とも呼び，その起源は，僧侶が仏に花を供えた儀式にあり，16世紀頃，芸術として確立しました。華道の歴史が進むにつれ，多くの流派が生まれ，創立者はそれぞれ立花，投入れ，生花のようなさまざまなスタイルを唱道しました。華道の最も古い流派として知られる池坊は立花を専門にしています。投入れは，茶道が流行した16世紀後半に盛んになりました。伝統的な生花スタイルの華道においては，3本の主要な枝または茎が天・地・人を象徴してこの3つが自然の調和をなし，全宇宙を表わすように生けられます。1920年代には，小原流とか草月流のような新しい流派が起こり，現代的生け花を生み出して，生け花の芸術的側面をいっそう強調しました。新しい流派は，必ずしも3つの象徴概念にとらわれることなく，現代的な趣味に訴えるために，もっと自由な生け方を創り出しています。前衛派の中には，プラスチック，鉄，ガラスなど無生物材料さえ用いる派があります。葉や枝を人目を引く色に塗ることまでする派もあります。女性は適齢期になるとたいがい茶道とともに華道のけいこをします。

they brought forth "modern *ikebana*", which puts more emphasis on artistic aspects of flower arrangement. Newer schools do not always follow the three-symbol concept, but create a freer style of arrangement to appeal to modern taste. Some avant-garde schools even use 'lifeless' materials such as plastic, iron, and glass. Others go as far as to paint the leaves and branches in attractive colors. Many young girls in anticipation of marriage in a few years' time take lessons in flower arrangement as well as lessons in the tea-ceremony.

(O)

kagome-kagome the 'bird-in-the-cage' game. Japanese children have a variety of games accompanied by specific songs. These songs, handed down for generations, are simple and unsophisticated, often varying with the locality. One of the most popular outdoor games with songs is *kagome-kagome*. A number of children walk in a circle, singing: "Bird in the cage, when are you getting out ?" One child who plays the role of the bird in the cage squats down in the center, with eyes closed. To get out of the cage, the child must guess who happens to be directly in back when the other children finish the whole song. If the guess is right, the child in back becomes the bird. (T)

kaimyō also **hōmyō** a posthumous Buddhist name. Originally it is a Buddhist name given to devout believers who receive the commandments of Buddhism. More generally, however, it is a posthumous Buddhist name given to the soul of a newly departed person by the priest at a funeral. The name

かごめかごめ　　日本の幼児には，歌を歌いながらする遊戯がいろいろあります。このような歌は昔から伝承されてきたもので，単純にして素朴な歌です。歌を伴う遊戯のうちで最も人気があるのはかごめかごめです。「かごめかごめ，かごの中の鳥はいついつ出やる」と歌いながら，何人かの子供たちが輪になって歩きます。1人が鳥になって，輪のまんなかにしゃがみ，目を閉じます。かごから出るためには，他の子供たちが歌い終わったとき自分のまうしろにいるのはだれか言い当てなければなりません。うまく当たると，今度は当たった子供が鳥になります。

戒名・法名　　本来は仏教の戒律を受ける敬虔な信者に与えられる名前ですが，もっと一般的には，葬儀にあたって僧侶から死者の霊につけられる死後の仏教徒名です。死者が生前に呼ばれていた名前は俗名です。それぞれの宗派には独自の戒名のつけ方がありますが，一般的にはいくつかの漢字からできています。戒名は

by which the deceased was called in his lifetime is *zokumyō* (a secular name). Each sect has its own way of giving *kaimyō*, but as a rule it is made up of several Chinese characters (*kanji*). *Kaimyō* is written on a wooden memorial tablet (*ihai*) and sometimes engraved on the gravestone. (S)

kairo   a body warmer. Years ago when there was no effective way of heating a house in the cold season, people put a small body warmer inside a waist sash (*obi*) to keep themselves warm and comfortable. Solid fuel or benzine was used as the source of heat. Recently new throw-away chemical *kairo* pads have appeared. It is used by sufferers of backache or winter sports fans. (K)

kakushigei   a hidden talent. It refers to a person's special skill, one that is likely to be unknown to other people. It is often demonstrated upon request at various social gatherings. Such displays of hidden talent are meant to solidify a group relationship, as people get to know concealed aspects of each other. Among the wide repertoire of hidden talents are singing, dancing, poem recitation, instrument playing, magic, etc. (Y)

kamakura   a small round hut made of snow (similar to an igloo). It is popular in the snowy areas of northern Japan, where children enjoy making snow houses for fun. They take meals and play inside the *kamakura*, sometimes inviting parents and grandparents to join them. Sitting around a

位牌に書いたり墓石に刻んだりします。

懐　炉　　数十年前，冬に部屋全体を暖める暖房器具がなかった頃，人々は帯の間に小さな懐炉を入れて寒さをしのぎました。燃料には固形燃料やベンジンが使われました。最近では，使い捨てカイロが出回り，腰痛の人や，ウインタースポーツ愛好家の間で使われています。

隠し芸　　人知れず身につけている芸のことです。宴会などでしばしば他人からせがまれて，座興として披露する芸でもあります。お互いに隠しもつ芸を見せ合うことで仲間意識が一層深まると考えられています。隠し芸には，歌，踊り，詩の朗読，楽器の演奏，奇術などといろいろあります。

かまくら　　東北地方の豪雪地帯に見られる雪小屋で，子供たちが雪を固めて作ります。中で食事をしたり遊んだりします。両親や祖父母を呼んでは，火鉢を囲んで，家族や地方にまつわる昔話を聞いてくつろぎます。

hibachi (charcoal brazier), they enjoy listening to old tales of family and local traditions. (K)

kamidana   a household Shinto shrine. Traditional families have their own home shrines to worship Shinto deities every morning. The *kamidana* usually is set on a shelf built above a lintel in the living room. It typically houses talismans of gods to protect the family from evils. *Sake* (rice wine), food, and candles are offered for the deities enshrined there. (HO)

kami-shibai   a picture-story show. Many of the pastimes which used to be popular among Japanese children have almost disappeared from their world, owing to the spread of TV throughout the country. One of the most typical examples is *kami-shibai*, a show of large pictures that depict scenes in a story, accompanied by a showman's narration. Before *kami-shibai* began to lose its popularity some twenty years ago, such showmen were seen going by bicycle from street to street, with a box of picture-story cards on the carrier, and performing *kami-shibai* before a crowd of children on the roadside. Nowadays it barely survives in kindergartens. (T)

kamiza   an upper seat. When having a party, Japanese people are very concerned about where to sit, because they differentiate *kamiza* from *shimoza* (a lower seat). *Kamiza* is the place where a guest or the most important

神　棚　　伝統的な家庭には毎朝神道の神様に祈りをささげるために神棚というものがあります。神棚はふつう鴨居の上に作られた棚の上に置かれています。神棚には，悪霊から家族を守るために魔よけが置いてあります。そして，酒，食べ物，ろうそくなどが，そこに祭られている神様のために献納されます。

紙芝居　　カラーテレビの普及にともなって，かつて日本の子供たちに人気があった楽しみの多くが子供の世界からほとんど消えてしまいました。その典型的な例が紙芝居です。これは，物語の場面を描いた絵を見せながら，紙芝居のおじさんが話をして聞かせるものです。今から20年ほど前に紙芝居は人気を失い始めましが，それ以前は，紙芝居のおじさんが自転車の荷台に絵の入った箱を積んで，路地から路地へとまわって来て，道端で大勢の子供たちを前にして紙芝居を演じている姿をよく見かけました。今日では幼稚園などでやっと生き残っているにすぎません。

上　座　　上座・下座の区別があるため，日本人は宴会の折，たいそう座席に気を遣います。上座はお客さんかその会の座長が座る席で，下座は地位の低い者が座る席です。では，どうやって席の上下が決まるのでしょうか。上座は入口から最も遠い所にあ

person of a gathering is seated, while *shimoza* is the seat where the inferior sits. How does one know whether a seat is upper or lower ? The upper-most seat is usually located farthest from the entrance, whereas the bottom seat is generally closest to the door. In a Japanese-style room, the top seat is closest to the *tokonoma* (alcove in the room). The rest of the seats are also arranged in a way that reflects the strict hierarchical organization of the gathering. (HA)

kanchū-suiei a mid-winter swim. It is a traditional custom practiced by some Japanese-style swimming schools to demonstrate their heritage and to entertain the public. The custom has also been adopted by some youth groups to show off their ability to bear the cold. Usually this event takes place sometime between the beginning of January and the beginning of February, the coldest season called *kan* by the old lunar calendar. During the same period, many schools of ancient Japanese martial arts start their practice for the new year, known as *kangeiko*. This practice, which is usually held early in the morning every day for a couple of weeks, places emphasis on acquiring self-discipline. (Y)

kandō disinheritance or disownment. In the Edo period (1603-1867) when the family system was wholly patriarchical, the parent could disinherit a disobedient, prodigal, or delinquent son. The disinherited son was to be dressed in a kimono made of paper (*kamiko*) and turned out of the house. However, a mere declaration of disinheritance made by the parent had no legal force, unless it was registered

り，下座はドア寄りの所にあります。和室では，床の間のすぐそばに上座があります。そして，その他の席も，参会者の社会的上下関係をそのまま反映するように序列化されているのです。

寒中水泳　日本古来の泳法を伝える各流派の水練道場がそれぞれの伝統に基づく泳法などを庶民に披露する行事です。また，この習慣をまねて，元気のよい若者が寒さをものともせず初泳ぎをします。一般に1月の初めから2月にかけて，旧暦でいう寒中に行われます。この時期には，日本古来の武道の門下生が寒稽古と称して，新年最初の練習を開始します。これは早朝稽古となります。主眼は精神修養ならびに自己鍛練です。

勘　当　江戸時代には，家族制度は完全に家父長制で，父親は，言うことをきかなかったり，放蕩であったり，不良であったりする息子を勘当することができました。勘当された息子は，紙でできた着物（紙子）を着せられて家から追い出されました。しかし，ただ父親が勘当を宣告するだけでは法的効力がなく，町奉行所と呼ばれる役所に登録し，認可を受ける必要がありました。法的効力のない勘当は内緒勘当と呼ばれ，私的な勘当となりまし

at and sanctioned by the public office called *machi-bugyō-sho*. The unauthorized *kandō* was called *naisho-kandō* or private disinheritance, a milder punishment inflicted out of parental affection. *Kandō* generally involved a moral as well as an economic sanction, for the disinherited son was branded as a disgrace to the family and completely cut off from it. Today the word *kandō* usually means disownment rather than disinheritance. A well-meaning but misguided father, disapproving of his daughter's proposed mate, might threaten her to disown her unless she broke off the match. Disownment is, however, more often declared than practiced. (S)

kankeri a children's game known as "Kick the Can" in America and "Tin can Tommy" or "Kick can Bobby" in England. It is a variation of hide-and-seek. One player kicks a tin can out of a circle drawn around it. While the seeker is putting it back to the center of the circle and counting to one hundred, other players hide themselves. The seeker then goes looking for them, keeping an eye on the can. When he finds a person, he hurries back to the can and putting one foot on it calls out, "I spy so-and-so, one, two." Players named in this way become captives and stand around the can. If a player kicks the can before the seeker can call his name, the captives get free and the seeker must start all over again. (S)

kanreki the celebration of a person's 60th birthday. According to the Chinese zodiac system, it takes 60 years for a man to finish a cycle on this earth. People mark their 60th birthday with a great celebration, as the completion of this

た。これは親の愛情から加えられる穏やかな罰です。勘当はたいてい経済的な制裁ばかりでなく精神的な制裁も含みました。というのは，勘当された息子は一家の恥という烙印を押され，家族から完全に絶縁されたからです。今日では，勘当ということばは，たいていは相続権の廃除よりもむしろ親子の縁を切ることを意味します。善意からですが考え方の違った父親が，娘の花婿候補を是認せず，破談にしなければ勘当にすると脅すこともあるようです。しかし，勘当は宣言されるだけで実行されることは少ないようです。

缶けり　　アメリカでは「キック・ザ・キャン」，イギリスでは「ティン・キャン・トミー」とか「キック・キャン・ボビー」として知られている子供の遊びで，隠れんぼうの変種です。1人が，円の外へブリキ缶を蹴り出し，鬼がその缶を円の中心に戻して100まで数える間に，他の者は隠れます。鬼は缶に注意しながら探しに行きます。だれかを見つけたら，急いで缶まで戻り，その上に片足を乗せて，「だれだれ見つけた，イチ・ニー」と大声で言います。こうして見つけられた者は捕虜になり，缶の周囲に立ちます。鬼がその名前を言うより先にだれかが缶を蹴れば，捕虜は自由になり，鬼は最初からやり直さなければなりません。

還　暦　　古代中国の十二支によると，人間はこの地上で60年かけて一つのサイクルを通過するとされています。人々は60歳の誕生日を盛大に祝いますが，それはこの60年のサイクルの完了であると同時に新生の年でもあるからです。60歳の誕生日をむかえ

sixty-year cycle symbolizes "rebirth". People who have reached the age of sixty are presented with a red *chanchanko* (padded sleeveless *kimono* jacket for a baby), because they are supposed to become infants again then. Other specially celebrated birthdays are *koki* (70th), *kiju* (77th), *beiju* (88th), *sotsuju* (90th), and *hakuju* (99th).　(K)

kanten　Japanese gelatin. *Kanten* is a pure form of gelatin made from red seaweed called *tengusa*.　It is generally used for sweets and jams, though it has no nutritious value at all.　As a jellying agent, it is similar to conventional gelatin, but its texture is more delicate and yet does not so easily break.　*Kanten* is usually sold in dry, light sticks.　Before being cooked, it is torn into small pieces and soaked in water. Small cubes of cooked *kanten* jelly are an important part of *mitsumame*, a sweet, cold snack particularly nice in summer and popular with girls.　(T)

kappa　a water spirit. There are several different regional variations of the *kappa* figure.　Most commonly, it is described as having a dish full of water on the top of its head around which its hair hangs. Without this water, it is said to lose its supernatural power.　It also has webfeet and leaves behind footprints on the sands of a river bank similar to those of a big bird.　It is usually friendly to children.　As it is believed to be a good swimmer, a child who can swim well is called a *kappa*.　(K)

た老人には，赤いちゃんちゃんこが贈られます。もう一度赤ん坊に戻るということなのです。他の寿賀のお祝いに，70歳での古稀，77歳の喜寿，88歳の米寿，90歳の卒寿，そして99歳の白寿があります。

寒 天　　てんぐさという赤い海藻から作るゼラチンのような食品です。栄養価はまったくありませんが，菓子やジャムなどを作るのに使います。働きはゼラチンに似ていますが，きめはもっとなめらかで，しかも形がくずれにくいのです。寒天は普通は棒状の軽い乾物として売っています。調理する前にほぐし，水に浸します。できあがった寒天を四角に小さく切ったものは，特に夏期に女の子が好む冷たいおやつの蜜豆には欠かせません。

かっぱ　　かっぱの正体は地域によっていろいろにいわれています。最も一般的なものは，頭のてっぺんに水のたまった皿があり，その周囲に髪をたらしている，というものです。皿の中の水がないと超能力を失うといわれています。足には水かきがあり，土手に残す足跡は大きな鳥の足跡のようでもあるそうです。子供には親切です。泳ぎが大変に得意なことから，水泳の上手な子供のことをかっぱといいます。

karaoke　　singing to a cassette-recorded orchestra tune. Japanese people like singing.　Thanks to the development of audio technology, they can now enjoy singing like professional singers accompanied by an orchestra.　The gimmick is a cassette tape of a recorded orchestra and a tape recorder with a mixing device.　Almost all popular songs have *karaoke* tapes.　Music companies produce current ones as soon as they hit the pop chart.　Japanese people enjoy all kinds of music, but when it comes to *karaoke* singing, they tend to prefer *enka*, Japanese original songs of sad poems and melancholic melodies.　Many drinking establishments have very sophisticated *karaoke* singing facilities.　Some of them are so well equipped that customers are presented with a cassette tape or even a video tape of their performance immediately after they get off the stage.　(HO)

katori-senkō　　a mosquito-repellent incense.　In the shape of a flat spiral coil, it is burned on an ornamental porcelain dish in a room to keep mosquitoes away.　Made of pyrethrum, it has proved harmless to the human body and is still popular.　A new device (called *denki-katoriki*) which uses electricity to produce mosquito-repellent chemical vapor is also available now.　(K)

kaya　　an anti-mosquito net. Designed to prevent mosquitoes from disturbing sound sleep, it was widely used in houses across the country until quite recently. It was available in several different sizes, made for use in either a 3-, 4. 5-, 6-, or 8-*tatami*-mat room.　As it was made of hemp, it

カラオケ　　日本人は歌を歌うことが大好きです。音響技術の発達のおかげで，だれもがプロの歌手のようにオーケストラの伴奏で歌うことができます。仕掛けはオーケストラのカセットテープとミキシング装置のついたカセットコーダーです。ほとんどすべての歌はカラオケのテープになります。音楽会社はヒット曲がでるとすぐにカラオケ版を製作します。日本人はあらゆる種類の音楽を楽しみますが，カラオケとなるとまず演歌です。これは日本の歌謡曲で，悲しい詩と哀愁をさそうメロディーを特徴としています。お酒を飲む場所にはたいてい精巧なカラオケ装置があります。なかにはものすごい装置をもったところがあり，お客は歌い終わってステージをおりるやいなや，今歌った歌のカセットテープや，ビデオテープがプレゼントされます。

蚊取線香　　平たい渦巻状にしたもので，室内の蚊を除くため素焼の皿に置いて焚きます。除虫菊から作られ，人体に無害とされていることから現在でも使われています。電気蚊取器といわれている化学的な気体を発散させて蚊を退治する新製品もあります。

蚊　屋　　蚊に睡眠を邪魔されないようにと考案されたもので，つい最近までは全国の家庭で使われていました。3畳，4畳半，6畳，8畳用とあります。麻布で作られているところか

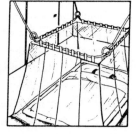

most likely served as an electric insulator as well. During an electrical storm, some people put one up for this purpose. Children were told to run into it to prevent the Devil of Thunder from taking away their navals. In olden days, a woman's effort in making a *kaya* was regarded as equal to a man's effort in building a house, and the finished object was held to be very precious. (K)

kaze   the wind.   The wind as well as the rain has been more than a mere natural phenomenon with the Japanese. There was an ancient belief that the wind was caused by comings and goings of invisible gods. With ancient people, therefore, all winds except ill and nasty winds were literally *kamikaze* (divine winds). The word for "a cold" is a homophone of *kaze* and written in two Chinese characters meaning "the evil wind". This fact suggests that ill winds were believed to be the work of the malevolent god. The god of the wind (*fūshin* or *fūjin*) was also worshiped. He was traditionally depicted in the figure of a fierce-looking demon sitting on a cloud with a large bag containing winds on his shoulder. Many poets of the medieval ages composed short poems (*waka*) about the wind, which was considered one of the chief charms of nature. Phrased as *ka-cho-fū-getsu*, flowers—especially cherry blossoms—, birds, the wind, and the moon were regarded as the most meaningful objects of artistic description. Many different names are given to the wind according to the direction and the season in which it blows—to cite a few examples, *kochi* (an east wind or a spring wind), *hae* (a south wind), and *kogarashi* (a cold wintry wind).

ら，絶縁体の役割もはたしたのでしょう。雷がなると，子供は，雷様におへそを取られたくないなら急いで蚊屋の中に入りなさいといわれたものでした。昔は，女性が蚊屋を作ることは男性が家を建てるのに匹敵するとまで考えられていました。そして，できあがった蚊屋は貴重品のあつかいを受けました。

　風　雨と同じように，日本人は風も単なる自然現象以上のものと考えてきました。古代には，風は目に見えない神々の往来によって起こるものと信じられていました。だから，古代人にとっては，悪い風以外はすべて文字どおり神風だったのです。風邪は風の同音異義語で，悪い風という意味の2字の漢字で書かれます。この事実は，悪い風は邪神によって起こされると信じられていたことを示しています。風の神（風神）に対する信仰もありました。風神は伝統的に，風の入った袋を肩にかついで雲の上に座った恐ろしい鬼の姿に描かれています。中世の多くの詩人は風についての和歌をよんでいますが，風は自然美の主要なものの一つと考えられていたのです。花鳥風月と称せられ，花（特に桜），鳥，風，月は，最も意義深い芸術的対象とみなされていました。風向きや季節によって，多くの異なった名前が風につけられています。少し例をあげると，東風（東から吹く風，または春風），南風（南から吹く風），木枯（冷たい冬の風）などです。これらの名前は古風で，口語ではほとんど使われませんが，日本人は今でも自然現象一般に対して敏感であり，風を比喩的に把握することにたけています。比喩的には，風は雰囲気，様子，様式，態度といった意味を持っています。この意味での風をあらわす漢字は，和風とか洋風という複合語の場合のようにフウと発音されます。

Most of these names sound archaic and are seldom used in colloquial speech, but the Japanese remain sensitive to natural phenomena and metaphorical conceptualization of the wind. Figuratively, *kaze* means an air, a look, a style, or a manner. The *kanji* (Chinese characters) for *kaze* in this sense is usually pronounced *fū* as in the compounds *wafū* (Japanese style) and *yōfū* (Western style). (S)

Keirō-no-hi　Respect-for-the-Aged Day. It falls on September 15. In the middle of the 1960s, there was much criticism in the U. S. A. and Europe of Japan's exports allegedly based on cheap labor policies. Part of the Japanese Government's response to this was to increase the number of national holidays. This holiday is one of those established in this way. On this day, young people wish the elderly a long life and express gratitude for all they have done for them. Various cultural and sports events are held for the entertainment of senior citizens. Some cities and municipalities present them with a cash bonus of about five thousand yen. (K)

Kenkoku-kinenbi　National Foundation Day. In prewar times February 11 was the day when people celebrated the birth of the country. According to Japanese legend, it was the day when the First Emperor Jinmu started the nation of the rising sun. Mythology mixed with history, the celebration of this day was a symbolic representation of the emperor system (tennoism) of Japan. As Japanese imperialism was relinquished with the advent of the post-war constitution, this

132

敬老の日　　9月15日にあたります。1960年代の中ごろ，欧米では，日本のいわゆる低賃金労働政策による輸出品に対して激しい非難がありました。これに対して日本政府のとった策の一つは，国民の祝日を増やすことでした。敬老の日もこうしてできたものの一つで，この日に若者はお年寄の長寿を祈り，今までの努力に対して感謝の意を表わします。各地で文化的行事や運動会が開かれ，お年寄をもてなします。長寿のお祝いとして5千円ほどの現金を贈呈する市町村もあります。

建国記念日　　戦前の日本では，2月11日に建国の祝いを行っていました。言い伝えでは，この日に，わが国初代の神武天皇が即位し，日の昇る国すなわち日本国を始めたそうです。歴史と神話があいまって，この日は，まさに日本の天皇制を象徴する祝日となったのでした。第2次大戦後，帝国主義の崩壊と同時に，この祝日も廃止されました。しかし，1966年に，政府は建国記念日という名のもとにこの日を復活しました。政府のこの決定には各方面で強い反対がありました。日本が再び昔の帝国主義・軍国主

celebration was abolished. In 1966, however, the Japanese Government decided to establish this date again as National Foundation Day. There was strong opposition in some quarters against this decision, as there was a fear that it might trigger Japan's return to the old imperialism and militarism. It seems that many people are still wondering whether this is the right date to celebrate their national foundation. (K)

kenkyo   humility or modesty. *Kenkyo* is one of the most important concepts of virtue in Japan. In Japanese society, people are expected to be humble and modest regardless of their social position. They are supposed to modulate the display of their ability, talent, knowledge, or wealth in an appropriate manner. Self-assertiveness, aggressiveness, and ambitiousness are all more or less discouraged, and consideration for others encouraged. Even a person who is responsible for a certain job is not supposed to have his own way, but to create consensus in a harmonious way. This attitude seems to come from the assumption that everybody's honor is as good as anybody else's. In other words, everyone has a right to have his honor respected. For example, if an elderly leader lacks effective leadership, others are expected not to force him out, as that could disgrace his honor. To protect his honor, they should help him go out with honor. This code of behavior is extremely important for any group leader in Japanese society. (K)

kigan   a prayer. People sometimes visit shrines and temples to offer prayers. Some people pray for religious or

義に戻るのではないかと懸念されたからです。多くの人々は今でも，この日が建国を祝う日として適当かどうか自問しているのです。

　　謙　虚　　日本の社会で最も重要な美徳の一つです。日本では，人々は社会的な地位に関係なく謙虚であるべきだとされています。能力，素質，知識，富などを表に出すときには控え目にすることが賢明とされています。自己主張をし，進取の気象を持ち，大志を抱くことは，どちらかというと歓迎されず，他人に対して思いやりを持つことの方が奨励されます。ある仕事の責任者でさえも，まったく自由に行動するのではなく，常に全員の調和に基づいて行動することが望まれます。この態度は，人間はみな名誉というものを持っているので，1人1人の自尊心を大切にしたいという考えに基づいているようです。例えば，もしある年輩者に指導者としての能力が欠けているとしたら，まわりで彼をやめさせるようなことをしてはなりません。そんなことをすれば彼の名誉を傷つけることになるのです。彼を傷つけないためには，彼が自分から名誉をもってやめることができるように，いろいろと手はずをととのえてあげるのです。このような配慮は，日本社会の指導者にとってきわめて重要なことなのです。

　　祈　願　　人々は時に祈りをささげるために神社やお寺を訪れます。ある人々は宗教的，精神的な理由により祈りますが多くの

spiritual reasons. But more people pray simply for secular and materialistic purposes. When days of entrance examinations are nearing, for example, many students go to holy places specially dedicated to gods of wisdom or learning and pray for their assistance. People also pray to a god for the fulfilment of their wishes with a vow to abstain from one of their pleasures (such as drinking or smoking). When they have their prayer answered, they visit the god's place for thanksgiving and are liberated from the vow. (HO)

kikkyō fortune and misfortune. There are many ways of fortune telling in Japan. One of the most popular is a six-day divination (*rokuyō* or *rokki*) marked on the calender designed for ordinary people. Each day is noted with one of the six prophecies adopted from China. They are:

Senshō (early win)   Lucky in the morning but unlucky in the afternoon.

Tomobiki (friend trailing)   Lucky in the morning and evening but unlucky at noon.

Senpu (early losing)   Slowdown. Unlucky in the morning, but lucky in the afternoon.

Butsumetsu (Buddha's death or all things' nullification)   Most unlucky. Maximum precaution required.

Taian (great safety)   Very lucky. All shall go well.

Shakkō (red mouth)   Very unlucky. A little better at noon.

Many people usually like to hold wedding ceremonies on *Taian* days and rarely on *Butsumetsu* days. They also shy away from conducting funeral services on *Tomobiki* days. (HO)

人々は，世俗的，物質的な目的のために祈ります。例えば，入学試験の日が近づいてくると，多くの学生は，特に知恵や学問の神様がまつられている神聖な場所に行き，助力をあおぎます。また，ある人は，お酒やたばこのような楽しみの一つを断って，自分の願いが達成されることを神に祈ります。願いがかなうと，神様のところへお礼に訪れ，禁を解くのです。

吉　凶　　日本にはたくさんの占い術があります。最も一般的なものの一つは六曜（六輝）で，普通のカレンダーにのっています。それぞれの日に次の6つの吉凶のどれかが記入されています。これらは中国から取り入れたものです。

先勝……朝良し，午後悪し

友引……朝・夕良し，午後悪し

先負……平静に，朝悪し，午後良し

仏滅……最悪，最大の用心が必要

大安……最良，万事良し

赤口……悪し，午後少し良し

多くの人々は，たいてい大安の日に結婚式を行い，仏滅の日にはほとんどしません。また，友引の日に葬式を行うことをためらいます。

kiku-ningyō   a "chrysanthemum" doll. At chrysanthemum festivals held on September 9 across the country, dolls made of fresh chrysanthemums in a wide variety of colors are displayed.   Bunches of chrysanthemum flowers and leaves are shaped into life-size dolls and clothes and then elegantly arranged to portray famous characters in dramas and folk stories. (K)

Kimigayo   the Japanese national anthem .   The poem which starts with "Kimigayo-wa..." expresses hope for the longevity of the reign of the current emperor.   Originally found in *Kokinshū* (*Collection of Ancient and Contemporary Poetry*), compiled in the early tenth century, this poem has been handed down to the modern age.   In 1869, an English musician composed the melody, which was later slightly rearranged by a Japanese musician of the Ministry of the Imperial Household.   In 1893, the Ministry of Education started to use this music as the national anthem to be played for national celebration.   Now there are various criticisms against the imperial institution, especially with regard to its role in the expansion of militarism during World War II.   Some teachers, for example, are against playing *Kimigayo* on school grounds.   Generally speaking, however, this anthem is still popular and arouses feelings of solemnity in the Japanese heart. (K)

kimodameshi   a courage-testing ritual for children.   Adults hold some ritualistic competitions to develop children's courage or "guts".   For example, they send them along a dark

菊人形　9月9日に各地で開かれる菊祭では，いろいろな色の菊で作られた菊人形が展示されます。菊の花や葉で，あでやかな等身大の人形や衣装を作ります。たいていは，民話や劇の主人公を形どったものです。

君が代　日本の国歌で，「君が代は……」で始まる歌詞は，天皇の治世が長く続きますようにという願いをうたったものです。もともとは，10世紀初頭に編纂された『古今集』にある和歌です。1869年に，英国の音楽家によってメロディーが作られ，後に宮内省の楽官によって少し手直しされました。1893年には文部省が，祝祭日の儀式用唱歌として公布しました。今日，天皇制に対してさまざまな批判があります。特に，第2次大戦において軍国主義を伸長させた責任に対しては，厳しいものがあります。このようなことから，学校で『君が代』を演奏することに反対する先生もいます。しかし，一般的にいえば，この国歌は依然として人々の心に訴えるものを持っています。これを聞くと，たいがいの日本人は厳粛な気持ちになるものです。

肝だめし　子供たちに度胸をうえつけるために大人が行う，ある種の儀式的な意味合いを持つ競技です。例えば，夕方の薄暗い山道を歩かせたり，夜中に墓地を通る道を歩かせたりします。

mountain trail in the evening or on a designated route through a graveyard at night. In high schools or colleges, senior students hold initiation ceremonies to test the courage of freshmen by ordering them to carry out various frightening tasks. (K)

kimono　Japanese clothes. *Kimono* in its broadest sense refers to all types of clothing, but most commonly to *wafuku* (Japanese clothes), as opposed to *yōfuku* (Western clothes). In spite of various changes in style, the *kimono* has basically remained unchanged for centuries. As it is not practical for modern life, Japanese people today do not wear it in their daily lives but only for very special occasions such as weddings and funerals. Wearing a *kimono* is not easy. Unlike Western clothes, which are made so as to fit the wearers, a *kimono* must be adjusted according to the manner in which it will be worn. It requires some specific undergarments, including *naga-juban* (a full-length undergarment) shaped like the *kimono* itself. The *kimono* and its undergarments are all fastened with a number of cords and sashes wound around the waist. *Obi* (an outer sash), usually about a foot wide, with gorgeous embroidery, is tightly wound and tied on the back to serve as a decorative finish. Many other accessories are indispensable to the formal *kimono*. Many women accustomed only to Western clothes cannot put on a *kimono* by themselves, and attend a *kimono* school to learn how to wear it properly. Women's formal *kimono* for festive occasions, made of high quality silk fabrics with exquisite patterns and colors, are accepted as one of the most beautiful

高校や大学では，上級生が新入生の歓迎会で度胸試しに恐ろしい場所を歩かせることがあります。

　着　物　　最も広い意味ではあらゆるタイプの衣類を指しますが，普通は洋服に対して和服を意味します。着物はこれまでスタイルにいろいろな変化がありましたが，基本的には何百年もずっと同じです。現代生活においては実用的でないため，ふだん着物を着る人はあまりなく，結婚式とか葬式など特別の機会にしか着ません。着物の着方は簡単ではありません。洋服は着る人の体型に合うよう作られますが，着物は着付け方によって体に合わせていかなければなりません。上に着る着物と同じような形の長じゅばんなど着物専用の下着を必要とします。着物と下着はすべて，何本ものひもや帯でウエストのまわりを締めて固定します。女帯は通常1フィート位の幅で，豪華な刺繍がほどこしてあります。しっかりと締め，背中で結び，結び目が装飾の役をはたします。他にもいろいろなアクセサリーをつけます。洋服しか着なれていない女性が多くて，1人で着物を着ることができず，着付け教室へ通って正しい着方を習ったりします。女性の正装の着物は，模様や色彩が見事な高級絹織物で仕立てられ，世界でも最も美しく優雅な民族衣装に数えられています。着物は既婚女性と未婚女性とでは，色や模様，袖の長さにはっきりとした区別があります。男性の正装は着物，羽織，袴からなり，すべて地味な色のものです。

　和服がどれも複雑で着付けが難しいというわけではありません。気楽に着られるものもいろいろあります。例えば，ゆかたは夏に愛用され，丹前は寒い季節には快適です。半てんとはっぴ

and elegant national costumes in the world. There is a clear distinction in color, design, and the sleeve-length between married and unmarried women's *kimono*. Men's most formal outfit consists of *kimono*, *haori* (a short coat), and *hakama* (a long, divided skirt), all of dark, somber colors. Not all Japanese clothes are so complicated and difficult to wear. There are many casual types such as *yukata* (a light, cotton *kimono*) popular in summer and *tanzen* (a padded, large-size *kimono*) comfortable in cold weather. *Hanten* and *happi* are both overcoats similar to *haori* in shape, but used for working wear. (T)

kitsune a fox. When the Japanese think of a fox, two distinct images come to mind. One is a cunning, deceitful, goblin-like creature, and the other is a benevolent guardian. Japanese folklore is full of stories about foxes. The fox is commonly believed to have the ability to bewitch or possess a person. In this connection, it is often contrasted with a racoon dog (*tanuki*) which is also believed to be capable of bewitching or possessing a person, but in a rather stupid and humorous way. The *kitsune* is, unlike the *tanuki*, worshiped as a messenger of the gods of the mountains and rice-fields, and even as the very god of harvest. Therefore, stone statues of foxes are seen squatting in pairs on the grounds of *Inari* (a harvest god) shrines throughout the country. Customarily, the offering to the fox spirit is *aburage* (thin pieces of fried bean curd). (T)

kiza a cultural deviation that disturbs the present

は，共に形が羽織に似ていますが，働き着です。

狐　日本人が狐に対して抱いているイメージには，2つのまったく違ったものがあります。その一つは，ずる賢く，人をだまし，悪さをする動物であり，もう一つは，情深い守護者です。日本の民話には狐にまつわる話がたくさんあります。狐は人をだましたり，とりついたりすると広く信じられています。この点に関しては，狐はよく狸と対比されます。狸も人をまどわしたり，とりついたりしますが，同時に間が抜けていて，滑稽な動物とされています。このようなイメージとは別に，狐は山の神や田の神の使者として，また収穫の神そのものとしてあがめられます。全国各地の稲荷神社の境内には，座った狐の石像が対で見られます。狐には油揚を供える風習があります。

き ざ　世間一般の文化的行動規範からはずれたある種の型

mind-set. Particular types of deviations from the prevalent cultural norm of behavior sometimes irritate certain kinds of people and are called *kiza* (mind-disturbing). It is particularly so when an act of deviation is perceived as the outcome of an effort to imitate patterns of another culture that is seen as "higher" than that of the community. This evaluation seems to apply most conspicuously to persons who are perceived to be obsequiously following Western patterns of behavior. Thus, persons who profusely praise American ways of life, persons who frequently use English words while speaking Japanese, or persons who adopt typically Western gestures (who shrug their shoulders or wink) are apt to be branded as *kiza* and sanctioned in various ways. (HO)

kodakara   a treasure of children. As an eighth-century Japanese poet says, there is no treasure more precious than children. According to Japanese folk beliefs, children are Heaven's gifts, and those under seven years of age deserve special attention. These beliefs have had a deep influence on child-rearing, resulting in close contact between mother and child. The concept of *kodakara* is also closely related to the old Japanese family system which was based on the continuity of each family by its direct descendants. This family system was legally abolished over thirty years ago, but the underlying idea of the family and therefore the importance attached to a child's birth still prevail throughout the country. (T)

kōden   an obituary gift. It is presented by relatives and acquaintances at a funeral to the family of the deceased.

は時に人々をいらだたせ、きざ（気に障ること）と呼ばれます。逸脱行為が、そのグループの文化よりも高いと思われる文化の型を模倣した結果とみなされるときに、特にそうなります。なかでも、西洋のものまねをしているとみなされる人がきざといわれるようです。だから、アメリカの生活様式をやたらにほめる人、日本語の中にひんぱんに英語を入れる人、西洋風のジェスチャー（肩をすくめたりウィンクしたり）をする人などは、きざという烙印をおされ、いろいろな方法で制裁を受けます。

　　子　宝　　8世紀の日本の歌人がよんでいるように、子供にまさる宝はありません。日本の民間信仰によると、子供は天からの授かりもので、7歳以下の子供は特別の保護を受けるべきものとなっています。この考え方は育児に深い影響を及ぼし、母と子の強い結びつきを生みました。子宝の概念はまた、直系子孫による家の継承を基盤とする日本の古い家族制度と密接なつながりがあります。この家族制度は30年以上も前に法的に廃止されました。しかし、その根底にある考え方と、その結果として子供の誕生が重要視される傾向は、今なお全国的に残っています。

　　香　典　　昔は米や麦などの食糧も香典として贈られましたが、今日では一般に金銭で、喪に服した家族の経済的負担を軽く

In ancient times, foods such as rice and wheat were presented as an obituary gift. Today *kōden* is generally a monetary offering, which is originally intended as a contribution to lightening the financial burden of the family in mourning. *Kōden* is put in an envelope tied with black and white strings used exclusively for mournful occasions. When people attend a funeral service, it is considered to be a very important social courtesy to make this monetary offering. The names of the donors and their donations are taken notes of so that courtesy may be returned on a future occasion. (S)

Kodomo-no-hi Children's Day. It falls on May 5, and is one of the most popularly celebrated national holidays. Although it is called Children's Day, it is actually celebrated as the Boys' Festival. (The Girls' Festival is March 3, which is called *hinamatsuri* or the Doll Festival.) It is also a seasonal festival called *tango-no-sekku* (Iris Festival), because May 5 marks the beginning of summer on the old lunar calendar. To drive away bad spirits and celebrate the future of their sons, families hoist *koinobori* (cloth coustructed carp streamers) from balconies and flagpoles, and indoors display *gogatsu-ningyō* (*samurai* dolls and their armaments) on layered ledges. Children take *shōbuyu* (a bath with a bunch of floating iris leaves), and eat *kashiwa-mochi* (a rice cake wrapped in an oak leaf) and *chimaki* (a dumpling wrapped in bamboo leaves). Carp, *samurai*, irises, oak trees, and bamboos all symbolize strength. Parents prepare these decorations and foods with the earnest wish that their children may grow up to be healthy and robust. (K)

146

するためという意図によるものだったのです。香典は，哀悼の意を表わす専用の白黒の紐で結んだ封筒に入れます。葬儀に参列したときに香典を贈るのは重要な社会的儀礼と考えられています。喪家では，返礼をするときに備えて，贈り主の氏名と金額を記帳します。

子供の日 　5月5日にあたり，最も楽しい国民の祝日の一つです。子供の日とは呼ばれるものの，厳密には男の子のお祭りです（女の子のお祭りは3月3日で，ひな祭りと呼ばれます）。この日は旧暦によれば夏の始まりであることから，端午の節句とも呼ばれます。悪霊を追い払い，子供の未来を祝福するために，戸外には空高く鯉のぼりを掲げ，室内には棚に五月人形を飾るのです。子供は，菖蒲湯につかり，柏餅やちまきを食べます。鯉，武者人形，菖蒲，柏の木，そして竹などはすべて，力強さを象徴しています。両親は，子供の健康と成長を願いつつ，これらの飾りや食べ物を用意するのです。

kōhaku red and white. This color contrast symbol-izes the simple beauty such as that of the red and white blossoms of the Japanese plum trees. A red-and-white-striped curtain is used on such an auspicious occasion as a commence-ment ceremony. A pair of red and white *manjū* (bean-jam buns) are presented to participants. In accordance with the historical fact that between 1180 and 1185 the Genji clan fought under white flags against the Heike clan under red flags, opposing teams are often divided into the reds and the whites. For example, the *Kōhaku* Singing Contest is an annual compe-tition between male and female popular singers. One of the most popular events in Japan, it is held on New Year's Eve and is broadcast by NHK (Japan Broadcasting Corporation). (K)

koi a carp. The *koi* is a fresh-water fish living in rivers, ponds, and lakes. It is raised to be eaten or kept as an ornamental fish. *Arai* (raw slices washed in cold water) in summer and *namasu* (raw slices seasoned in vinegar) in winter are popular delicacies. The *koi* is also known as a symbol of success, strength, courage, and perseverance in attaining high aims, because it is believed to be the only fish that can swim up rapids supposedly through its determination to overcome any obstacle. It is thus customarily served on auspicious occa-sions. *Koinobori* (carp streamers) for Children's Day on May 5 reflect parents' wishes for boys to grow up as strong as the *koi*. (Y)

kokeshi a limbless doll. It is a simple wooden doll,

紅　白　　この対照的な色合いは，日本の梅の花に見られる簡素な美しさを象徴しています。卒業式のようなめでたい行事には，紅白の縦縞の入った幕が張られ，参加者には紅白饅頭が配られます。1180年から1185年に及んだ歴史的にも有名な源平合戦では，源氏側が白旗，平家側が赤旗の下で戦ったことから，紅白に分かれた対抗試合が現在でもよく行われます。例えば，毎年大晦日の晩にNHKが放映する紅白対抗歌合戦では，男女の有名歌手がそれぞれ紅白に分かれて勝負を競い，年末の最も人気のある行事の一つとされています。

鯉　　川，池，沼などに住む淡水魚で，食用と観賞用とがあります。夏はあらい，冬はなますで食べるのが代表的調理法です。鯉は，大きな目的を成し遂げる強さと勇気と忍耐力とを備え持つ魚としても知られています。これは，鯉だけが激流をさかのぼり，あらゆる障害を克服できる唯一の魚であると信じられていることに由来します。したがって鯉は祝い料理に使われます。また，5月5日の子供の日には，この故事にあやかり，男児のために鯉のぼりを立てる習慣があります。

こけし　　素朴な木製の人形で，丸い顔と円筒形の胴でできて

made up of a wheel-turned body and a ball-shaped head. It usually represents a female figure, with the eyes, eyebrows, nose, mouth, and hair painted on the head, and the body decorated with floral or other simple but bright designs. It has neither arms nor legs. Having originated in northern Japan, *kokeshi* dolls are now popular throughout the country. Each locality has its own style of carving and painting them. They are usually sold at gift shops as souvenirs for tourists. The value of *kokeshi* is said to be decided by how delicately the face is painted. （Y）

konjō　　fighting spirit or "guts". As it suggests strong willpower and determination, this word has been highly prized by sportsmen and businessmen, and has thus often been in their mottoes. Indeed, their invincible military-like spirit is often associated with *konjō*, i. e. in the sense that it is a source of great stamina, tenacity, or perserverance. In this respect, *konjō* is a key word in understanding Japanese stoicism, which has been practiced by the male population since feudal times. Even today, whether a man has *konjō* or not is significant in evaluating his character. A man who possesses *konjō* is highly praised, for he would stop at nothing in the course of duty, willingly subjecting himself to unbearable circumstances in the process. A man who lacks *konjō*, however, is regarded as contemptible and cowardly, because in difficult situations, he would give up easily. Thus, *konjō* is a symbol of masculine spirit. （HA）

konnyaku　　devil's tongue jelly. *Konnyaku* is a jelly-

います。一般に，女性の姿をかたどっていて，顔には，目，眉，鼻，口，そして髪が描かれ，胴体には花柄や明るい色の模様が描かれています。こけしには手足がありません。日本の東北地方が発祥地とされていますが，現在では全国にいろいろな形のものがあり，地方色を出しています。こけしは一般に旅行者のみやげ物として，みやげ物売場で売られています。こけしの価格は顔の描き方によって決まるとされています。

　根　性　　このことばは強靭な意志力と決断力を連想させるので，スポーツ選手やビジネスマンのあいことばになっています。たしかに彼らの不屈な戦闘心は，このことばと結びついて考えられています。根性は持久力を暗示します。この点で根性は，封建時代以来男性が実践してきた日本的禁欲主義を理解する上で重要なことばといえましょう。現在でも，根性があるかないかは，人物評価の上で重要になっています。根性のある男は，いったん仕事となればどんな逆境にもひるまず，期待された職責を貫徹します。その反対に，根性のない男は，困難なことに出会うとすぐに降参してしまうので，卑劣な臆病者であると見下げられます。こうしてみると，根性は，いかにも男の魂を象徴しているといえましょう。

　こんにゃく　　こんにゃくいもの粉で作った食品です。栄養価

like food made from flour of devil's tongue, a kind of yam. Though it has little or no nutritive qualities, nor any taste of its own, it is favored by many Japanese because of its appetite-stimulating texture, and is used in a variety of dishes. There are two kinds in color : black and white. There are also two kinds in form : rectangular and noodle-like. The black and rectangular one is one of the most common ingrendients in *oden* (Japanese hotchpotch), which is popular in winter. The white noodle-like one, called *ito-konnyaku* or *shirataki*, is indispensable to *sukiyaki* (a pot dish of meat and vegetables). (T)

kotatsu a leg warmer with a coverlet. *Kotatsu* is a device used in winter to keep the legs and feet warm. Traditionally a fire was made with charcoal or briquettes and put in a fireproof sunken area, over which was set up a latticed wooden frame with a thick quilt covering it. In recent decades, however, a special electric warmer usually attached to a table-like, portable frame is more popular because of its cleanliness and convenience. The *kotatsu* is inferior to central heating system, or even to a stove, in that it does not warm the upper part of the body or the room itself. However, it is more energy-saving, and brings about a feeling of closeness among the people sitting together with their legs in it, sharing a coverlet large enough for all of them. The scene in which all the family gather around the *kotatsu* to talk over a cup of tea is indeed a typical one of a happy home in Japan. (T)

はほとんどなく、それ自体の味もありません。しかし、食欲を促す歯ざわりがあって、多くの日本人が好物とし、いろいろな料理に使います。色は黒白の2種類があります。形も長方形とうどん状の2種類があります。長方形のこんにゃくは、冬場に好まれるおでん料理の中で最も人気のある材料です。うどん状のものは、糸こんにゃくとしらたきと呼ばれ、すきやきには欠かせない材料です。

こたつ　冬に足を暖めるよう工夫されたものです。伝統的なやり方では、炭や練炭をおこし、床に四角の穴を掘って不燃性にした場所に置きます。その上に格子作りの木枠をのせ、こたつ布団ですっぽりくるみます。しかしここ二、三十年は、持ち運び可能なテーブル状の枠に電気暖房器を取り

付けた電気こたつが、清潔さと簡便さのために広く用いられています。こたつでは上半身や部屋そのものが暖まることはなく、その点では集中暖房装置やストーブに劣ります。しかし、こたつはエネルギー消費が少なく、しかも皆いっしょに寄り集まって一つのこたつに足を入れ、1枚の大きな布団を共用することができるので、親密感が生まれます。家族全員がこたつを囲んで座り、お茶を飲みながら話をしている場面は、日本の典型的な一家だんらんの風景です。

kuiawase   the ill effect of foods eaten together. It used to be a popular belief that certain kinds of food, when eaten together, had an ill effect because of a poisonous substance produced by chemical reaction during digestion. The combination of eels and pickled plums (*umeboshi*), for instance, was believed to cause a fatal illness. That of potatoes and mint was another example. Clams taken together with mushrooms were said to cause a stomach-ache. The list of foods not to be eaten in combination goes on and on. *Kuiawase* was also believed to cause fever, erruption, nausea, and diarrhoea. Scientific research has proved, however, that there is little ground for the *kuiawase* theory, demonstrating that the ill effects are produced in fact by causes other than combinations themselves. Nevertheless, some people still hold the belief and avoid eating certain foods in combination. (S)

kujira   a whale. The hunting of whales has a long history in Japan. The word *kujira* appears even in *Kojiki* (*The Record of Ancient Matters*) compiled in 712. For Japanese people living in a land surrounded by the water, marine products are indispensable food resources, and in particular, whale meat is an important source of animal protein. Whales are used in a variety of ways in Japan : whale oil for lubricants, detergents, and cosmetics ; the teeth, baleen, and bones for various artifacts ; and the tendons for the gut of tennis rackets. (Y)

kyōdaibun   a sworn brother. It refers to a brotherly

154

食合せ ある種の食物はいっしょに食べると，化学反応で胃の中に生じる毒物のために，体に悪い影響を及ぼすと，かつて一般に信じられていました。例えば，鰻と梅干の組合せは致命的な病気を起こすと信じられていました。じゃがいもとハッカというのもあります。はまぐりと茸をいっしょに食べると腹痛を起こすともいわれていました。このような食合せの例は数多くあります。食合せは，発熱や吹出物を起こしたり，吐き気や下痢の原因となったりするとも考えられていました。しかし，科学的調査によって，食合せ説はほとんど根拠がないこと，悪い作用は実際には食物の組合せ以外の原因によるものであることが証明されています。しかし，なかにはまだこの説を信じて，危険な組合せであるとされていた食物を食べるのを避けている人々がいます。

鯨 日本における捕鯨の歴史は古く，『古事記』（712年）にも鯨の文字が記されています。四方を海に囲まれている日本人にとり，水産物は欠かすことのできない食料であり，とくに鯨肉は重要な動物性蛋白源です。日本では鯨は多方面に利用されています。例えば，鯨油は工業用油や洗剤，そして化粧品の原料に，歯，骨，ひげなどは工芸用に，そして筋はテニスラケットのガットに，というぐあいです。

兄弟分 血縁関係のない者どうしが結ぶ兄弟関係のことで

relationship, formed between persons who have no blood connection.   One such relationship exists among craftsmen, such as carpenters, blacksmiths, plasterers, scaffolding men, and other professionals of traditional artisanship.   When an apprentice becomes adequately skillful after his period of hard training, he is offered a cup of *sake* (rice wine) by an older colleague.   They pledge loyalty and enter into a new relationship of mutual understanding and obligation, thus being bound to each other by a sense of brotherhood.   Gamblers and gangsters also develop this relationship.   (Y)

ma　　the effective use of time and space intervals.   This concept often refers to the aesthetic sense of an artistically placed interval in time or space.   This sense originally came from traditional music and subsequently spread to various other arts.   In traditional music, *ma* signifies the effective use of intervals between notes or chords. Musicians avoid adhering to an exact rhythm or beat, thus producing variations in accordance with the performers and the situation.   Furthermore, a pause is often inserted in traditional singing and dancing, especially when accompanied by such instruments as the *koto* (a horizontal harp with 13 strings) and *shamisen*(a three-stringed banjo-like instrument).   In *nō* music, in particular, *ma* is highly valued and applies to several different aspects : (1) the rhythm itself, (2) a good/bad sense of rhythm, (3) a beat, (4) rest, (5) an interval between two neighboring phrases of a song.   Why then is this aesthetic notion important to the Japanese mind ?   The best answer is given by the Zen ideal of nothingness and imcompleteness : things

156

す。このような関係は，大工，鍛冶屋，左官，鳶職その他の職人の間にみられます。弟子がある期間の修業を終えて一人前になると，先輩から杯をもらい，お互いに忠誠を誓って，兄弟分という絆で結ばれるのです。また，賭博師ややくざの間でもこの現象がみられます。

間（ま）　間とは，時間・空間を巧妙に操作する間隔という美的感覚の問題です。この感覚は，伝統音楽に端を発し，後に他の諸芸術に転用されました。伝統音楽では，間とは音と音との間の効果的なつなぎをさします。演奏者はリズムや拍子にぴったりと乗ることを嫌いますので，奏者とか状況によっていろいろなバリエーションが生じることになります。休みを入れたり伸ばしたりすることは，琴や三味線の伴奏する唄や踊りの場合，ごく普通に行われていることです。特に能楽では，間は大いに尊重されていて，さまざまな側面で使われています。すなわち，(1)リズムそのもの，(2)リズム感の良し悪し，(3)拍，(4)休拍，(5)謡の句と句の間の休拍，などがそれです。それでは，いったいなぜこのような美的観念が日本人にとって重要なのでしょうか。この問いに対しては，無と不足を良しとする禅の理想を持ち出して答えるのが一番的確でしょう。貴いものは，口に出すことも，演じられることもないのです。だから，音と音の間の休拍には特別な意味が加わるのです。禅の老師は，自然が論理的展開をするとは考えません。宇宙は不合理のものと考えます。そして，時間と空間の非対称的な組合せという日本芸術の特質を賞賛するのです。今日，多くの

157

precious are unsaid and unperformed. Thus, a rest between sounds conveys its own special significance. Zen philosophers do not accept a logical sequence of nature, for they see the universe as irrational. They praise asymmetrical arrangements of time and space, such qualities that constitute the essence of Japanese arts. Many Japanese today fail to realize that their value system is strongly influenced by Zen Buddhism. However, their appreciation of arts is still oriented toward the recognition of *ma*, the effective use of time and space intervals. (HA)

machiai   a high-class hotel-cum-restaurant. In the seventeenth and eighteenth centuries, *machiai* (short for *machiai-jaya*) was a place where people—especially wealthy merchants—held meetings, received guests, and had *geisha* sprees. In the mid-nineteenth century, they increased in number and flourished. Particularly, political wirepullers and businessmen with political affiliations met influential statesmen at the *machiai* by appointment, and, while entertaining them, made behind-the-scenes political dealings (*machiai-seiji*). Today no restaurant professes itself to be a *machiai*, but some high-class Japanese restaurants do serve as such.   It also refers to a place where participants of a tea party arriving before the appointed hour wait for other participants and make preparations for attending the tea ceremony. It is usually a portico or a room close to the tea-ceremony room. (S)

maiko   a dancing girl. Among the innumerable attractions of the ancient city of Kyoto is *maiko* dressed in her characteristic costume : a colorful, long-sleeved *kimono*, a

日本人は，自分の価値観が禅の強い影響下にあることに気づいていません。しかし，日本人は芸術を観賞するにあたって，今なお間を重視しているのです。

待　合　　17～18世紀には待合（待合茶屋の短縮形）は，特に富豪の商人たちが寄合いを持ったり客を接待したり芸者遊びをしたりする場所でした。19世紀中頃にはその数も増え，待合は大いに繁盛しました。特に，政界の黒幕や政商が有力な政治家と待合で会合し，接待をしながら，政治的な裏取引き（待合政治）を行ったものです。今日では，待合であると公言する料理屋はありませんが，高級な料亭にはそのような役割をはたしているところもあります。待合とはまた，茶会のときに，時間前に到着した人が他の参加者を待ったり茶席に出る用意をしたりする場所のことでもあります。たいていは，玄関先かまたは茶室に近い部屋が待合となります。

舞　子　　古都京都の数多い魅力の一つに舞子があります。舞子は，華やかな色彩と長い袂の着物，だらりの帯，ぽっくりと呼ばれる高い下駄など，独特の装いをしています。将来芸者になる

dangling sash (*obi*), and high clogs (*pokkuri*). The *maiko* is a teen-aged *geisha*-to-be peculiar to Kyoto, who is trained in not only dancing but also singing, playing the *shamisen* (a three-stringed musical instrument), and other traditional Japanese arts to entertain male customers at prestigious Japanese-style restaurants. Formerly some girls at an early age were apprenticed to *geisha* house owners to be trained as *maiko*. Now they become *maiko* of their own will, choosing to live in a world quite different from that of the average girl. In recent years, however, they have rapidly decreased in number, partly because bars or other places readily available for pleasure are drawing more customers. It is said that there are currently only about twenty *maiko* in Kyoto. (T)

mājan　mah-jong. Mah-jong is an indoor game usually played by four persons with 136 pieces shaped like small tiles, called *pai*. Each *pai* is inscribed with a symbolic picture or Chinese character on its face. The game begins with the players sitting around a square table. Each of them has a "hand" of 13 *pai*, while the rest of the *pai* are placed face down in the center of the table. The players take turns picking up a *pai* from the center pool and discarding an unwanted one from their hand in order to build up various combinations. The first player to complete a combination wins the game and gains a certain number of points. This is repeated as long as the players wish. Mah-jong was first brought to Japan by people returning from China or the U. S. around the end of the Meiji period (1868-1912). Mah-jong today is the most popular pastime among university students and businessmen. Small

十代の少女で，京都にだけいます。踊りだけでなく，歌や三味線，その他日本の伝統的芸事を仕込まれ，高級料亭で男性客をもてなします。以前は，幼時から置屋に徒弟に出され，舞子になるよう仕込まれましたが，今では，自分から舞子になることを希望し，普通の少女とはまったく違う世界に生きることを自分の意志で決めているようです。しかし最近は，バーその他簡単に遊興を求められる場所が客を集めていることもあって，舞子になる少女はぐんと少なくなりました。現在京都には20名ほどの舞子がいるにすぎないといわれています。

　　麻　雀　　4人のプレイヤーが，136枚の牌と呼ばれる小さな駒で，勝負を競う室内遊戯です。それぞれの牌の表面には漢字や図柄が刻まれています。4人のプレーヤーはそれぞれ13個の牌を手元に持ち，正方形のテーブルに座ってゲームを始めます。残りの牌は全部テーブルの中央に裏返しに並べておきます。4人が順番に，並んだ牌から1個ずつ引き，同時に不用の牌を手元から1個ずつ捨て，手持ちの牌をある形に整えていきます。最初に組合せのできあがった者が勝ちとなり，定められた得点を得ます。同じゲームの繰返しが何回でも続きます。麻雀が日本に初めて持ち込まれたのは明治末期で，中国やアメリカからの帰国者によるものでした。今日，麻雀は大学生やサラリーマンに最も人気のある娯楽の一つです。これは小遣い銭かせぎのギャンブルになっています。

money is usually gambled in this game. (Y)

majinai   an incantation or a charm. Supposed to have a magic power for good, *majinai* takes both verbal and nonverbal forms. It is mostly practiced on the basis of wishful thinking and has been observed since primitive ages. Some people recite incantations to protect themselves against accidents, such as personal misfortunes and natural disasters. They believe that a magic power resides in the words themselves. For example, when foot goes to sleep, they say, "*Shibire, shibire, kyō e nobore* (Numbness, numbness, go up to Kyoto)." There is also a set of gestural-behavioral charms. An old example is that a person could not be bewitched or befooled by mischievous foxes, if he kept his eyebrows moist with saliva. In its broadest sense, the term *majinai* also refers to talismans (*omamori*) for dispelling evil spirits and demons that are believed to cause illnesses and accidents. (Y)

maneki-neko   a beckoning cat. In some parts of the country it is believed that when a cat uses its forepaw to rub its face, its keeper will have visitors. This belief is said to date back to ancient Chinese literature. At any rate, the cat has come to be regarded as an omen of good luck in the form of *maneki-neko* (a beckoning cat). The *maneki-neko* is a replica of a white cat, in part painted in bright colors, made of either papier-mâché or porcelain, with one paw raised in a beckoning gesture. For the Japanese, this gesture is similar to that of beckoning for someone to come, though to Westerners it is the opposite—that of waving good-by. The

まじない　まじないは，福をもたらす神秘的な威力が秘められているとされ，呪文によるものと，なにか他の形によるものとがあります。まじないは，いわば原始的願望に基づくもので，古代から行われています。病気や交通事故などの災害からの身の安全を願っておまじないを唱えますが，これは，神秘的な威力が呪文の中にあると信じているからです。例えば，足がしびれたときには「しびれ，しびれ，京へのぼれ」と呪文を唱えます。他に動作を用いるまじないもあります。古い例としては，つばをまゆ毛につけると狐につままれることがない，というのがあります。また，病魔などを退散させる魔除けのお守り礼などもあります。

招き猫　日本のある地方では，猫が前足で顔をなでると飼主のところに客が来ると信じられています。このような俗信は古代中国にまでさかのぼるといわれています。こんなことから，猫が，招き猫として幸運をもたらすものとみなされるようになりました。招き猫は，体の一部を鮮やかな色に塗っ

た白猫の張り子または陶製の置物で，人を招き寄せる格好に前足を上げています。この格好は欧米人にとっては別れを告げるときの身振りですが，日本人にとっては逆で，だれかを招き寄せる身

maneki-neko is often seen sitting on a shelf that faces the entrances of Japanese-style shops, inns, and restaurants throughout the country. Those engaged in such business use it as a good-luck charm, expecting it to attract more customers. (T)

manjū   a bun with a bean-jam filling. *Manjū*, originally the meat bun, was introduced from China into Japan in the fourteenth century. The buns soon began to be stuffed with sweet bean jam instead of meat, and they were eaten with tea at temples by Buddhist priests, who made meat-eating a taboo. The bean-jam bun, made in a variety of ways, became popular among the common people in the seventeenth century. There are many different recipes for *manjū*. Generally, the dough, made of a mixture of flour, baking powder, and sugar is kneaded, torn into pieces, stuffed with various kinds of red-bean jam, and then is steamed. *Manjū* and *yōkan* (sweet-bean jelly) are among the most popular Japanese-style sweets. (S)

manzai   a comic stage dialogue. *Manzai* is a vaudeville act performed by a pair of comedians. There are two types of *manzai*, old and new. The old form of *manzai* is performed by two persons during the New Year season: one sings cheerful songs while the other dances to a hand drum. They visit in the neighborhood bringing good wishes for the New Year season. The new form of *manzai* features a comical dialogue exchanged by a duo. Hanabishi, Achako (1897–1974) and Yokoyama Entatsu (1896–1971) are known to be the pioneers of today's *manzai*. Recently these vaudevil-

振りに似ています。招き猫は，全国いたるところで，和風の商店，旅館，料理店などの入口に面した棚によく見かけます。これらの商売を営む人々は，招き猫が客を集めてくれることを期待して，縁起物として置いています。

饅　頭　もとは肉入りの饅頭で，14世紀に中国から日本に伝わりました。まもなく肉のかわりに甘いあんがつめられるようになり，肉食を禁じていた仏教の僧侶が寺院で食べていました。いろいろな製法によるあん入りの饅頭は17世紀には庶民の間に広まりました。饅頭の製法にはいろいろありますが，一般には，小麦粉，パン粉，砂糖を混ぜ合わせてこねて作った皮に，さまざまな種類のあずきあんをつめて蒸します。饅頭とようかんは最も一般的な和菓子です。

漫　才　2人のコンビが滑稽なかけあいやしぐさをする寄席芸です。伝統的な万歳と現代の漫才とがあります。万歳では，2人組が正月に家々を訪れ，祝言を述べて，1人が鼓を打ち，もう1人がそれに合わせて舞い歌うのです。一方，万歳の現代版である漫才では，2人の滑稽な対話が中心となります。花菱アチャコや横山エンタツはこの分野のパイオニアといわれています。最近は漫才ブームで，常時テレビで放映されています。出し物にも新しい工夫がなされています。楽器を使うグループもいれば，2人以上のメンバーをもったグループもあります。

lians are appearing more and more on TV and gaining increased popularity with the public. Many new comic styles and actions have been introduced. Some groups use musical instruments, and others have more than two actors or actresses. (Y)

matsuri an annual local festival. *Matsuri* originated from the ancient rites related to the agriculture and the spiritual well-being of local communities. It is basically a religious observation whereby participants enter a state of active communication with the deities ; this act is accompanied by socializing among participants through feasts and festivities, such as carrying *mikoshi* (a portable shrine), dancing *kagura* (sacred dances), pulling *dashi* (floats), and marching in parade. While the religious rite is carried out with ceremonious formalities, the festivities following it are a performance of vitality, free from strict rules. Although they are conducted by Shinto priests and a group of community leaders, annual festivals are thoroughly enjoyed by all the people in the community. Since village festivals evolve around the cycle of rice growing from preparation of seedlings to harvesting, they center on agricultural rites in spring and fall, celebrating an anticipated good crop or giving thanks for a rich harvest. They emphasize a man-god communion. On the other hand, city festivals, characterized by playful elements and commercial interests, occur mostly in summer, stressing human comradeship. Notable examples are *Hakata Dontaku* in Fukuoka, *Gion-matsuri* in Kyoto and *Awa-odori* in Tokushima. (HA)

祭　祭は，農作物の豊穣とムラの
精神的安寧を祈る古来の祭礼に由来し
ています。基本的には宗教行事で，参
加者は神々と積極的に交わるのです。
これに，ごちそうや，みこし，神楽，
山車，氏子の行列といった催しが加わ
り，祭につどう者たちの間にも親しい
交わりが生じるものです。初めに行わ
れる宗教的儀式は堅苦しく儀式ばったものですが，後に続くお祭
騒ぎは，厳しい規則もなく，活力に溢れたものです。祭の運営は
神主と氏子代表の手でとり行われますが，地区の人々が総出で祝
います。ところで，ムラの祭は，苗の準備から稲刈りに至る稲作
の過程に沿って行われてきました。とくに春祭と秋祭は予祝と豊
作の儀礼として年中行事の中心をなすものであり，ムラビトとカ
ミとの交わりが強調されています。それに対して，都会の祭は，
遊びと商売の要素が濃厚で，夏によく行われ，人と人との交歓が
強調されます。福岡の博多ドンタク，京都の祇園祭，徳島の阿波
踊りなどはその代表例といえましょう。

matsutake   the most valuable mushroom in Japan.   It is scientifically named *Armillaria Matsudake*.   It grows in groups mostly in Japanese-red-pine groves in mid-October.   It is among the largest kinds of edible fungi, and its brown cap has a diameter normally of four or five inches.   It is highly valued in Japan for its pleasingly sweet smell.   The two most popular ways of cooking *matsutake* are (1) roasting it in a covered casserole (*mushi-yaki*), and (2) boiling it in a broth in an earthenware teapot (*dobin-mushi*).   Hiroshima, Okayama, Kyoto, and Nagano are the main growing districts, but recently the *matsutake* crop has fallen short on account of deforestation and overhunting.   Consequently, the native *matsutake* is now too expensive a food for the family table.   *Matsutake* mushrooms are also imported from Korea, and they are available at lower but nevertheless prohibitive prices.   (S)

meishi   a name card.   The *meishi* plays an important role in Japan, especially in the business world.   People usually exchange their cards at their first meeting.   Because Japanese people often adjust their behavior and language depending on people with whom they are speaking, knowing the social position of someone with whom they are dealing is of vital significance.   One's *meishi* provides this information, as it includes one's occupation or company and position as well as one's name and business address.   With a few words written on its back, the *meishi* can also be used as a short letter of introduction.   (K)

menko   a children's card dashing game.   In one of the

松 茸　　学名はアルミラリア・マツダケで，10月中旬に，主として赤松林に群生します。食用きのこのうちでも最も大きな種類に属し，その褐色の笠は平均で直径4〜5インチになります。その芳香のために，松茸は日本で非常に珍重されています。最も代表的な調理法は蒸し焼きと土瓶蒸しです。広島，岡山，京都，長野などが主な産地ですが，最近は伐採と乱獲のために松茸の産出は非常に少なくなっています。その結果，国内産の松茸は，一般家庭の食卓に乗るにはあまりにも高価になりすぎています。松茸は韓国から輸入もされています。こちらはより安いのですが，それでもやはり手が出ないくらいの値段です。

名 刺　　名刺は日本では特に仕事の上で重要な役割をはたします。普通，初対面で名刺を交換します。日本人は話す相手によって態度を変える傾向がありますので，相手の肩書を知る必要があるのです。名刺はこの点で便利です。名刺には，氏名，住所の他に，職業，会社名，肩書などが記されています。各刺の裏に一言書き添えれば，簡単な紹介状としても活用できます。

めんこ　　子供の遊びで，遊び方はいくつかあります。そのう

several versions of the game, it is played by two or more persons, who put one card each on the ground and then by turns throw another of their cards on to the ground, trying to turn over the others' cards. If a card is turned over by one of the players, it goes into his possession, and the loser must place another card on the ground to continue the game. Cards are made of pasteboard. They vary in size, shape, and design, but the most popular ones are circular or rectangular cards with famous *sumō* wrestlers, baseball players, movie stars, and comic characters printed on them. *Menko* originated in the eighteenth century, and in the early days, the cards were made of clay, wood, or lead. The game is now almost out of fashion. (S)

menrui　noodles. Japanese noodles can be divided into two distinct types : *soba* made of buckwheat flour and *udon* made of wheat flour. Traditionally, *soba*, thin and brownish, is favored in Tokyo and eastern Japan, while *udon*, fat and white, is popular in Osaka and western Japan, though both *soba* shops and *udon* shops usually use both types of noodles and serve a wide variety of noodle dishes. Besides *udon*, there are three other kinds of Japanese noodles made of wheat flour, all different mainly in shape : wide and fat *kishimen*, thinner *hiyamugi*, and delicately fine *sōmen*. *Hiyamugi* and *sōmen* served cold are popular especially during the hot and humid summer season. Moreover, *rāmen* (Chinese noodles) is in great demand throughout the year. When eating any of these noodles, it is quite proper to make slurping noises, though they seem to displease many Western visitors to Japan.

ちの一つは，2人以上の子供が，それぞれ1枚のカードを地面に
置き，順番にもう1枚のカードを地面に投げつけて，他の者のカ
ードをひっくり返そうとします。カードをひっくり返したら，そ
のカードは自分のものになります。とられた人はゲームを続ける
ためには，また別のカードを1枚地面に置かなければなりませ
ん。カードはボール紙製で，大きさや形やデザインはさまざまで
す。最も一般的なのは円形や長方形のカードで，有名な力士や野
球選手や映画俳優や漫画の主人公が印刷されています。18世紀に
始まったものですが，初期には，カードは粘土や木や鉛でできて
いました。この遊びは今ではほとんどすたれかけています。

めん類　日本のめん類は2種に大別できます。そば粉で作る
そばと，小麦粉で作るうどんです。伝統的に，細くて茶色っぽい
そばは東京や東日本で好まれ，太くて白いうどんは大阪や西日本
で人気があります。しかし，通常，そば屋もうどん屋もともに2
種のめん類を用い，豊富なメニューを用意しています。うどん以
外に，小麦粉で作る日本のめん類は3種類あり，それぞれ主に形
状に違いがあります。平たいきしめん，細い冷麦，さらに細いそ
うめんです。冷麦とそうめんは冷たくして出すと，蒸し暑い季節
には特に好評です。これらの他にラーメンが一年中たいへん需要
があります。めん類を食べるとき，すすりこむ音をたてるのを，
日本を訪れる欧米人の多くが不快に思うようですが，少しも無作
法ではありません。めん類は音をたてずに食べると風味が失われ
ます。

It is believed that noodles do lose flavor if eaten silently. (T)

miai-kekkon an arranged marriage. Until the end of World War II, most marriages were arranged. Today, this custom accounts for approximately 30 percent of marriages. One reason for the high rate of arranged marriages is that these arrangements generally provide people with opportunities for finding a compatible spouse. In fact, well-matched marriages are often the outcome of the *miai* system, which involves those who take a more realistic or less romantic view of marriage (the go-between, parents, and relatives) than the prospective couples themselves. *Nakōdo* (a go-between) helps with the exchange of information between the two families. Important information is always exchanged in writing and photos are included. If both parties agree to go to the next step, the go-between introduces the prospective couple along with their parents. After this initial meeting called *miai*, the couple see each other periodically, until they decide, giving proper consideration to the other's suitability as a partner, either to get married or not to. It is customary for the man to send gifts (usually an engagement ring and some money) to the woman, when his proposal is accepted. This engagement ceremony is called *yuinō*. Usually a few months later, a wedding takes place, conducted in the style of Shintoism or, less commonly, Buddhism or Christianity. (O)

mimi-kaki an ear pick. Traditional Japanese *mimi-kaki* is designed as a cleaning tool as well as a comforter to soothe itchiness of the ear. A commercially sold ear pick

見合結婚　　第2次世界大戦末までは，ほとんどの結婚は見合によりました。現在では，約30パーセントの結婚が見合です。見合結婚の割合が大きい理由の一つは，概して見合が良縁を得る機会となっているからです。実際，うまくいっている結婚はしばしば見合の結果なのです。見合には，若いカップル当人よりも，結婚に対して現実的な見方をする人たち，すなわち仲人とか両親とか親類の者が間に入ります。仲人は，両家の間の情報交換の手はずを整えます。重要な情報は常に文書で交換し，写真を添えます。もし双方が次の段階に進むことに同意すれば，仲人は結婚の見込みがある2人を両親ともども引き合わせます。見合と呼ばれるこの初対面の後，2人は定期的に交際し，相手が伴侶としてふさわしいかどうかじっくり考えたうえ，結婚するかどうか決めます。男性の申込みが受け入れられると，男性が女性に贈物（普通は婚約指輪とお金）をするのがしきたりです。この婚約式を結納といいます。通常，数カ月後に，神道式で，あるいはまれに仏教式かキリスト教式で，結婚式が行われます。

耳かき　　伝統的な日本の耳かきは，耳のかゆみを和らげるとともに，耳掃除もする道具として作られていま

usually is a narrow bamboo stick which is about 20cm (8 inches) long. One end of this tool is curved to pick up wax in the ears. To the other end of *mimi-kaki* is attached a small pompon, which is mainly designed to soothe ear itchiness. Unlike disposable cotton swabs, it is used repeatedly. As well as cutting hair, Japanese barbers provide the service of shaving, and sometimes cleaning the customer's ears using *mimi-kaki*. (O)

min'yō a folk song. The Japanese folk songs may be classified into the following three groups: (1) the song of celebration, (2) the work song, and (3) the song for the folk dance. Songs of celebration are sung on happy occasions in praise of gods and in commemoration of a festival, a good harvest, or a large catch. Work songs were originally sung by people engaged in physical work. There are a great many work songs concerning various kinds of occupations and industries ranging from agriculture, fishery, and mining to building and engineering. Songs for the folk dance, deriving from songs of celebration, have largely become the Bon Festival dance songs, whose words are strong in local color. The audience often responds to the song, putting in short cheering notes between phrases and beating time with the hands. The traditional instruments accompanying a folk song are a flute made of bamboo (*fue*), a banjo-like, three-stringed instrument (*samisen* or *shamisen*), and a drum (*taiko*). (S)

miren a feeling of lingering attachment. Lingering attachment is a feeling one develops when, for example, one is

す。市販の耳かきは，普通，長さが約 20 cm の細い竹の棒です。
この道具の一方の端は，耳あかが取れるように曲がっています。
もう一方の端には小さなポンポンがついています。これは主に，
耳のかゆみを和らげるためのものです。使い捨ての綿棒と違っ
て，何度も使われます。日本の床屋は，散髪するだけでなく，ひ
げそりも，そして時には耳かきを使って客の耳掃除までしてくれ
ます。

　民　謡　　　日本の民謡はつぎの 3 種類に分類できるでしょう。
(1)祝儀唄，(2)作業唄，そして(3)踊り唄です。祝儀唄は，おめでた
い行事のときに，神を讃えたり，祭を楽しんだり，豊作や大漁を
祝して歌われます。作業唄は，もとは肉体労働に従事する人たち
によって歌われました。農業，漁業から建築，土木に至るまで，
さまざまな職業や仕事に関係する非常に多くの作業唄がありま
す。祝儀唄から発達した踊り歌は多くは盆踊り唄となりました
が，その歌詞は地方色豊かなものです。聴衆は，歌の間に合いの
手を入れたり手拍子を打ったりして歌を景気づけます。民謡の伴
奏に使われる伝統的な楽器は，竹製の笛，バンジョーに似た 3 弦
の三味線，そして太鼓です。

　未　練　　　未練とは，例えば世間の圧力で愛する人と別れなけ
ればならないようなときに，もえあがる感情のことです。基本的

forced to part with one's beloved due to the pressure of social circumstances. It basically is part of the emotional category of sorrow. In accordance with display rules of emotion in Japanese culture, a man is said to be effeminate and unreliable if he cannot suppress his lingering attachment to his sweetheart once he has decided he had better leave her. A woman, on the other hand, is considered to be vulnerably attractive when she nonverbally expresses her lingering affection for her lover, though she knows she has no choice other than to let him go. As it is natural that both men and women should find it terribly heart-breaking to part with their beloved, *miren* is a characteristic theme of *enka*, Japanese popular songs that describe tragic lovers torn by destiny (*sadame*) and the world (*seken*). (HO)

miso　soybean paste. A fermented, high-protein seasoning which can be used in various dishes, *miso* is one of Japan's most important soybean foods. Since it is rich in flavor and aroma, it can be used as bouillon, dressings, dips, and so on. *Miso* originated under the name of *chiang* in China about 2,500 years ago, and was brought to Japan by Buddhist priests during the seventh century. It took hundreds of years to transform the original Chinese *chiang* to the present unique and distinctive Japanese *miso*. It is made from boiled and crushed soybeans mixed with wheat, barley, or rice, and salt. The mixture is injected with a yeastlike mold and is allowed to mature for months or even as long as three years. Well made *miso* keeps for a long time, even if not refrigerated. *Miso* is either brownish or whitish, the whitish type being the

には悲しみの感情にはいります。日本文化の感情表現ルールによれば，男性はいったん恋人と別れたほうが良いと決めたからには未練がましくあってはならないとされています。さもないと，めめしい，頼りがいがないといわれます。一方，女性は，恋人と別れる以外に選択の余地がないとわかっていても，未練たっぷりの表情を示すと，傷つきやすい可愛らしい人と考えられます。当然のことながら，男女ともに愛する人との別れはつらい心の痛手となるので，未練は演歌のテーマとなります。演歌は，定めや世間によって引き裂かれた悲劇の男と女をうたう日本の歌謡曲です。

味　噌　　味噌は日本の最も重要な大豆食品の一つです。醸造した高蛋白の調味料で，いろいろな料理に使われます。風味と香りが強いので，スープの素，ドレッシング，漬け床などに用います。味噌は約2,500年前に中国でチャンという名称で生まれ，7世紀に仏教僧が日本に伝えました。それから数百年かかって，元来の中国のものから，現在の日本のユニークで独特の味噌になりました。味噌は，煮てからつぶした大豆に，小麦，大麦または米と塩を加えて作ります。この混合物にイーストのような発酵菌を注入し，数カ月から，長い時は3年もそのまま熟成させておきます。上等の味噌は，冷蔵庫に入れなくても，長く保存できます。赤味噌と白味噌があり，白味噌の方が薄味です。

milder.　(O)

mochi　a rice cake.　Steamed glutinous rice is pounded into a cake and made into balls or cut into squares.　The simplest way to serve *mochi* is to grill it and dip it in sweetened soy sauce.　*Kinako-mochi* (a rice cake grilled, moistened, and rolled in sweet soybean flour) is another of many ways to enjoy *mochi* as a confection.　It is customary to eat a soup containing rice cakes (*zōni*) on New Year's Day.　*Mochi* was formerly regarded as food for festive and ceremonial occasions.　Rice-cake making used to be among the most important household work to be done in preparation for the New Year.　In old times, families in the rural districts enjoyed and took pride in making their own home-made rice cakes, though pounding steamed rice into cake was a hard and time-consuming task.　Since rice cakes are now available at any super-market all the year round, fewer and fewer people take the trouble of making home-made rice cakes.　(O)

momijigari　an excursion for viewing scarlet maple leaves.　It is a traditional event in autumn when the hills and mountains are aflame with autumnal tints.　Many families visit these areas on holidays to see the fall colors and enjoy food and drinks in the midst of natural beauty.　This recreational event, along with another similar one in spring known as *hanami* (cherry-blossom viewing), has its origin among the court aristocracy in the Heian period (794-1185).　The nobles enjoyed playing music, composing poems, and gathering beautifully colored leaves.　While *hanami* is a lively spree

餅　餅は蒸したもち米をついて作ります。形は丸いのと四角のがあります。最も簡単な食べ方は，焼いて砂糖じょう油につけて食べることです。きなこ餅は，菓子として餅を食べる多くの方法の一つです。お正月には雑煮として食べる習慣があります。以前は，餅は祭礼や儀式のときの食物とされていました。餅つきは，新年を迎える準備として行う家事の中で最も重要なものに数えられたものです。昔は，いなかの家庭ではそれぞれ餅つきをし，自家製の餅を自慢しました。しかし，蒸した米をつく作業は時間がかかる重労働です。今では餅は一年中どこのスーパーマーケットでも買えるので，わざわざ自宅で餅つきをする人はどんどん減っています。

紅葉狩　紅葉狩とは，山や丘が秋色で一面に彩られる季節に紅葉を眺め楽しむ伝統的な行事のことです。休日には多くの家族づれが山々を訪れて，食事などをしながら紅葉を楽しみます。紅葉狩は春の花見と同様に，平安時代の貴族社会における行事でした。当時の貴族は，音楽を奏し詩歌を作し，美しく彩られた紅葉を集めて楽しみました。花見は，浮かれ騒ぐ人たちの祝宴の場ですが，紅葉狩はむしろ，自然界の変わりいくさまを鑑賞するための静かな行事です。

with lots of merry-making, *momijigari* is rather a quiet pastime allowing one to dwell upon how things change. (Y)

mon also **kamon**   the crest of a family. It originated in the eleventh century when court nobles (*kuge*) and warriors (*buke*) used emblems as symbols of their families. Military families of the feudal age marked with their crests not only banners, curtains, and clothing but also furnishings and household things. In the Meiji period (1868-1912), many of the common people adopted family crests bearing some connection with their newly assumed family names. The designs were drawn from a variety of objects—the sun, the moon, stars, plants, animals, geometrical patterns, and letters. Clothing marked with the family crest is called *montsuki*, which literally means "a thing with a crest". A crested *haori* and *hakama* form the traditional formal dress. The crest of an open chrysanthemum (*kiku-no-gomon*) is the crest of the Imperial family and that of hollyhock leaves (*aoi-no-mon*) represents the Tokugawa Shogunate family. (S)

mono-no-aware   pathos. The word *mono-no-aware* generally means a feeling of sympathetic pity aroused by the pathos of things. In its more technical sense, it refers to an element in experience or in artistic representation evoking compassion, and/or to a capacity for appreciating such an element. It has been established as a literary concept, since Motoori Norinaga (1730-1801) employed it in describing the sentiment prevalent in literature of the Heian period (794-1185), and typically in *Genji-monogatari* (*The Tale of Genji*)

紋・家紋　家紋は，11世紀に宮廷の貴族や武士が一族の象徴として紋章を使ったのが起源です。封建時代の武家は，のぼりや幕や衣服ばかりでなく，家具や家庭用品にも紋をつけました。明治時代には，平民の多くが新しく苗字を名乗るようになりましたが，同時に，苗字と何らかの関係のある紋も持つようになりました。模様はさまざまで，太陽，月，星，植物，動物，幾何学模様，文字などを表わしたものがあります。家紋のついた衣服は紋つきといわれますが，それは文字どおり紋のついたものという意味です。紋つきの羽織・袴は伝統的な正装です。開いた菊の花の紋章（菊の御紋）は皇室の紋で，葵の葉の紋は徳川将軍家の紋です。

もののあわれ　もののあわれという語は一般に，物事のしめやかな情趣に触れて起こる同情的な哀感を指します。より専門的には，現実の体験や芸術作品の中で同情心を呼び起こすような要素のことであり，またそのような要素を理解できる能力のことでもあります。本居宣長が，平安時代の文学，特に紫式部の『源氏物語』に顕著な情緒について述べるのにこの語を使って以来，それは文学上の概念となりました。彼は，『源氏物語』はもののあわれが何であるかを読者に教えてくれる傑作だと考えました。この概念は，現世の生命が基本的に無常であることに対する同情的

written by Murasaki-Shikibu (798?-1014?). He considered *Genji-monogatari* to be a masterpiece that shows the reader what *mono-no-aware* really is. The concept may be defined as a sympathetic understanding of the basically transient nature of earthly existence. It is often contrasted with the term *okashi*, which is applied to another characteristic of the Heian literature as represented by *Makura-no-Sōshi* (*The Pillow Book*) written by Sei-shōnagon (b. 967?). While *okashi* refers to the intellectual interest or pleasant sensation a person feels when he discovers hidden beauty by direct contact with the outside world, *mono-no-aware* constitutes reflective contemplation and aesthetic appreciation of natural beauty and human existence. (S)

mushi-no-ne　　the chirping of insects. In autumn *suzumushi*(bell ring insect), *matsumushi* (a kind of cricket), and *kōrogi* (common cricket) start singing. This singing of these insects strikes the right chord in the heart of Japanese people. They find something sad and lonely in these chirpings, realizing the end of the hot summer, the coming of the severe winter, the short lives of the insects, and by association the mutation of life. This sentiment called *mono-no-aware* (the pathos of things) has been portrayed quite often in traditional Japanese poetry. In Japanese-style water paintings, this melancholy is portrayed by an old man listening to these insects. Also, in *kabuki* theater, *mushi-no-ne* is produced through a combination of several instruments. (K)

musubi　　a rice-ball. *Musubi*, which is usually called *o-*

な理解であると定義できるでしょう。もののあわれは，おかしという語とよく対照されますが，これは清少納言の『枕草子』に代表される平安文学のもう一つの特質を指すのに使われます。おかしは，外界との直接の接触によって隠れた美を発見するときに感じる知的な興味や快い興奮のことですが，もののあわれは，自然美や人間存在に対する省察や審美的理解から生じるものです。

虫の音　秋になると，鈴虫，松虫，こおろぎなどの鳴き声が一斉に聞こえてきます。この虫の音は，まさに日本人の心に深くしみとおるのです。何かもの悲しく，わびしい思いが感じられ，同時に，夏の終りと厳しい冬の訪れ，そして虫の短い命とともに，この世の常ならぬことが思い起こされるのです。このような情感は，もののあわれとして日本古来の詩歌によくうたわれています。日本の水彩画でも，この悲しく寂しい情景は，虫の音を聞く老人の姿に象徴されています。また歌舞伎でも，虫の音はいろいろな楽器を使って作り出されます。

むすび　むすびは，敬語の接頭辞「お」をつけて，おむすび

musubi with an honorific prefix *o-*, is also referred to as *o-nigiri* or *nigiri-meshi*. The original variety of *o-musubi* is a handful of boiled rice, pressed and shaped with salt-smeared hands into a round, triangular, or oval ball, and containing *ume-boshi* (a soft pickled plum) in its center. There are many variations of *o-musubi*. Some are wrapped with *nori* (a thin sheet of dried seaweed) or contain, instead of *ume-boshi*, a pinch of grilled salmon fillets or dried bonito flakes seasoned with soy sauce. Simple in taste and easy to make and carry, *o-musubi* is the most popular food for traveling, picnics, and many other outdoor activities. *O-musubi* is not only made at home by hand, or more conveniently with a wooden or plastic mold, but also sold at fast-food shops, Japanese-style restaurants, and department stores, especially at lunchtime. (T)

nabemono a one-pot dish. *Nabemono* (literally "things cooked in a pot") is a general term for a one-pot dish cooked right at the table. *Sukiyaki*, *mizutaki*, *yosenabe*, and *shabu-shabu* are some examples of the *nabemono*-type dishes. These are very popular in winter, because people can warm themselves by eating the heated foods directly from a boiling pot. It is also an ideal dish for a party. All the preparation can be done in advance, and the portions to be cooked can be adjusted quite easily. At the center of the table, a pot, filled with broth, is set on some kind of heating unit such as a gas ring. Beside the pot, fresh vegetables, slices of fish, chicken, meat, and often *tofu* (soybean curd) are beautifully arranged on a platter. Diners cook for themselves, choosing their favorite foods from the platter and putting them in the pot at

となります。また，おにぎりとか，に
ぎりめしという言い方もあります。お
むすびの原型は，一握りの御飯を手に
塩をつけて握り固め，丸型か三角形か
俵型にし，中心に梅干を入れたもので
す。また，これにいろいろな変化をつ
けたものもあります。海苔でくるんだ
り，梅干の代わりに，焼いた鮭の身
や，しょう油で味つけしたかつお節のひとつまみを中に入れるこ
ともあります。味は素朴で，作るのも持ち運びも簡単なので，ピ
クニックや旅行その他戸外活動の際に最も人気のある弁当となり
ます。おむすびは，家庭で手で握ったり，簡便な木型やプラスチ
ック型を利用して作るほかに，弁当屋，和風料理店，デパートな
どで，とりわけ昼食時に売れています。

　鍋　物　　食卓の上に鍋を置いて作る料理の総称です。鍋料理
の例として，すき焼き，水炊き，寄せ鍋，しゃぶしゃぶなどがあ
ります。煮えている鍋から直接熱い食物を取って食べるので，体
が暖まり，冬には大変好まれます。これはまたパーティーには理
想的な料理です。準備はすべてあらかじめしておくことができ，
しかも調理する分量を人数に合わせて調整することが楽にできま
す。食卓の中央に，ガスこんろなどの熱器具を置き，わりしたを
入れた鍋をかけます。鍋の横の大皿には，生野菜，薄切りした
魚，鶏肉，牛肉，そして豆腐などをきれいに並べておきます。そ
して，自分の好きなものを選び，食卓の上の鍋に入れて，煮なが
ら食べます。

the table.　(O)

naniwabushi　the art of tale-telling by narration and singing.　Also known as *rōkyoku*, it is accompanied by the *shamisen*, the three-stringed banjo-like instrument.　Originally, *naniwabushi* developed from a funeral memorial address (*sekkyo-saimon*) in the Kansai area during the Edo period (1603 -1867).　It was after the Meiji period (1868-1912) that *naniwabushi* became a popular art style.　Its tales are made up of popularly known historical events.　They emphasize *giri* (mutual obligations) and *ninjō* (human feelings).　Today it is still loved by old people, although it is becoming out of fashion. There is an expression *naniwabushi-teki*, which is sometimes applied to a man who is governed by the old concepts of *giri* and *ninjō*.　(Y)

nattō　fermented soybeans.　In Japan soybeans have been of vital importance as a major source of protein.　There are various soybean products such as *miso* (fermented soybean paste), *shōyu* (soy sauce), and *tōfu* (soybean curd). *Nattō* is also an important soybean food valued not only for its nutritious qualities but also for its easy digestion and absorption.　Some Japanese say that a Japanese-style breakfast without *nattō* can never satisfy them.　Because of its peculiar smell and sliminess, however, even those foreigners who are very fond of Japanese cuisine seem to find it extremely difficult to enjoy *nattō*.　(T)

nawanoren　a straw-rope curtain.　A small folksy-

浪花節　　浪曲としても知られ，物語風の叙事詩で，バンジョーに似た3本弦の三味線の伴奏が付きます。もともと浪花節は説経祭文から発達したものであり，江戸時代に大坂で始まりました。その盛りを見るに至ったのは明治以後です。有名な武勇伝などを材料とし，義理・人情に触れています。今日ではあまりはやらなくなってきてはいるものの，年輩の愛好者は依然として多いようです。浪花節的という表現がありますが，これは，古い義理・人情にとらわれている人を指します。

納　豆　　日本では大豆は蛋白源としてとても重要です。味噌，しょう油，豆腐など多くの大豆製品があります。納豆もまた大豆を用いた重要な食品で，栄養価が高いだけでなく消化吸収も容易な点で優れています。日本人の中には，朝食に納豆がなかったら満足できないという人がいます。しかし，納豆には特有の臭いがあり，ぬるぬるしているため，日本料理が大好きな外国人でも納豆を喜んで食べる人はあまりいないようです。

縄のれん　　小さな庶民的な雰囲気をもった飲み屋は縄のれん

looking drinking place is often called *nawanoren* as it has a straw-rope curtain hung over its entrance to show that it is open. (When the curtain is missing or it is inside the sliding glass-door, the place is either closed or preparing to be open soon.) Such a place is also called *aka-chōchin*, if it has a large lighted red-lantern at its entrance. A *nawanoren* place is patronized by ordinary people living or working in its neighborhood. In most cases, customers know one another. If they meet as strangers, they soon become friends. On their way home after work, people sometimes drop by one of those places to enjoy their *banshaku* (evening drinks). When in a festive mood, they may hop around from one place to another. This act is caricatured as climbing up step by step on a ladder into raptures (*hashigo-zake*). (HO)

nemawashi behind-the-scenes efforts for securing a consensus. According to a dictionary, *nemawashi* means "the act of digging around the root of a big tree one or two years before its scheduled transplantation, and clipping off all but the main root and the large branch-roots, and allowing new hairs to grow, thus facilitating the transplantation, and also enabling the tree to bear better fruit" (translated by M. Matsumoto). From this arises a figurative meaning : the ground work to obtain support or to secure informal consent from people concerned prior to a formal debate or vote. Since Japanese society operates on group decision or consensus, *nemawashi* is an indispensable process in achieving this general agreement. It avoids open confrontation as well. Another notable characteristic is that a proposal can be

と呼ばれます。入口に縄で作ったのれんがつるしてあるからです。それは店が開いていることを示します（これが見あたらないか，ガラス戸の内側にあるときは，閉店か準備中かのいずれかです）。入口に大きな赤いちょうちんがともされているならば，赤ちょうちんとも呼ばれます。縄ののれんは，近所の住人や勤め人がひいきにしています。多くの場合，お客はお互いに顔見知りです。見知らぬ者どうしがであっても，すぐに友達になります。人々は仕事のあと帰宅する途中で，晩酌を楽しむために，こういった店に立ち寄ります。つい浮かれると場所を変え，はしご酒になりますが，これは，はしごを1段ずつのぼっていい気持ちになっていく姿をいったものです。

根回し　辞書には，「大木を移植する1，2年前に，その周囲を掘って，主根と側根の大きいものを残し，その他の根を切り，新しい根を発生させて，移植を容易にすること。果樹の結実を良行にするためにも行う」と出ています。ここから，正式な討論か議決に至る前にあらかじめ関係者の支持を取り付ける行為という比喩的な意味が生じます。日本の社会は集団決定とコンセンサスで動いていますから，根回しは合意を得るための不可欠な過程なのです。この根回しゆえに，対立を避けて全会一致の実を結ばせることができるのです。それから，根回しの段階で，全員に受け入れられる理想的なものになるよう提案を修正しうるということも，特筆に値します。実際，会議における正式な議決というのは，あらかじめ準備された暗黙の決定を確認する儀式にすぎません。

revised in the process of *nemawashi* until it is molded into an ideal form which is acceptable to everyone. In effect, the formal decision on the floor is little more than a ceremony to confirm the decision already reached behind closed doors. (HA)

nenbutsu   the prayer to Amida Buddha (Amitabha). Originally the word meant "to meditate on Buddha", but now it usually means chanting a prayer to Amida Buddha. It is written in six Chinese characters which read "Na-mu-a-mi-da-butsu", and implies, "I sincerely believe in Amida Buddha," or as the Shinshū sect interprets it, "I submit myself to Amida Buddha to ask for salvation." According to the teachings of the Jōdoshū and Shinshū sects, rebirth in Paradise or the Pure Land (*jōdo*) can be insured by repeating this prayer. (S)

nihon-buyō   Japanese dancing. *Nihon-buyō*, or simply called *nichibu* in short, is comprised of three types: *mai, odori*, and *furi*. *Mai* refers to a traditional dance such as a *nō* dance involving a quiet, controlled form. *Odori*, also a dance, is a more dynamic form associated with *kabuki* (traditional theater). *Furi* is a set of conventionalized gestures and postures of dancing, through which symbolic expression is conveyed. *Nihon-buyō* usually means *odori*, which grew out of various folk dances while incorporating some aspects of *mai*. It is often contrasted with the Western ballet. The former usually keeps a lower posture with the feet sliding on the floor, and thus, is described as being inward and earthbound, while the latter is outward and skybound with

190

念　仏　　この語は，もともとは，仏陀について瞑想することを意味しましたが，今ではたいてい，阿弥陀仏への祈りを唱えることを指します。それは南無阿弥陀仏という6つの漢字で書かれます。南無阿弥陀仏とは，一般的には「心から阿弥陀仏を信じます」，または真宗の解釈では「救済を求め阿弥陀仏に私自身を任せます」という意味です。浄土宗や真宗の教えによれば，この祈りを繰り返し唱えることで，天国つまり浄土での再生が確実になるとされています。

日本舞踊　　略して日舞ともいい，舞い，踊り，振りの3つの要素から成り立っています。舞いは，能に見られるような，感情を抑えた静かな踊りです。踊りは，歌舞伎に見られる躍動的な踊りです。振りは，慣例化された手のしぐさや姿勢などで，象徴的表現を生み出します。日本舞踊は一般には，民俗舞踊から生まれた歌舞伎の踊りを指しますが，その発展過程で能の舞いの要素も取り入れています。日本舞踊はしばしばバレエとも比較されます。日本舞踊が，腰を入れ姿勢を低くして摺り足をする内向的かつ地上的なものであるのに対し，バレエは，跳躍や体の回転などを取り入れた外向的かつ天上的なものです。今日存在する多くの流派は家元制度によって自派の伝統芸を守っています。中でも知名度の高い流派としては，藤間，西川，若柳，花柳などがありますが，これらはすべて家元の名前です。

a lot of dynamic leaps and bounds, and spins and turns. Today there are many different schools of Japanese dancing, each controlled by its own *iemoto* or head master of a family who has handed down its traditional form and style. The Fujima, Nishikawa, Wakayagi, and Hanayagi schools are the most popular ones at present. Their names are those of the *iemoto* families. (Y)

nihon-gami　Japanese-style hair-do. *Nihon-gami* usually refers to the women's hair set in the traditional Japanese style, as opposed to Western style. Hairstyle in Japan has undergone numerous changes. The most striking one took place in 1870s, when the Government, as part of its modernization policy, prohibited men from wearing old hairstyles. They clipped off their topknots (which, popularly called *chonmage*, are worn today by *sumō* wrestlers). Women, who had developed various elaborate hairstyles differing according to the class, age, marital status, occasion, etc., continued to wear them until much later. They began to arrange their hair in Western ways for practical reasons. Nowadays *nihon-gami* calls to mind *geisha* girls or performers of traditional theater arts. Most Japanese women rarely wear it, probably only once in their lives—at their wedding. The bride wears the most decorative *nihon-gami*, which is, however, not her own hair, but a wig she rents for the occasion. (T)

nihongo　the Japanese language. Also called *kokugo* (national language), Japanese belongs to the Ural-Altaic

日本髪　　日本髪とは普通，西洋風の髪型に対し，日本の伝統的な髪型で結った女性の髪を指します。日本の髪型はさまざまな変化を経てきました。中でも最も顕著な変化は1870年代に起こりました。政府は近代化政策の一環として，男子が従来通りの髪型に結うのを禁止したのです。このため，男性はチョンマゲを切り落とすことになりました（チョンマゲは今では力士が結っています）。女性は，階級や年齢，既婚か未婚か，どんな社会的状況かなどによって異なる，手の込んだいろいろな髪型を作り出しました。それらの髪型は1870年代以後も続いていました。しかし，後になって実用的な理由から，洋風に髪を結うようになりました。今日では日本髪ときくと，芸者とか伝統的な舞台芸術の演技者を連想します。ほとんどの女性は日本髪を結うことはまずありません。おそらく一生に一度，結婚式に結うだけでしょう。花嫁は最も華やかな日本髪姿になりますが，しかしそれも自分の髪ではなく，この時のために借りたかつらなのです。

日本語　　日本語はウラル・アルタイ語族に属していますが，その起源は未だ完全に確定されていません。文法的には，主語—

language family, but its origin is still undetermined completely. Syntactically it is characterized by a subject-object-verb order, with a modifier preceding a modified unit. It also has a set of postpositional particles specifying a grammatical function and a modal elaboration. The Japanese writing system utilizes four different kinds of symbols: (1) *kanji*, (2) *katakana*, (3) *hirakana*, and (4) *rōmaji*. *Kanji* is a set of ideographs principally borrowed from classic Chinese characters. Both *katakana* and *hirakana* are Japanese original syllabaries invented in the eighth or ninth century based on Chinese characters. They differ in orthographical form, but have a syllabary of 48 letters each. *Romaji* is an alphabet of 28 Roman letters. All Japanese are supposed to learn how to read and write 996 *kanji* characters specially selected for educational purposes and all other syllabic and alphabetic letters during their 6 years of elementary education. (HO)

nihon-teien a Japanese garden. The history of Japanese gardening started more than a thousand years ago. In the eighth century, gardens were usually kept as natural as possible by planting flowers, trees, and shrubs around the house. A pond containing live fish was also tastefully arranged in the center of the garden. By the end of the ninth century, they came to be landscaped in a style which symbolized natural beauty. With an artificially made hill, *tsukiyama*-style gardens had a central pond which symbolized the sea, and banks of earth and stones which represented the mountains. Shrubs and trees were still kept natural. In the twelfth century, Zen Buddhism exerted a great influence on the style of Japanese

目的語—動詞の順序になり，修飾語が被修飾語の前にきます。後置詞である助詞・助動詞があり，一定の文法上の機能と意味上の変化を示します。日本語を書くには4種の文字を使います。(1)漢字，(2)かた仮名，(3)ひら仮名，(4)ローマ字です。漢字は表意文字で，主として古典中国語から借用したものです。かた仮名とひら仮名は日本独自の文字体系で，8〜9世紀に漢字を基礎に発明されました。2つの体系は書体が違い，両方とも別種の48文字からなっています。ローマ字は，ラテン文字のアルファベットです。すべての日本人は6年間の初等教育のうちに，996語の教育漢字と，他の3つの文字体系の読み書きを学ぶことになっています。

日本庭園　　日本庭園の歴史は，千年以上前に始まりました。8世紀には，花，高木，低木を家の周囲に植え，できるだけ自然に近い庭が一般的でした。また，生きた魚を放った池が趣よく庭の中心に設けられました。9世紀末には，自然美を象徴する様式で造園されるようになりました。人工の丘を設けた築山式庭園には，中心に海を象徴する池と，山を表わす土と石で作った丘がありました。低木や高木は自然のまま保たれました。12世紀になると，禅宗が造園法に大きな影響を及ぼしました。庭は平らな土地に設計され，木や石は，庭全体が自然の風景を表わすように，人工的に造形されました。この独特な庭園様式は枯山水と呼ばれ，空間に人工美と自然美の調和を作り出すことをねらいとしました。白い砂の層が海を象徴し，砂の上のすじ模様が水の流れを表

garden landscaping. The garden was laid out on a flat area, and the trees and stones were artificially shaped so that the entire garden represented a natural landscape. This particular style of garden called *karesansui* (the dry garden) aimed at creating a harmony between the artificial and natural beauty of space. The sea was symbolized by a layer of white sand, and the flow of water was represented by a pattern of sand furrows. Waterfalls were designed by arranging rocks. Gardens were made on a great scale by influential warriors in the sixteenth century, but at the same time, small and simple gardens were designed for tea-houses. Running water, paths with stepping stones, lanterns, and trees were arranged to complement a tea-house. This style of garden has been well adapted in modern Japanese houses. Japanese gardens differ from Western gardens in two respects. While Japanese gardens are designed to be enjoyed from within the house, Western gardens focus on the beauty from the outsiders' point of view. Furthermore, the former emphasize mainly the natural scenic beauty, while the latter present a more geometrical beauty. (O)

ninjō   human feelings. Japanese people believe that love, affection, compassion, and sympathy are the most important feelings that all human beings should nurture. This assumption emanates from the fact that one of the virtues that Japanese society emphasizes is cooperation among people. In daily life, Japanese people are bound by the code of *ninjō* in their attitudes toward others. For example, imagine that you have run out of salt while cooking. You can visit your

196

わしました。岩を配置して滝としました。16世紀には，勢力のある武士が大規模な庭を作らせました。しかし同時に，茶室に合うように，小さく簡素な庭も設計されました。流水，踏石のある小道，灯籠，樹木が茶室を引き立てるように配されました。この様式の庭は，現代の日本家屋にうまく取り入れられています。日本庭園は，2つの点で西洋の庭園と異なっています。日本庭園が家の中から眺めて楽しむように設計されているのに対し，西洋の庭園は外から見たときの美しさを強調します。さらに，前者が主として自然の風景美を大事にするのに対し，後者は幾何学的な美を表現しようとします。

人 情　　日本人は，愛，いつくしみ，哀れみ，そして思いやりの心を，人間が育むべき最も大切な感情であると信じています。この考えは，日本の社会が人間どうしの調和に重点を置くところからきているのでしょう。日常生活でも，他人に対して人情をもって接することを信条としています。例えば，料理中に塩が切れたとします。隣に塩を借りに行けば，もちろん喜んで貸してくれるでしょう。同様に，親戚からリンゴをたくさん送ってもらったら，たいがい，近所におすそ分けしたいという気持ちになるも

neighbor to borrow some. The reaction next door should certainly be very cooperative. Likewise, suppose that you are sent many apples by your relative. Then you will want to give some to your neighbors. This "give and take" attitude is based on the belief in the wisdom of mutual reliance. Thus, when all is well with you, you are expected to help others, and when you are in need of help, you can count on them. This sense of interdependence in the community is what constitutes *ninjō*. (K)

Niō also **Kongō- rikishi** a pair of statues of the guardian gods standing at a temple gate. The fierce-looking, powerfully-built, and hard-muscled statues represent the guardian gods of Herculean strength, who in Indian mythology are believed to protect Buddha's teachings from corruption by earthly desires. One of the statues holds in its right hand an ancient Indian weapon called *kongō-sho* and is supposed to be saying *"a"*, and the other with its right hand open saying "hum". They are Sanskrit alphabets. *"A"* is alpha and *"hum"* is omega, and thus *"a-hum"* represents every being in the universe. Temple gates furnished with these statues are generally called *niō-mon*. (S)

nō a noh dance or classical Japanese dance-drama. *Nō* is the oldest of all classical dance-dramas in Japan that developed in the fourteenth century from religious sources and folk myths. It is a combination of drama, music, and dance (*mai*). In older days, *nō* was patronized by the warrior class, whereas *kabuki* (traditional theater) and *bunraku* (classical puppetry) were

のです。このようなもちつもたれつの態度は，人間はお互いに助け合うものであると信じているところから生まれるのです。うまくいっている時には困っている人を助け，つまずいた時にはまわりの人に助けを求めることができるわけです。このような共同体の中での相互依存という感覚が人情のもとになっています。

仁王（金剛力士） この恐ろしい形相をした，頑健な体格で筋骨逞しい一対の像は，怪力の守護神を表わしています。彼らは，インド神話で，煩悩による腐敗から仏陀の教えを守るものと信じられています。一つの像は，右手に金剛杵という古代インドの武器を持ち，「阿（あ）」と言っています。もう一つの像は，右手を開いて，「吽（うん）」と言っています。これらは梵語のアルファベットです。阿はアルファ，吽はオメガですから，「阿吽」は宇宙の万物を指します。これらの像が立っている寺院の門は，一般に仁王門と呼ばれています。

能 日本最古の舞踊劇であり，14世紀頃に民衆神話や宗教的儀式などから発展しました。これは，劇，音楽，そして舞いを一体化したものです。かつて，歌舞伎や文楽が大衆演芸であったのに対して，能は武士階級のものとされていました。能は，象徴性と簡単な舞台装置を特徴としています。舞台と客席を隔てる幕はありません。シテと呼ばれる主役とその助演者であるシテヅレ

for the common people. *Nō* is characterized by some symbolic features and simple sets. There is no curtain between the stage and the audience. The chief actor (*shite*) and his associates (*shitezure*) wear various kinds of masks (*nō-men*) to denote the characters they represent, such as an old man, a young woman, a demon, an animal, and a supernatural being. They express a wide range of feelings and emotions through their dances, which are accompanied by flutes, drums, and chants of *utai*. There is a one-act comic interlude called *kyōgen* (literally, crazy words), which is of simple construction and is performed to fill the intervals between the *nō* plays. It serves as a relief from the solemnity of the *nō* drama. (Y)

noren　a split curtain. It is a short, split curtain hung at the entrance or the doorway of a shop or a restaurant to show that it is in business. It is also used in private homes as a space divider or decoration. It was originally used to keep out the sun and dust in front of the shop's doorway. With the development of commercialism in the fourteenth century, the *noren* curtain was installed instead of the door in order to make it easy for customers to enter and exit the shop. At the same time, the name and/or the symbol of the shop came to be dyed in a light color on the normally dark background of *noren*. The word *noren* also refers to a shop's reputation. When an apprentice or an employee is freed and allowed to open his own shop, he may be endowed with a reputed *noren* curtain of his master's shop. It is considered not only honorable but also profitable to inherit the *noren* of a highly

は，能面と呼ばれる面をつけ，それぞれ老人，女，鬼，動物，神などを表現します。あらゆる感情表現は，役者の舞いと，笛や鼓などの楽器，そして謡と呼ばれる歌唱によってなされます。また，能劇と組み合わせて演じられる滑稽で素朴な狂言は，能のもたらす一種の緊張感をほぐす役割をします。

のれん 切れ目が入った短いカーテンで，商店や料理店の戸口につるし，営業中であることを示すものです。個人の家でも，空間の仕切りとして，あるいは装飾として使います。元来は，店の軒先に日よけ，ちりよけとして使ったものです。14世紀に商業が発展すると，客の出入りが簡単になるようにと，戸の代わりにのれんを設けました。同時に，濃い色で染めたのれんの布地に，薄い色で店の名前や商標を染め抜くようになりました。また，のれんという語は店の信用を指します。奉公人の年期があけ，自分の店をもつようになると，主人はのれん分けをします。評判の高い店ののれんを譲り受けることは，名誉なことであるばかりか，実利的でもあるのです。

prized shop.   (O)

nori   seaweed.   It specifically refers to laver or any seaweed of edible kind, known as *asakusa-nori* or *ao-nori*.   It is either boiled in soy sauce (*tsukudani*) or dried and made into blackish purple paper (*hoshi-nori*).   *Nori* is highly nutritious, containing protein, vitamins A and B, minerals, and iodine.   It is in dispensable to many Japanese-style dishes.   For example, it is used for wrapping *maki-zushi* (*sushi* rolls) and *o-musubi* (rice balls) or for garnishing noodles such as *soba* and *udon*. The cultivation of *nori* has long been practiced on the many laver farms laid out inside the bays on the Pacific coast. (HA)

noshi   a strip of dried abalone used as a gift decoration. The Japanese have various elaborate methods of wrapping and decorating gifts.   The most common gift decorations are *noshi* and *mizuhiki*, whose uses vary with the occasion.   *Noshi* is abbreviated from *noshi-awabi* (stretched abalone), which is valued as a symbol of long life.   A long, thin strip of dried abalone is wrapped in specially folded red-and-white paper and pasted on the upper right of a congratulatory gift.   *Mizuhiki* is a pair of strings tied around a wrapped gift and finished up with a decorative knot.   The colors of the strings are red and white for ordinary gifts, gold and silver for wedding gifts, and black and white for funeral offerings.   In Japan it is quite common to give cash as presents.   However, it is never presented unwrapped, but is always enclosed in a proper packet.   Envelopes with *mizuhiki* and *noshi* printed on them

海　苔　　特に食用になる海藻のことで，浅草海苔とか青海苔として知られています。しょう油で煮るか（佃煮），乾燥して黒っぽい紫色の紙状にします（干し海苔）。海苔は栄養価が高く，蛋白質，ミネラル，ビタミンA・B，ヨードを含んでいます。多くの日本料理に海苔は欠かせません。例えば，巻きずしを巻いたり，おむすびを包んだり，そばやうどんの薬味に使われたりします。太平洋岸の湾内の養殖場で海苔の養殖が昔から行われています。

の　し　　日本には贈物の包装や装飾についてさまざまな技巧をこらしたやり方があります。最もよく見られる飾りはのしと水引で，これは時と場合により違った用い方をします。のしは「のしあわび」を省略した語で，長生きの象徴として貴重なものとみなされています。乾したあわびを細長く薄く

延ばしたものを，独特の折り方をした紅白の紙に包み，慶事の贈物の右上に貼付します。水引は1組のひもで，包装した贈物にまわして両端を飾り結びするものです。ひもの色は，普通の贈物では赤と白，結婚の贈物には金と銀，葬儀用には黒と白です。日本では贈物として現金を出すことはまったく普通の習慣ですが，むき出しということはなく，きちんとした袋に入れて出します。便宜上，水引とのしが印刷してある袋をよく使います。

are often used for convenience's sake. (T)

nure-en　a closed-in veranda outside the house shutters. Usually made of wood, it is under the eaves of the roof. A veranda inside the house shutters is called *engawa*. In rural areas, houses are generally large enough to have both. These serve a variety of purposes as do other rooms in a Japanese house. In winter, people sit in these verandas and enjoy the sunshine. In summer, they relax there in the cool of the evening breeze. They also receive and entertain their neighbors or friends there on informal occasions. Nowadays, in the cities, an average house has no space for either of them. (K)

obake　a goblin, a monster, a ghost, or an apparition. One well-known *obake* figure is called *hitotsume-kozō* (a one-eyed monk-dwarf). Another is *rokurokubi* (a long-necked female monster). People enjoy *obake* shows in summer. Visitors go through a designated route set out within a pitch-dark make-shift house, and on the way, encounter many frightening tricks played on them by these imaginary creatures. Such an experience is considered to be an effective way of forgetting the summer heat. The word *obake* is also used to describe anything extraordinary. Thus *obake-kabocha* is a mammoth pumpkin and *obake-yakan* is a giant kettle. (K)

oden　Japanese hotchpotch. *Oden* is a hotchpotch of Japanese radishes, taros, hard-boiled eggs, *hanpen* (fish-paste cakes), *chikuwa* (bamboo-shaped fish-paste cakes), *konnyaku* (paste cakes made from the starch of the devil's tongue plant),

濡　縁　　雨戸の外側にあるベランダみたいなものです。普通
は木で作られていて，ちょうど軒下にあたります。雨戸の内側の
ものは縁側と呼びます。田舎の家は大きいので，両方ともありま
す。これらは日本家屋の他の部屋と同様に多目的に使われます。
冬はそこで日なたぼっこをしますし，夏は夕涼みにちょうどよい
わけです。たいがいのことは隣人，友人ともそこで用を足しま
す。都会の家は一般に狭いので，どちらもほとんどありません。

　　おばけ　　どんなおばけがいるかと
いうと，一つ目小僧やろくろ首が有名
です。夏にはおばけ大会というのがあ
ります。まっくらな小屋の中の決めら
れた通路を通って行くと，いろいろな
妖怪が出てきて，恐ろしい目にあうの
です。これは夏の暑さをしのぐのによ
い方法とされています。おばけという

ことばは，何か異常な形をした物を表現するときにも使います。
例えば，大きなカボチャをおばけカボチャと呼んだり，大きなや
かんをおばけやかんといいます。

　　おでん　　おでんは，大根，里芋，ゆで卵，はんぺん，ちく
わ，こんにゃく，がんもどきなどのごった煮です。辛子か味噌を
つけて食べます。19世紀中頃に盛り場の屋台で最初に売られてか
ら，おでんはすぐに広い人気を得ました。今では特に寒い季節の

ganmodoki (fried soybean curd mixed with bits of vegetables), and so on. It is eaten either with mustard or with
miso (a paste made by grinding a mixture of steamed rice,
cooked soybeans, and salt, and fermenting it in brine). *Oden*
became popular in the mid-nineteenth century, when it was
first served at open-air stalls at pleasure resorts. It has
become one of the representative home-cooked dishes served
especially in the cold season. It is also a good accompaniment
of hot *sake* (rice wine). In the western districts, *oden* is called
kantō-daki (eastern-style hotchpotch). (S)

ohajiki　　marbles. Though it is not known when this
game originated, it was most popular among girls in the Edo
period (1603–1867). A number of small marbles are used in
this game, which is usually played indoors by girls. Players
sit down on the floor and scatter marbles in front of them.
One girl flips a marble in an attempt to hit another without
touching other marbles. If successful, she can get the one she
hit. She can continue flipping her marble until she misses, or
until more than one marble is contacted per flip. Her playing
hand or fingers must not touch any other marble than the one
she is flipping. When she fails, the turn is passed to another
girl. The player who gains the most marbles by the end of the
game is the winner. (O)

oharai　　the Shinto ceremony of purification. In
Shinto ways of life, "purity" is an indispensable concept.
Impurities are believed to invite evil spirits and thereby lead to
calamities. If a person encounters someone's death, for

代表的な家庭料理となっています。また，熱燗の酒のよい肴ともなります。関西地方では，おでんは関東だきと呼ばれています。

おはじき　　この遊びの由来は不明ですが，江戸時代に女の子に最も人気があった遊びです。この遊びは，小さなおはじき玉をたくさん使い，女の子が家の中でします。遊びに加わる者は床に座り，おはじき玉を前にまき散らします。1人が，他の玉に触れずに，一つの玉を指先ではじいて，もう一つの玉に当てようとします。もしうまくいけば，当たった玉は自分のものになります。当てそこなうか，はじいた玉が2つ以上の玉に当たると，次の子に順番が移ります。はじこうとしている玉以外の玉に手や指が触れても交替します。一番たくさん玉を取った者が勝ちです。

お祓い　　神道の生活様式では，清浄ということはとても大切な概念です。不浄は悪霊を呼び，災難を引き起こすと信じられています。例えば，他人の死に遭遇すると，けがれるといわれます。そこで，清めの儀式を行うことになります。この儀式は自分

example, he is believed to become impure. So the person is supposed to perform the rite of purification. He may do it himself by observing a certain symbolic procedure (such as scattering a pinch of salt at the entrance upon coming home from a funeral). He may also visit a shrine to receive a special purification service from a priest. Once he has made his mental absolutions, he might even expect to have made reparation for his moral misconduct. This is a Japanese way of saying that repentance wipes out sin. (HO)

okonomiyaki　 a Japanese pancake. It is a very economical Japanese food served for lunch or snacks. It is highly nutritious, containing a variety of ingredients. The main ingredients for *okonomiyaki* are flour, eggs, vegetables (such as cabbage and onion), and meat or fish and shellfish. A mixture of these is flattened and shaped into a round pizza-like form on a hot plate and cooked in the same way as are pancakes. It is served with mayonnaise, Worcestershire sauce, ketchup, or any combination of these three. The sizes of *okonomiyaki* vary, but it normally measures seven or eight inches in diameter. There are many *okonomiyaki* shops where you can enjoy cook-it-for-yourself-in-your-own-way facilities. Most shops also provide take-out service. (O)

omamori　 an amulet or a charm. Many Japanese people still carry a religious amulet or charm which they buy at a shrine or a temple. It is made of a strip of paper, plastic, or wood, on which some blessing or prayer from the shrine or the temple is written. It is put in a small attractive cloth bag

で行うこともできます。葬式から家へ帰ってきたとき，玄関で塩をひとつまみふりまくというような，一定の象徴的儀式を行うのです。神社を訪れて神主から特別なお清めを受けることもあります。みそぎをすませば，不徳行為の償いがなされたとさえいわれます。これが日本式にいうところの，悔い改めれば罪が許されるということです。

お好み焼　　お好み焼は，昼食または間食として食べる大変経済的な料理です。いろいろな材料を使うので，高い栄養価があります。主な材料は，小麦粉，卵，キャベツや玉ねぎなどの野菜，それに肉か魚貝類です。これらを混ぜ合わせたものを熱い鉄板の上にのせ，薄くのばして，ピザのような円い形にし，ホットケーキを作るのと同じやり方で焼きます。マヨネーズ，ウスターソース，ケチャップ，あるいはこの3種のどれかを混ぜ合わせたソースをかけて食べます。お好み焼の大きさはいろいろですが，普通は直径20センチほどの大きさです。お好み焼屋はたくさんあり，客が自分の好きなように焼いて食べる設備をもっています。たいていの店は持帰りサービスもしています。

お守り　　多くの日本人は今でも，神社や寺でお守りを買って身につけています。お守りは紙やプラスチックや木でできた細長いもので，その上にはお祈りが書いてあります。きれいな布製の小さな袋に入れて，首にかけたり，ハンドバッグや財布にしまったり，車の中にぶらさげたりします。お守りを身につけるのは，

to be worn around the neck, carried in a purse, attached to a wallet, or hung in a car. People carry *omamori*, believing or expecting that it will protect them from various kinds of misfortune, or that it will bring forth divine help in realizing their specific wishes. Since different gods and deities are worshiped at different shrines and temples, people get their specific *omamori* talisman at a specific place. For example, drivers who wish to stay away from traffic accidents go to a shrine where the god controlling traffic safety is worshiped. Pregnant women get their *omamori* from a shrine where the guardian god of infants is worshiped. Some businessmen obtain theirs from the god of commerce, and some high-school students, wishing to pass university entrance exams, get *omamori* from the god of learning. (O)

ōmisoka　　the last day of the year or New Year's Eve. Preparations for the New Year are to be made by *ōmisoka*. General house-cleaning (*ōsōji*) and rice-cake (*mochi*) making used to be among the most important work to be done before the New Year. After the house-cleaning, the New Year decorations made up of pine-tree branches (*kadomatsu*) are put up at the gates, and a sacred straw festoon (*shimenawa*) is hung above the front door. Round mirror-shaped rice cakes (*kagami-mochi*) are offered on the household altar (*kamidana*) or placed in the alcove (*tokonoma*) of the main room. On New Year's Eve, temples ring the watch-night bell (*joya-no-kane*) 108 times, wishing to relieve the human sufferings caused by men's earthly desires, which amount, according to Buddhist belief, to 108. Adult members of the family may sit around a *kotatsu*

神様があらゆる不幸から守ってくれるとか，特別な願いをかなえてくれると信じていたり期待しているためです。いろいろな神々がいろいろな神社や寺でまつられているので，人々は特定のところで特定のお守りを手に入れます。例えば，車の運転をする人は自動車事故にあわないことを願って，安全をつかさどる神様がまつられている神社へ出かけます。妊婦は子供の守り神がまつられている神社でお守りをもらいます。商人は商いの神から，大学入試にパスしたい高校生は学問の神様からお守りをもらうといったぐあいです。

大晦日　　新年を迎える準備は大晦日までに済ますことになっています。大掃除と餅つきが，かつては新年を迎える前にする最も重要な仕事でした。大掃除の後に，松の枝の飾り（門松）を門のところに立て，わらで作った飾り（しめ縄）を玄関に飾ります。そして，丸い鏡の形の餅（鏡餅）を仏壇や神棚や床の間にそなえます。大晦日の夜には，寺院は除夜の鐘を108回つき，仏教の教えによる108の煩悩によって生じる人間の苦悩が除かれるよう祈願します。家庭では大人たちがこたつに座って，除夜の鐘の鳴るのを聞いて祝杯をあげます。この夜の食事は地方によってさまざまです。関西や中部地方では，伝統的なおせち料理を食べ，関東地方ではそばを食べます。

(fire-place with a coverlet) and toast the New Year at the stroke of the watch-night bell. Meals taken on this night vary widely with the locality ; *osechi* or customary dishes for the New Year are served in the western and central districts, and *soba* or buckwheat noodles in the eastern districts. (S)

omiyage a souvenir. In old times, people traveled long distances to visit famous shrines. The custom of giving souvenirs was originally meant for sharing gods' blessings with people who stayed home. Therefore, most souvenirs were local products which were produced in the area of a shrine. Today the religious implication of a souvenir has been lost, but it is still customary for travelers to give gifts to their relatives and neighbors on their return. Visitors also bring presents to the host's home. Depending on the purpose of the visit, souvenirs are carefully chosen. There are a few rules and taboos. For example, when visiting a sick person, it is considered inappropriate to give those flowers that wilt quickly or drop their tops easily. (O)

on moral indebtedness. It refers to the social and psychological indebtedness one incurs upon receiving a favor from those in superior positions. The concept of *on* derived from Chinese philosophy and Japanese feudal society. In feudal Japan, when the society was strictly hierarchically arranged, those in the top ranks were expected to show toward their subordinates a kind of favorable paternalism, including a personal concern for their private lives. In return for such benevolence, inferiors were expected to demonstrate respect

おみやげ　昔，人々は有名な神社にお参りをするために遠いところまで旅をしました。おみやげをあげる習慣は，もともとは，家で待っている人に神様の祝福をわけてあげることを意味したのです。だから，おみやげといえばたいがい，神社のある地域でつくられた物産でした。今日，おみやげのもつ宗教的意味合いは失われましたが，旅行から帰ってくると親類や近所の人たちにおみやげをあげる習慣はそのまま残っています。よその家を訪問するときもおみやげを持って行きます。訪問の目的によって，おみやげ品を慎重に選びます。きまりやタブーもいくつかあります。例えば，病気のお見舞いに行くときは，すぐに枯れたり落ちたりする花を贈ることは不適当とされています。

恩　目上の人から受ける恩恵に対して，社会的，心理的な義理を負うことです。恩の概念は中国思想と日本の封建社会に由来します。日本の封建的階級社会では，目上の者が目下の者の面倒を公私にわたりみていました。その見返りに，恩恵を受けている者が目上の者に対して忠誠を誓っていたのです。これこそ恩のもつ意味なのです。世話になった人に対してその恩に報いる方法はいろいろあります。武士は戦場にでかけ，必要があれば主君のために命をも投げ出します。子供たちは年老いた両親の面倒をみ，親孝行するのです。また，年に2回ほど定期的に行われている贈

and loyalty. Out of this code of behavior developed the concept of moral indebtedness. *On* takes several forms of service for its repayment. The *samurai* warrior fulfilled his obligations to his lord in battle, risking his life if necessary. Sons and daughters exercise acts of *kō* (filial piety) and take care of their aging parents. The gift-giving custom, which is practiced nationwide at least twice a year to benefactors (superiors, teachers, customers, etc.), is also a product of the socio-psychological pressure to repay indebtedness. Japanese society is still governed by the concept of *on*, and human relations are bound by a complicated network of mutual responsibilities and obligations. (Y)

oni   an ogre. The most commonly-found image of *oni* is a human-like figure with a horned head and an ugly red face. A loincloth of a tiger's skin covers its naked body. The *oni* are rather familiar beings in the life of Japanese people, and often appear in folktales, legends, and proverbs as a symbol of evil with violent and cruel natures and of Herculean strength. Parents often tell children that if they misbehave, *oni* will come and eat them. On the day of *setsubun* (a time-honored Buddhist festival of bean throwing held on February 2 or 3), people drive away the *oni* from the household by throwing roasted beans at them. These beans have been used as a charm against demons since ancient times. In Akita Prefecture, young men dressed as *oni* go from house to house, scolding lazy children who do not do their best in their work. In Aichi Prefecture, there is an annual event called *oni-matsuri* (the Ogre Festival) to drive away evil spirits and pray for

答の習慣も恩返しの行為とみることができます。事実，日本の社会はいまだに恩の上に成り立ち，人間関係は相互に対する責任感と義務感に基づく複雑なネットワークのなかに築き上げられています。

鬼　鬼のイメージで最も一般的なものは，人身で角を持ち，醜い赤ら顔をした怪物です。裸で虎の皮のふんどしをしめています。日本人の生活には身近な存在で，民話や伝説などでは，怪力で性質の悪い悪神として描かれています。親が子供に，よい子にしていないと鬼がきて食べられちゃうぞ，などと言います。2月の節分の日には，炒り豆をまいて鬼を追い出します。炒り豆は古来から悪霊を追い払う魔除けに用いられています。秋田県では，鬼に扮した若者が家から家へと訪れて，怠けている子供たちを戒めます。愛知県には鬼祭りという年中行事があり，悪霊を追い払い，来る年の豊作を占います。

abundant farm crops in the coming year. (Y)

onsen   a hot spring. There are many hot springs in Japan and most of them are developed as tourist spots. Japanese people are fond of hot spring bathing. The water is hot enough (more than 25°C or 77°F) and contains various kinds of mineral elements and/or natural gasses. People consider it as an ideal means of relaxation. Vacationers visiting spas usually stay in hotels, inns (*ryokan*), or family-run lodging houses (*minshuku*), and spend several days enjoying their hot spring bathing facilities. Deep in the mountains, local people may relax in a public open-air spa (*rotenburo*). Hot springs have also been recognized as medically effective. They are used not only for recuperation and rehabilitation but also for therapeutic treatment of many chronic diseases (such as rheumatism, gout, neuralgia, hypertension, etc.). (HO)

origami   the art of folding paper. The making of various figures from a piece of paper is one of the unique Japanese arts. Traditionally, *origami* products were commonly used for decorating ceremonial tools at shrines. Even today, the *sake* (rice wine) server and cups used at a Shintoist wedding ceremony are tied with ritualized *origami* decoration. Since the Meiji period (1868–1912), *origami* has been a popular pastime among children. Commercially-sold, colorful, square papers are used for making a variety of figures—stylized cranes, turtles, ships, flowers, hats, balloons, etc. Since *origami* can stimulate and enrich imagination and develop dexterity of hand, it is highly prized by Japanese people. (O)

温　泉　　日本にはたくさんの温泉があり，その多くは観光地として開発されています。日本人は温泉につかるのが好きです。お湯はあたたかく（摂氏25°，華氏77°以上），いろいろな種類の鉱物質や天然ガスを含んでいます。人々はこれを理想的なくつろぎの手段と考えています。休暇をとって温泉を訪れる人々は，普通，ホテルや旅館や民宿に滞在し，温泉浴を楽しみながら数日をすごします。山奥では，土地の人々が露天風呂でくつろぎます。温泉は医学的に効果があると認められてきました。病後の健康回復やリハビリテーションのためだけでなく，多くの慢性病（リューマチ，痛風，神経痛，高血圧など）の治療にも使われています。

折り紙　　1枚の紙からいろいろな形をつくりだす折り紙は日本特有の芸術の一つです。古くは折り紙は神社で儀式用具を飾るために使われました。今日でも，神前結婚で使われる酒の入れ物や盃は儀式用の折り紙で飾られます。明治以降は折り紙は子供の遊びになりました。色とりどりの四角い折り紙を買い，鶴，亀，舟，花，帽子，風船などのいろいろな形を作ります。折り紙は想像力を刺激し豊かにするだけでなく手先を器用にするので，日本人は折り紙を評価しています。

oshibori   a hot, hand towel. It is a damp towel for cleaning hands at the table. Though table napkins or serviettes are rarely used at Japanese-style meals, *oshibori* serves almost the same purpose. A white or light-colored towel just about the size of a Western washcloth is commonly used for *oshibori*. The towel is soaked in either cold or hot water, wrung out thoroughly, rolled tightly, and offered on a plate-type container. *Oshibori* is especially appreciated when it is provided during the hot summer weather. Most Japanese-style restaurants and coffee shops offer *oshibori* all the year round. (O)

ōsōji   general house-cleaning. Among a great many annual events, *ōsōji* (general house-cleaning) is one of the essential preparations for the New Year. It is not merely a thorough cleaning, but has a religious significance of purification. Traditionally, this cleaning, known as *susu-harai* (soot sweeping), took place each year on December 13 as a rite for preparing to welcome the God of the Year. Nowadays, people give their houses a thorough cleaning much later, during the last few days of the year, and furnish them with New Year decorations. In addition to the year-end clean-up, *ōsōji* was customarily done by the entire neighborhood in spring and autumn, on the day fixed by the local government. Even heavy *tatami* mats were all taken up to be aired and dusted off. However, such large-scale cleaning has been made either unnecessary by vacuum cleaners and other effective devices, or difficult by changes in living modes of the Japanese. (T)

おしぼり　　　湿らせたタオルのことで，食卓についたときに手をふくのに使います。和食の場合はテーブルナプキンをめったに使いませんが，おしぼりがその代わりをします。白か淡い色のタオルで，西洋の洗顔タオルほどの大きさのものです。タオルは冷水かお湯のどちらかに浸し，十分にしぼってしっかりたたみ，お皿のような形をした入れ物にのせて出します。おしぼりは夏の暑いときに大変喜ばれます。たいがいの日本料理店や喫茶店では，1年中おしぼりを出してくれます。

大掃除　　　非常にたくさんの年中行事の中で，大掃除は新年を迎える準備として絶対に欠かせないものです。大掃除は，ただ単に徹底的にきれいにすることだけでなく，浄めという宗教的な意味を持っています。伝統的にこの掃除は煤払いとして知られ，歳の神を迎える準備の儀式として，毎年12月13日に行われました。今日での大掃除はもう少し遅く，年末の数日の間に行われ，家々には新年用の飾りつけがされます。年末の大掃除の他に，以前は春と秋に近隣の地区が役所の定めた日にいっせいに大掃除をする習慣がありました。重い畳をすべてあげて風を通し，パンパンとたたきます。しかし，このような大がかりな掃除は，電気掃除機やその他の有効な掃除法のおかげで不要となったり，あるいは日本人の生活様式が変わったために困難になりました。

otedama   a game of beanbags.   It is an old game using small cloth bags filled with beans.   This game originated in the ninth century and has been popular mainly among girls. The word *otedama* refers to both the beanbags and the game. A bag, slightly smaller than a tennis ball, is made of four small pieces of cloth sewn together and filled with beans, rice, or beads.   There are two ways of playing *otedama*.   One involves tossing several beanbags upward with both hands, in a fashion similar to juggling.   In the other, the player manipulates several bags according to a certain rule, while tossing up one main bag called *oya*.   In both cases, the game is played to a song accompaniment.   (O)

oyabaka   a "foolish" parent.   This term refers to a parent who is so fond of his/her own child as to do a "foolish" thing for its sake.   "Foolish" things that such indulgent parents might do for their dear children vary depending on how "foolish" they are.   For example, some may buy their children every toy they show interest in, however difficult it might be financially.   Others may spend every weekend going fishing with their children, although they have something else to do for themselves.   Many are willing to sacrifice themselves in their own way for the wellbeing of their children. Nor can those parents punish their children for any misbehavior, although they often know that they should.   (HO)

oyabun-kobun   the relationship between a boss and one who works for him.   Based on a metaphorical extension of the

お手玉　　お手玉は昔からある遊び
で，豆をつめた小さな布の袋を使って
します。9世紀に始まりましたが，主
に女の子の遊びになっています。お手
玉というと，豆の袋とゲームの両方を
意味します。お手玉は，テニスのボー
ルよりも少し小さく，4枚の小さな布
切れをはぎ合わせ，中に豆や米やじゅ

ず玉を入れて作ります。遊び方は2通り。一つは，両手を使って
数個のお手玉を順ぐりに空中へほうり上げ，取ってはまた上に投
げるという遊びです。まるで奇術のようです。もう一つは，親と
呼ばれる1個のお手玉があがっているうちに，ルールにそって数
個のお手玉をあやつります。両方とも歌に合わせて遊びます。

親ばか　　かわいさのあまりに，子供のためならどんなばかな
ことでもしかねない親のことをいいます。子供に甘い親がかわい
い子供のためにどんなばかなことをするかというと，親のばかさ
加減によっていろいろあります。例えば，ある親は，やりくり算
段をしてでも，子供のほしがるものはなんでも買い与えます。ま
た，ある親は，他にどんなに用事があっても，毎週のように子供
と釣りにでかけます。多くの親は，子供の幸せのためなら自分の
生活を犠牲にすることをいとわないでしょう。別の面からいう
と，このような親は，子供が間違いをおかしても叱ることができ
ないのです。ここは叱らなければいけないと思っても，なかなか
そうできないのです。

親分・子分　　日本社会の特徴となっている親密な家族制度の延
長上にある親分・子分の関係は，相互の経済的・社会的利益のた

closely knit family system of Japanese society, this relationship is meant for these persons' reciprocal economic and social benefits. It is still prevalent (though submerged frequently) in many sectors of Japanese society : political, economic, or even academic. Possessing a greater economic, political, or social power, the superordinate *oyabun* (literally, person who plays the role of a parent) is supposed to take care of the subordinate *kobun* (literally, person who plays the role of a child) in all aspects of his social existence. In return, the *kobun* feels under moral obligation to accept the total authority of the *oyabun* and work for him in every respect. (HO)

oyakōkō   filial piety. In old days, filial piety was one of the most valued codes of ethics binding children. In their childhood, they were taught to be obedient and loyal to their parents. On a daily basis, they were encouraged to help parents with various kinds of errands. If parents were too sick to work, elder children were supposed to take their place to support the family. Although cases to the contrary are often reported in the newspaper, children are still expected to be at least civil to parents. When parents age, affectionate and dutiful sons and daughters very often volunteer to live with them and take care of them in return for their unselfish parenting. (HO)

pachinko   a pinball game. One of the post-war manias which swept the country, it still remains a very popular game today. Virtually every town has several large *pachinko* parlors furnished with more than one hundred machines. A

めにできたものです。それはしばしば裏に隠れることがあります
が，いまだに日本社会の多くの分野においてうかがわれます。こ
のことは，政界，経済界はいうにおよばず学界においてさえいえ
ます。巨大な経済的・政治的・社会的勢力をもつ上位の親分は，
下位の子分の面倒をその社会的存在のすべての面において見るも
のとされています。そのお返しとして，子分は親分の権威を受け
入れ，すべての面で義務を感じ，親分のために働きます。

親孝行　昔は親孝行というのは子供にとって最も大事な道徳
律の一つでした。子供の時に，親のいうことをよくきき，親を大
切にすることを教えられました。日常生活においては，親の手伝
いをいろいろとするよういわれました。反対の例がしばしば新聞
で報道されていますが，子供は今でも親に対して最低限親切であ
ることが期待されています。親が老いると，愛情豊かな，そして
従順な息子や娘は，無心に自分を育ててくれたお返しとして，自
分から，親と同居し世話をすることを申し出ます。

パチンコ　パチンコは戦後日本中
に大流行したものの一つで，現在でも
非常に人気のあるゲームです。どんな
町にも，100台以上の台を備えた大き

player buys a handful of small steel balls, puts them onto the loading tray attached to the vertical pin-table, and flips the lever which sets a ball in motion.   A more recent machine has a handle which automatically flips balls at a regular interval, so that the player has only to hold it at the angle he likes. The ball thus flipped goes down through pins on the table, and if it falls into one of the several winning holes, a dozen additional balls pour out onto the tray to the jingling of a bell. If not, it becomes lost, going into an outlet at the bottom of the table.   When the player succeeds in making a substantial increase in the number of balls, he is awarded prizes in exchange for the balls.   Some parlors keep a rich selection of goods as prizes.   (S)

rajio-taisō   a radio program for health exercise.   This daily program has been continuously broadcast by NHK (Japan Broadcasting Corporation) since 1928.   The regular ten-minute exercise routine consists of a dozen varieties of rhythmical body movements designed to be enjoyed by anyone, anywhere at anytime.   The broadcast is repeated three times during the day, but the 6 : 30 A. M. program has long drawn the biggest audience.   Following the rhythmic beat of *ichi-ni-san-shi* (1-2-3-4), groups of people engage in calisthenics in their neighborhood parks.   School children and their parents are encouraged to participate during their summer holidays. Exercising in unison is supposed to promote friendship and solidarity among the participants.   The exercise program is institutionalized and is practiced even when the radio program is not available.   Factory workers and school children have a

なパチンコ店がいくつもあります。パチンコをする人は，一握りの小さな鋼鉄製の玉を買い，垂直に立ったパチンコ台に付いている玉皿に入れ，玉をレバーではじきます。最近の台には，一定の間隔で玉を自動的にはじき出すハンドルがついているので，お客はそれを好きな角度に保っていればよいのです。こうしてはじいた玉は，台の釘の間を通って下に落ちて行きますが，いくつかある当り穴の中に入れば，12個ほどの追加の玉が，ジャラジャラと鳴るベルの音とともに玉皿に出てきます。そうでなければ，台の一番下にある打ち損じの穴に入っていって，玉はなくなります。玉を相当の量に増やすことができれば，玉と交換に賞品がもらえます。店によっては，さまざまな品物を賞品として置いてあります。

ラジオ体操　　この NHK のラジオ番組は，1928年以来，毎日放送されています。10分間に20ほどのリズミカルな運動を次々に行うようになっていて，だれでも，いつでも，どこでも楽しめる体操です。この放送番組は1日に3度繰り返されますが，朝6時半の番組に人気が集まります。イチ，ニー，サン，シーの掛け声に合わせて，いろいろなグループの人々が近所の公園で体操に励みます。小学生は親といっしょに夏休みのラジオ体操に参加します。こうしていっせいに体を動かすと，友情と団結力が生まれます。ラジオ体操は社会的慣行となっており，番組に合わせなくても行われます。工場労働者や小学生は毎日この体操をしますし，運動会では必ずこの体操をすることになっています。

brief exercise period during the day.   At any athletic meeting
it constitutes an essential part of the event.   (HA)

rakugo   the art of comic story telling.   It is a traditional one-man talk show in which different figures are
distinguished by different voice qualities and head/body
orientations of the performing artist.   The stories are characterized by a humorous contrast of stupid (but sometimes
enlightening) and wise (but often trite) statements exchanged
by a young fool (*yotarō*) and an old master (*go-inkyo-san*).
The stories usually end up with some punning punch lines
(*ochi*).   There are two kinds of stories : classic comic stories
(*koten rakugo*), traditionally inherited by masters of the art,
and new comic stories (*shinsaku rakugo*), newly concocted to
describe current phenomena.   Professional comic story tellers
are called *hanashika*.   They start their career as an apprentice
to one of the masters of the art.   After many years of special
training and trial performances, they have to obtain a license
to be independent performers (*shin'uchi*).   Typically they
wear *kimono* and sit in a formal manner on a small cushion
(*zabuton*) when they tell *rakugo* stories at a special *rakugo*
theater called *yose*.   (HO)

reisui-masatsu   a rubdown with a cold wet towel.   It is
an old-type health exercise that many people still enjoy for
about 15 minutes every morning.   A rubdown with a cold wet
towel is considered to be good for health as it strengthens
the skin and facilitates circulation.   Since it is an uncomforta-
ble experience in the cold of winter, some schools use it for

落　語　　落語は伝統的な話芸で，1人で演じるものです。登場人物の違いは，演じる人が声質を変えたり，頭や体の方向を変えることによって表わします。噺は，若い与太郎のばかな（時には啓蒙的な）ことばと，年とった御隠居さんのかしこい（しかし常にありふれた）ことばというユーモラスな対照によってできています。噺はたいてい語呂合せによるおちで終わります。落語には2種類あります。伝統的に受けつがれた古典落語と，時代の現象を表わす新作落語です。プロの落語家を噺家といいます。彼らはこの職業に入ると，まず見習いとして師匠につきます。長年にわたる特別訓練と前座の修業後，真打ちの資格をとってはじめて一人前になります。落語家が寄席と呼ばれる劇場で一席話すときは，着物をきて，座ぶとんという小さなクッションの上に正座ですわります。

冷水摩擦　　昔流の健康法で，今でも多くの人々が毎朝15分ほど行っています。冷たい水に浸したタオルで体をこすると皮膚が丈夫になり，血行もよくなるので，健康に大変良いといわれています。冬にするのは大変なことな

developing young children's mental discipline and physical endurance. In olden days some people poured cold well water over themselves early in the morning for the same purposes. (K)

rōnin a lordless *samurai* warrior. In the feudal times it often happened that *samurai* warriors would lose their lord in war or social upheaval. They had great difficulty finding another lord from whom they could receive a stipend for the service they would render. These lordless *samurai* warriors were called *rōnin*. They lived in a neighborhood of ordinary townspeople. Because they were poor, they had to work. Many taught children reading and writing. Thanks to their contribution, it is said, the literacy in Japan at that time was considerably higher than that in Europe. Today the term *rōnin* applies to a job-hunter who has resigned from a previous place of work. It also refers to high school graduates who have failed in university entrance examinations and are preparing for another attempt the next year. (K)

ryokan a Japanese inn. Today Western-style hotels are widespread in Japan. However, before hotels became popular, *ryokan* were the most common form of accommodation for travelers. They were an extension of the traditional Japanese living style—a *tatami*-matted room with a no-lock sliding door. They usually did not have a private toilet or bathroom. A maid came to the room to make up the Japanese bed (*futon*) and to serve a Japanese-style breakfast and dinner. Today they offer beautiful *tatami* rooms with all private

ので，子供の精神修養と忍耐力増強のために利用する学校もあります。昔は，同じ目的のために，朝早く冷たい井戸水を頭からかぶった人もいました。

浪　人　　封建時代に，いくさや社会的動乱などで主君をなくした武士はたくさんいました。新たに仕官し，禄をはむことは並たいていのことではありませんでした。このような主君のいない侍を浪人と呼びました。彼らは一般庶民に混じって住んでいました。生活は苦しく，働かなければなりませんでした。多くは子供たちに読み書きを教えましたが，そのおかげで，当時の日本人の読み書き能力はヨーロッパの人々に比べてかなり高かったそうです。今日，浪人といえば，会社をやめて新しい仕事を探している人や，大学入試に失敗して来年を期している学生を指します。

旅　館　　今日，どこへ行ってもホテルがありますが，以前は旅行者に一番よく利用されたのは旅館でした。伝統的な生活様式そのままで，部屋は畳敷き，戸は引き戸で鍵がついていません。個々の部屋には便所もなければ風呂もありませんでした。女中が部屋に来て寝床を延べてくれますし，和食の朝食と夕食を部屋まで運んでくれました。最近では，きれいな畳部屋に，必要な私的設備はすべて整っています。食事は昔と同じで，女中が部屋に運んでくれます。近代的なホテルに比べると，旅館は小規模な個人経営が多く，経営者も家族的な雰囲気を目玉にしています。

facilities, although meals are usually still served in the room by a maid as in old days. Compared with modern hotels, *ryokan* inns are managed on rather a small, private scale, and the owners are proud of their familial atmosphere. (K)

ryōtei　a high-class Japanese restaurant. It is principally a place where sophisticated Japanese cuisine is served. It sometimes serves as an establishment where traditional artistic performances are presented by *geisha* girls. Delicate and crucial business talks and political negotiations are often conducted there and, in many cases, the cost is put on the company expense account. (K)

sadō　tea ceremony. *Sadō*, which is also called *chadō* or *cha-no-yu*, is the traditionally ritualized way of preparing, serving, and drinking *matcha* (powdered green tea stirred in hot water). Tea drinking, introduced from China, was first practiced only by Buddhist priests, and then by *samurai* warriors in the early days. Later it gradually spread among common people. Sen-no-Rikyū (1522-1591) in the sixteenth century raised it to an art form, which lays the greatest emphasis on spiritual tranquility and simplicity of taste. Greatly influenced by Zen Buddhism, the tea ceremony has in turn influenced many aspects of Japanese culture such as architecture, fine arts, and ways of thinking and living. *Chakai* (tea parties) are held not only in *chashitsu* (tea rooms) but in the open air. Today there are a number of tea ceremony schools, including two major ones : Omote-senke and Ura-senke. Many girls study tea ceremony as part of their

料　亭　　主に高級日本料理を供する所です。時には，芸者を呼んで遊芸に興じる場所としても使われます。重要な商売上の取引きや政治的な折衝などにもしばしば利用され，その際の費用はたいていの場合に会社持ちとなります。

茶　道　　茶道とも茶の湯とも呼ばれます。これは，伝統的に儀式化された様式に従って，抹茶に湯を注いでお茶をたて，客にすすめ，味わうものです。お茶を飲むことは中国から伝わり，当初は僧侶だけがたしなんでいましたが，すぐに武士に及び，やがて庶民の間にも広まりました。16世紀に千利休がそれを芸術にまで高めました。茶道は，精神の静かさと趣味の簡素さを最も強調します。禅から大きな影響を受ける一方，建築，美術，思考，生活様式など日本文化の多方面に影響を及ぼしました。茶会は，茶室においてばかりでなく，戸外でも催されます。現在，茶道の流派はいくつもあり，二大流派は表千家と裏千家です。多くの若い女性が花嫁修行の一つとして茶道を学んでいます。

preparation for marriage.　(T)

sake　rice wine.　It is a traditional Japanese alcoholic beverage brewed from fermented rice and water.　There are about 2,600 *sake* manufacturers producing about 4,000 different brands across the country.　Local brands (*jizake*) are appreciated as much as national brands.　There are three different kinds of *sake* in terms of its manufacturing process : *seishu* (refined *sake*), *genshu* (crude *sake*), and *nigorizake* (unrefined *sake*).　*Seishu*, the kind most popularly drunk, has an alcoholic content of about 12-15% or as strong as grape wine.　Taste-wise, every brand is typically referred to as either *amakuchi* (sweet) or *karakuchi* (dry).　You can enjoy *sake* both cold and warm.　If you like it cold, the most common way is to sip it from a square wooden box (*masu*).　If you want it warm, heat it in a *tokkuri* (server) and sip it from a small cup (*sakazuki*).　It is usually said that you can enjoy *sake* at its best condition when warmed up to your body temperature (*hito-hada*).　Some people like it lukewarm (*nurukan*) at 30°C and others hot (*atsukan*) at 50°C.　The choice may depend on the weather or the dishes eaten with *sake*.　Based on the Liquor Tax Act, *sake* is classified by a national inspection agency as special, first, and second grade (*tokkyū*, *ikkyū*, and *nikyū*, respectively).　Almost all national manufacturers apply for a classification.　But many local brewers do not bother to, and put their products on the market as second grade.　Therefore, *sake* connoisseurs believe that local second graders are often as good as national special and first graders.　(HO)

酒　　日本の伝統的なアルコール飲料で，発酵させた米と水から醸造したものです。日本全国には2,600ほどの酒造会社があり，4,000ほどの銘柄を作っています。地酒も大手銘柄と同等の人気を博しています。酒は製造過程からいって3種類あります。清酒，原酒，そしてにごり酒です。清酒が最もよく飲まれます。アルコール分は12〜15％で，ワインとだいたい同じです。味の点からいうと，すべての銘柄は甘口か辛口かのどちらかです。酒は冷やかお燗をして飲みます。冷やの場合は，四角の木の枡で飲むのが一番普通のやり方です。燗の場合は，とっくりで温めて，盃でチビチビやります。人肌が適温とされています。30℃ぐらいのぬる燗を好む人もいれば，50℃ぐらいの熱燗を好む人もいます。どちらにするかは，その日の天候や肴によるでしょう。酒税法があるため，酒は国の等級決定機関によって特級，一級，二級に分類されます。全国銘柄の酒造会社はほとんどみな等級づけのために出品します。しかし，地酒メーカーの多くは出品せず，すべてを二級酒として売り出します。だから，通によれば，地酒の二級酒は全国ブランドの特級か一級なみにおいしいということです。

sashimi sliced raw fish. A plate of beautifully arranged *sashimi* has been considered a delicacy in Japan for centuries. The kinds of fish and shellfish enjoyed are *tai* (sea bream), *katsuo* (bonito), *maguro* (tuna), *hamachi* (yellowtail), *ebi* (shrimp), *ika* (squid), etc. Materials used for *sashimi* are always chosen with special attention, for it is extremely important that they be fresh. It takes particular skill to prepare *sashimi*, because the finest, boneless, skinless fillets of certain fish are sliced into bite-size pieces with an extremely sharp knife. Several kinds of fish slices are usually served together on a plate along with shredded white radish (*tsuma*). A small individual dish of soy sauce mixed with a little bit of hot horseradish (*wasabi*) is served for dipping *sashimi* just before eating. This traditional dipping sauce with the spicy condiment enhances the natural flavor of the fish. (O)

sasshi conjecture. *Sasshi* can loosely be translated as "conjecture", "understanding", "sensibility", "consideration", etc. It is an important concept in interpersonal relationship in Japan. According to the concept of modesty and sincerity that Japanese people esteem, direct self-expression is frowned upon. People are expected to guess what others intend to say. If they are not perceptive enough and dare to ask for information left unsaid, they are branded as rude. This communication pattern, often referred to as *ishin-denshin* (tacit understanding), is possible in a closely-knit community where people share a great many cultural assumptions. It also prevails in a tightly-ordered society where people tend to seek harmonious agreement while avoiding ideological confronta-

刺　身　　日本では昔から，お皿に刺身をきれいに盛りつけたのを御馳走としてきました。鯛，鰹，鮪，はまち，えび，いかなどの魚貝類が喜ばれます。刺身として使う材料は常に細心の注意をはらって選びます。新鮮であることが何よりも大切だからです。刺身をつくるには特別の技術が必要です。骨をとり皮をむきとった魚の最もよい切身を，よく切れる刺身包丁で一口サイズに切り分けます。数種類の魚の刺身を一皿に盛りあわせ，大根のつまを添えます。小皿にしょう油とわさびをまぜ，刺身にちょっとつけて食べます。このちょっぴり辛いわさびじょう油は，魚の持ち味をうんと引き立てます。

察　し　　意味は多義にわたり，日本社会の人間関係における一つの重要な概念になっています。謙遜や誠実さが美徳とされる日本社会では，自己主張は歓迎されません。人々は相手の心を読みとるものとされています。勘が鈍くて，話し手がわざと言い残したことについて質問などをすれば，無礼なやつといわれます。このようなコミュニケーション様式は時に以心伝心などとも呼ばれますが，成員間の関係が緊密で，多くの文化的前提を共有する社会で可能になるのでしょう。またそれは，整然とした秩序を持ち，イデオロギーの衝突を避け，調和を求める社会に生じることではないでしょうか。現在，日本は多種多様の文化的価値観を持った個人主義の社会になろうとしていますので，人々は昔ながらのコミュニケーションの様式をやめ，もっと自己主張を強くする言語使用の様式を身につけてきているようです。

tion. Since Japan is becoming an individualistic society with a diversity of cultural values, people are now abandoning the traditional communication style and acquiring more self-assertive language. (Y)

satori   spiritual enlightenment or awakening.   In the Buddhist philosophy, spiritual enlightenment or awakening constitutes attainment of transcendental wisdom by intuitive insight.   Implications of the enlightenment and methods of attaining it widely differ among the different Buddhist sects. According to the Zen sects, it is the realization of Buddhahood inherent in human beings.   They believe that the attainment of this wisdom will lead one to the state of freedom from karma and suffering (*bonnō*), or to the state of nirvana (*nehan*), which is the ultimate goal of Buddhism.   While the Zen sects emphasize deep meditation as a means of experiencing the enlightenment, the Tariki sects (the sects believing in salvation by faith) such as the Jōdoshū and Shinshū attach more importance to chanting *nenbutsu*, a prayer to Amitabha. (S)

Seijin-no-hi   Coming-of-Age Day.   January 15 is the national holiday when Japanese people celebrate the coming of age of all the youngsters who have reached the age of twenty during the course of that particular year.   The local government plays host to them at a ceremony held in the City Hall. Girls wear a *kimono* made up specially for this occasion.   Boys tend to prefer a Western-style formal suit.   Some people pay a special visit to a temple or a shrine in commemoration of the

236

悟　り　　仏教哲学でいう，直観的洞察によって超越的な知恵を得ることです。悟りの含意と悟りを開く方法は宗派によってさまざまです。禅宗では，悟りとは人間に内在する仏性を認識することであり，その知恵を得れば，人は業や煩悩から解脱した状態，つまり仏教の究極的目標である涅槃の状態に達することができると教えています。禅宗は，悟りを開く方法として深い瞑想を強調するのに対して，浄土宗や真宗などの他力宗（信心による救済を信じる宗派）は，念仏を唱えること，つまり阿弥陀仏への祈りをより重要視しています。

成人の日　　1月15日がその日にあたり，その年に満20歳になった若者を祝う国民の祝日です。市町村では，成人になる人を集めて祝典を催します。女性はこの日のために用意した晴れ着を着ますが，男性は背広を好むようです。神社仏閣に参拝する若者もいます。日本では20歳になると，選挙権が与えられますし，両親の承諾なしに結婚することもできるようになります。

day. At the age of twenty, a Japanese gains, among others previleges, the right to vote and the freedom to marry without parental consent. (K)

seiza   the formal way of sitting on *tatami*. There are basically two ways of sitting on *tatami* : sitting upright (*seiza*) and sitting cross-legged (*agura*). People are expected to sit upright on formal and ceremoninal occasions (for example, at a tea ceremony or a funeral service). People can sit with their legs crossed on informal and casual occasions (for example, at a drinking spree). When acquaintances meet, they often start with the *seiza* mode for an exchange of ritualistic greetings, and then change for the *agura* position. In fact, people seem to believe that they can achieve mental concentaration by straightening themselves up bodily. When they discuss serious matters, they are likely to assume the *seiza* position. Women will rarely sit cross-legged. When they sit at ease, they usually adopt a relaxed *seiza* variant. As the Westernization of houses continues, however, more and more Japanese young people are finding it difficult to sit upright without having their legs shaking under them. (HO)

seken-tei   decency or appearance. One aspect of the national character of the Japanese is what Ruth Benedict (1887-1948) called shame culture, in which people are more afraid of shame than sins. The idea of *seken-tei* derives from an individual's sense of shame, the feeling he experiences when his inferiority is disclosed to the public. Fear of being held in disrepute by society (*seken-tei ga warui*) gives the individual

正　座　畳にすわるには基本的に
2つの方法があります。正座とあぐら
です。正座は，格式ばった状況あるい
は儀式のときにします。例えば葬式や
お茶会の席などです。あぐらは，格式
ばらない気楽な状況でのものです。例
えば酒席などです。人々が会うとき，
まずは正座をして，儀礼的挨拶のこと

ばを交わします。それから，あぐらに変わります。背すじをきち
っと伸ばすすわり方は精神統一によいとされています。重要な問
題を話し合う際には，正座になりがちです。女性はあぐらをかく
ことはまずありません。くつろいでいるときは，正座をくずした
形ですわります。最近は家の中がますます洋風になってきている
ので，若い人たちは正座がなかなかできなくなっています。正座
をするとすぐ足がしびれるのです。

世間体　日本の国民性の一面をルース・ベネディクトが「恥
の文化」と呼びましたが，それは，罪よりも恥を恐れる文化とい
うことです。世間体という考えは，個人の恥の感覚，つまりその
人の劣等性が公けに暴露されるときに経験する感情からきていま
す。世間体が悪いということは，公共の道徳を侵害するような行
為をさし控える大きな理由になります。大切な自尊心を保つとい
うことは，世間に対して体面を保つことにもなります。人々は社

239

an adequate reason for refraining from acts offensive to public morals. People are anxious to keep their self-respect, which may be preserved so long as they appear decent to the public. They seek the approval of society, and consequently tend to act in strict conformity with the socially approved behavioral norms. Sensitive to criticism from others, Japanese people take much account of the public eye and mind what the world says about them. (S)

sekihan   rice steamed with red beans. It is served on festive occasions such as birthdays and weddings. While short grain rice is boiled for ordinary meals, glutinous rice is steamed for *sekihan* together with precooked *azuki* red beans. Both the rice and beans are soaked for many hours beforehand. Cooked with the water in which the red beans were soaked, the color of *sekihan* is light red. It is served hot in an individual rice bowl, or packed in a box if being eaten elsewhere. Toasted black sesame seeds mixed with salt are sprinkled over *sekihan*. (O)

senbazuru   one thousand paper cranes. The crane (*tsuru*) has been a symbol of longevity along with the tortoise (*kame*) for centuries. The former was believed to live for a thousand years, and the latter ten thousand years. In its contemporary sense, the word *senbazuru* commonly refers to strings of folded-paper cranes. Customarily, one thousand small paper cranes are folded with a prayer wishing for the quick recovery of a sick person. The folded paper cranes are meant to show the maker's care and concern for the sick

会の是認を求め，その結果として，社会的に認められた行動規範に厳密に従って行動する傾向が生まれます。他人の批判に敏感で，世間の目を重要視し，世間が自分について何をいっているかが重大な関心事になるのです。

赤　飯　赤飯は誕生日や結婚式のようなおめでたい日に作ります。日常の食事には普通の米を使いますが，赤飯にはもち米を使います。これを，ゆでたあずきと一緒に蒸しあげます。もち米もあずきも，料理する前に水につけておきます。蒸すときにその汁を使うので，赤飯はほんのりと赤い色をしています。赤飯は熱いうちに茶碗に盛って出します。別の場所で食べるのなら箱につめます。そして上からごま塩をふりかけます。

千羽鶴　昔から，鶴は千年，亀は万年も生きると信じられてきました。現代でいう千羽鶴は，折り紙の鶴をひもで通したものを意味します。千羽の小さな紙の鶴を折り，病いの床に伏している人が早くなおるようにと祈ります。折り鶴を作ると，病人のことを気にかけているという意味になります。

千羽の鶴ができあがると，ひもに通して結んで，病人に贈りま

person. When a thousand paper cranes are made, they are tied together with a few strings and presented to the sick person, who hangs them in the room for decoration. (O)

senbei   a Japanese cracker. It is a non-sweet confection enjoyed for snacks. The ingredients of *senbei* are flour, some sweetenings or seasonings, and eggs. Though it is often translated as "rice cracker", soybean flour and wheat flour are also used. It may be flavored with soy sauce, salt, or *miso* (soybean paste). The process of making *senbei* involves several steps. First, the ingredients are mixed. Second, the flour mixture is steamed. Third, the paste is cut into various shapes. Finally, the shaped paste is grilled. (O)

senbetsu   a farewell gift. Some money rather than a gift article is more commonly presented as *senbetsu*. In old times, when it was much harder to travel than it is nowadays, people went to a shrine to pray for a safe journey before leaving for a long trip. It was also customary to invite the relatives and the neighbors for a party. The invited people gave the traveler *senbetsu*, which was meant to be spent for necessities during the trip. The traveler on his return presented *omiyage* (souvenirs) to the persons who had given him *senbetsu*. Even today, this custom of giving a monetary gift is commonly practiced, especially when a person is setting out for a foreign country or when he is moving to a distant place. (O)

senkō   an incense stick used at a Buddhist ceremony.

す。贈られた人はそれを飾りとして病室につるします。

　煎　餅　　煎餅は辛党のおやつとして喜ばれます。煎餅の成分
は，粉と甘味料や調味料と卵です。煎餅は米でできたクラッカー
などと英語でいわれていますが，大豆の粉や小麦粉なども使われ
ます。しょう油や塩や，時には味噌で味をつけます。煎餅を作る
にはいくつかの過程があります。材料を混ぜ合わせ，蒸してか
ら，いろいろな形に切ります。最後にそれを焼き上げるのです。

　餞　別　　餞別には，品物よりも，いくらかのお金を贈ること
のほうがより一般的です。昔は旅行をすることが今よりもずっと
大変だったので，人々は出かける前に神社へお参りをして道中の
安全を祈りました。そして，親類や近所の人を招いて御馳走をす
る習慣もありました。招待された人々は旅に出る人に餞別を贈り
ました。それは旅行中の必要なときに使ってもらうためでした。
旅行者は餞別をくれた人に，お返しとしておみやげを買ってきま
した。現在でも，特に外国へ出かけるときや遠いところへ引っ越
すときには，なにがしかのお金を贈ることが習慣になっていま
す。

　線　香　　線香は江戸時代に発明されたといわれており，それ

The incense sticks are said to have been invented during the Edo period (1603-1867), and they took the place of the incense powder (*kō*), which had been in wide use, because they proved much easier to handle. The incense sticks are made from fragrant wood such as sandalwood, agilawood, benzoin, and clove and also from animal-derived perfumery such as musk and castor. These are blended, impasted, and pressed hard into sticks. Offering a candle (*tōmyō*) and burning *senkō* is an indispensable part of any Buddhist ceremony and service. The incense sticks are also burned when people visit a grave. (S)

sentō a public bath. As recent as several decades ago, many homes did not have bathing facilities. Thus, many people paid regular visits to the neighborhood public bath, which served also as a place where people could congregate to chat and gossip. Some professional talk-show entertainers collected their materials there, listening to conversations of average townspeople while taking a bath together. Today some people still go to a public bath, although the social aspect of these places has diminished. These days they enjoy merely the big bath rather than the conversation. (K)

seppuku suicide by self-disembowelment. Often known as *harakiri* in the Western world, *seppuku* was a death penalty to which a high ranking *samurai* warrior was condemned for a crime of great gravity. It was considered to be a less disgraceful punishment than beheading. It was a solemn, almost ceremonial suicide achieved by a man thrusting a short sword into the side of his belly and then moving it across, and

まで広く用いられた粉状の香にとって代わりました。というのも線香は取扱いがずっと楽であることがわかったからです。線香は，白檀，伽羅，安息香，丁字などの香木から，また麝香，海狸香などの動物性香料から作ります。これらの香料を混ぜ合わせ，糊料を入れて強く圧縮して棒状にします。

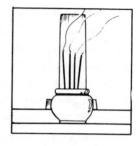

灯明をあげ，線香をあげるのは，仏教の儀式や礼拝に欠かせないものです。線香は墓参りのときにも焚きます。

銭　湯　　数十年前までは，風呂のない家がたくさんありました。そのような人々は銭湯に行ったものです。銭湯は一種の社交場でもあり，世間話や隣近所の噂話などをする場となっていました。噺家などは銭湯で庶民の会話を聞いてネタを集めていたようです。今日でも銭湯を利用する人はいくらもいます。しかし，お互いに親しいというわけではなく，おしゃべりを楽しむというよりも，単に大きな風呂につかることが楽しいといった感じのようです。

切　腹　　外国でははらきりなどといわれていますが，重罪を犯した上流武士に対する処刑の方法のことです。打ち首よりもまだ名誉が重んじられる刑でした。武士の切腹は厳粛で儀式的な行為で，男性は短刀で腹を横一文字に切り，女性は匕首を喉元につきさす

by a woman stabbing a dagger into her throat. By enduring the pain, the *samurai* was assumed to have made amends for his wrongdoing. To relieve the suffering, an aide would terminate his life moments later by beheading him with a long sword. One of the well-known historic cases of *seppuku* was the instance of the "forty-seven *rōnin* (masterlss *samurai* warriors)", who were sentenced to death by *seppuku* for the murder of Lord Kira in 1703. They had murdered him in the preceding year in revenge for the *seppuku* of Lord Asano, their master. In a similar way, at the end of World War II, several generals committed *seppuku*, though they were not ordered to do so. Since they led the nation to defeat, they felt they had failed to fulfill their responsibility to the Emperor. Another case was that of Mishima Yukio (1925-1970), an internationally famous novelist, who committed *seppuku* after he had failed to raise the Japanese Self-Defense Forces for a coup d'état against the contemporary government in 1970. This anachronistic act was a great shock to the Japanese people. People now use this term only metaphorically, implying how seriously they consider their responsibility for an error, say, in a business interaction. (K)

shabu-shabu　　a meat dish cooked at the table. The name *shabu-shabu* came from an onomatopoetic sound a slice of meat makes when it is dipped and cooked in a pot of boiling broth. The ingredients for *shabu-shabu* are very thinly sliced meat (beef or pork), *tōfu* (soybean curd), and vegetables such as Chinese cabbage (*hakusai*), mushrooms, and bean sprouts. Dipping sauces, such as a vinegary sauce (*ponzu*) and a sesame

ということをします。断末魔に耐えつつ，自分の犯した罪をつぐなうのです。無残な苦しみを早く終わらせるために，介錯人が長刀で首を切り落とします。歴史上有名な切腹には，元禄16年（1703年）の四十七士の例があります。彼らは，主君浅野内匠頭の仇をうつために吉良上野介を殺害し，切腹を命じられました。同様に，第2次大戦後，何人かの将校が自害しました。彼らは，日本を敗戦に導き，天皇に対する責任をまっとうできなかったことで，死んでお詫びをと考えたからです。別の事件としては，世界的にも有名な小説家三島由紀夫の切腹があります。1970年に当時の政府に対して自衛隊のクーデタを企てましたが失敗に終わり，自害したのです。この時代錯誤な行動は日本国民に衝撃を与えました。現在では，切腹ということばは比喩的にしか使われません。仕事で失敗した人は，その責任の重大さをかみしめて，腹を切らなければなどと言ってみるのです。

しゃぶしゃぶ　しゃぶしゃぶという名前は，薄切りの肉を熱いだし汁の中でゆすりながら煮るときの擬音からきたものです。しゃぶしゃぶの材料は，薄く切った肉（牛か豚），豆腐，白菜やしいたけやもやしなどの野菜類です。つけ汁としてポン酢やごまだれを小鉢に用意し，きざみねぎや大根おろしを添えます。料理は簡単です。薄切りの肉を最初に鍋に入れます。肉が煮えたら（好みにもよりますが，たいがい数秒間）すぐに鍋からとりだし，

sauce (*gomadare*), are served in individual bowls with chopped green onion and grated white radish (*daikon-oroshi*) for garnish. The cooking procedure is simple. The thin meat slices are always put in the pot first. As soon as the meat is cooked (usually in only a few seconds depending upon the diners' tastes), it is immediately removed from the pot and dipped into the sauce. When the meat has been savoured and enjoyed, the vegetables and *tōfu* are cooked in the same way. (O)

shamoji also **shakushi** a ladle or a rice scoop. It is a kitchen utensil for ladling out soup or boiled rice. Ladles for scooping up soup were formerly made of wood, bamboo, or shells, but they have been replaced by metallic ones. The rice scoop with a flat and oval head is mostly wooden, and it has been a symbol of the housewife since old times. Even today, members of the Housewives' Federation, when holding a demonstration, carry large rice-scoop-shaped placards. It is also a fetish sold at some famous shrines. It came to symbolize abundant crops because of its close relation to the staple food. (S)

share unconventional and unconstrained behavior or refined and stylish attire. The word is often considered synonymous with *iki* (chic and coquettish), which some people hold is a characteristically Japanese aesthetic concept. Traditionally *share* was considered to be the spirit characteristic of townsfolk and tradespeople rather than of the warrior (*samurai*) class. The derivative *o-share* always refers to personal adornment or to a person who smartens himself.

たれにつけます。肉を賞味したあと、野菜や豆腐を同じ方法で食べます。

　　しゃもじ・しゃくし　　汁をすくうしゃくしは，以前は木製，竹製または貝製でしたが，今日では金属製のものになっています。御飯をよそう平たい楕円形のしゃもじはたいてい木製で，昔から主婦の象徴でした。今日でも主婦連はデモをするときに，プラカードの代わりに大きなしゃもじを掲げます。
また，しゃもじは有名な寺院で呪物として売られてもいます。主食との緊密な関係のために，五穀豊穣の象徴となったのです。

　　しゃれ　　洒脱な行為や態度，または洗練され気のきいた身なりを指すこの語は，よく粋（シックで色気があること）と同意とみなされます。粋は日本特有の美的概念であると考える人もいます。伝統的にしゃれは，武士階級よりも町人，商人に特有な精神と考えられていました。派生語のおしゃれは，身なりを飾ること，または身なりを飾る人を意味します。やぼはしゃれの反意語です。しゃれには，また，座興のための機知のあることば，特に冗談や語呂合せという意味もあります。日本語には同音異義語が

Yabo is an antonym of *share*. *Share* is also a witty remark made to amuse one's company, such as a joke or a pun. Since the Japanese language abounds in homonyms, it is comparatively easy to make puns, which are, however, often looked down upon as *dajare* (poor jokes). (S)

shibumi austere elegance. The noun *shibumi* comes from the adjective *shibui*, the form that is more popularly used. The concept of *shibumi* covers many aesthetic properties. Its literal meaning is "astringency", commonly referring to the taste of an unripe persimmon. When it is applied to various other properties (such as color, design, taste, human character, manner, voice, etc.), it designates a subtle, unobtrusive and deeply moving pattern of beauty: *shibui iro* (an austere, elegant color), *shibui kōtaku* (a sophisticated luster), *shibui koe* (a low, well-modulated voice), *shibui engi* (a well-restrained performance), etc. The concept of *shibumi* has been fostered by artists and connoisseurs since the Muromachi period (1333-1568), and carefully preserved to this day in the vocabulary of the common people. In the meantime, it is often associated with such concepts as *wabi* (the beauty of simplicity) and *sabi* (the beauty of tranquility). (Y)

Shichi-fuku-jin the Seven Gods of Fortune. *Shichi* is seven, *fuku* is happy, and *jin* is a person, or in this case a god. Thus, *Shichi-fuku-jin* means the Seven Gods of Good Fortune. They personify the seven virtues of man in the form of seven deities symbolizing wealth and fortune. They always appear aboard a sailing ship, called *takara-bune* (the treasure ship).

多いので，語呂合せは比較的簡単にできますが，これはだじゃれといわれて軽く見られることもあります。

しぶみ　しぶみは名詞形で，もっと一般的な用法はむしろ形容詞形のしぶいです。しぶみという概念は多くの美的領域に関係します。本来，柿のしぶみのように，舌を刺激する味のことですが，色，デザイン，味，人格，行動，容姿，声などの描写の際は，地味で落ちついた深みのある趣きを表現しています。例えば，しぶい色とかしぶい光沢，しぶい声，そしてしぶい演技などといいます。しぶみの概念は室町時代にまでさかのぼり，芸術を愛好する人々によって大事にはぐくまれて，現在の一般庶民の語彙の中に入ってきたのです。同時に，しぶみはわびや，さびの概念に通じるところがあります。

七福神　直訳すると，7人の幸福な神々，すなわち幸福をもたらす7体の神々ということです。彼らは，人間の求める7つの福徳を擬人化したもので，皆いっしょに1隻の宝船に乗っています。毎年大晦日になると人々に幸

It comes into harbor every New Year's Eve to bring good luck to everyone. These seven gods are: *Ebisu* (the god of fishermen and tradesmen), *Daikoku* (the god of wealth and the patron saint of farmers) also known as *Ōkuninushi-no-mikoto, Benten* (the only goddess, who represents art, literature, music, and eloquence), *Bishamonten* (the god of war), *Fukurokuju* (the god of prophets), *Jurōjin* (the god of longevity), and *Hotei* (the god of contentment and happiness). They are believed to bring good luck and, therefore, are kept in shrines and houses throughout the country. (Y)

shichi-go-san   the seven-five-three festival. *Shichi, go*, and *san* literally mean seven, five, and three respectively. *Shichi-go-san* is the festival for boys and girls of three, boys of five, and girls of seven. In Japan these three ages are very important in the growing stages of children. On November 15, children of these ages are dressed in their best clothes and taken to a Shinto shrine by their parents. There they give thanks for their good health and pray for future blessings. Many girls wear colorfully patterned *kimono*, usually made specially for this occasion. The parents proudly take pictures of their children and buy them a stick of candy called *chitose-ame* (literally, 1,000-years-of-age candy) on the shrine grounds. This festival is said to have its origin in various customs of initiation observed in many parts of the country at certain prescribed points in the lives of children. (T)

shikishi   a square piece of fancy paper for writing a poem on. *Shikishi* is about a ten-inch-square paper on which

運を授けに港へと入って来ます。7人の神々とは次のとおりです。すなわち、漁師や商人の神である恵比須、福の神であり農民の守護神でもある大黒（またの名は大国主命）、唯一の女神であり、芸術、文学、音楽、弁舌の徳のある弁天、戦いの神である毘沙門天、予言の神である福禄寿、長寿の神である寿老人、そして最後に、満足と幸福の神である布袋です。彼らは幸運を招くものとして、全国の神社や家々で大切にされています。

七五三　七五三は文字通り7と5と3を表わし、3歳の男児と女児、5歳の男児、そして7歳の女児のための祭です。日本ではこの3つの年齢は、子供の成長段階において大変重要とされています。11月15日にこの年齢の子供は晴着を着て両親と神社へ行きます。神社では子供の健康を感謝し、将

来の加護を祈願します。女児の多くはこの日のために特別に仕立てた色鮮やかな模様の着物を着ます。境内で両親は誇らし気に子供の写真を撮り、千歳飴と呼ばれる棒状のキャンデーを買い与えます。この祭は、子供の成長のある一定の時期に、全国各地で行われていたさまざまな通過儀礼に起源を持つといわれています。

色　紙　色紙は約10インチ平方の大きさで、詩歌や日本画をかくための紙です。色紙の起源は、色のついた四角の紙に和歌を

to write a poem or to paint a Japanese-style picture.   It is said to have had its origin in the ancient practice of writing a *waka* (31-syllable Japanese poem) on a square piece of colored paper which is subsequently pasted on the *byōbu* (folding screen) or the *fusuma* (sliding screen) which has been painted with a landscape scene.   The present-day *shikishi*, made stiff and thick with linings, is usually white, but sometimes decorated with pale-colored patterns or sprinkled gold and silver dust. It serves independently as an interior decoration, or is presented as a token of remembrance.   It is popularly used not only for a poem or a picture but also for an autograph or *yosegaki* (literally, a collection of writings) in which a group of people each contribute a few words of congratulation or farewell as well as their signatures.   (T)

shikki   lacquer ware.   It refers to any artistically crafted article with a lacquer finish.   Since the introduction of refined lacquer techniques into Japan from China around the seventh century, various lacquer ware items with fine and distinctive local qualities have been produced throughout the country.   The lacquer ware of Japan excels in its durability because of its fine craftsmanship.   In particular, those of high quality can withstand high humidity and extreme changes in temperature.   Some of the more famous lacquer ware articles include : *makie*, manufactured in Kyoto and attractive for its graceful design and gold-and-silver-flaked surface ; *shunkei-nuri*, made in Gifu and characterized by thinly coated brownish lacquer ; *wajima-nuri* of Ishikawa, at present the most popular lacquer ware due to its durability and wide prac-

書き，風景画が描いてあるびょうぶやふすまに貼りつけた昔のしきたりにあるといわれています。現在の色紙は，裏打ちのある堅く厚い紙です。通常白色ですが，淡い色の模様がついているものや，金粉や銀粉を点々とあしらってあるものもあります。単独で室内装飾として用いたり，記念品として贈ったりします。色紙にかくものも詩や絵ばかりでなく，サインや寄せ書きなどもあります。寄せ書きとは，何人かの人々がそれぞれ自分の名前と，お祝いとかお別れのことばを1枚の色紙に書いたものです。

    漆　器　　表面に漆塗加工のしてある美術工芸品を指します。7世紀頃に中国より洗練された漆塗加工の技術が導入されて以来，国内全域でそれぞれ地方色豊かな作品が生まれています。日本の漆器は高度な職人芸から生み出され，耐久性に優れています。とりわけ高級品は気候の変化や高湿度にも十分耐えるものです。数ある中でも，優雅なデザインと金銀粉をまきつけてある京都産の蒔絵，岐阜の名産で褐色の漆を薄く塗りつけてある春慶塗，耐久性があり家庭用品としての実用性の高さから最も人気のある石川県の輪島塗，そして，あでやかな木彫りの上に朱漆や黒漆を塗った鎌倉彫などが有名です。

ticality for domestic use , and *kamakura-bori*, with elaborate chiseling and layers of lacquer in black and vermilion.　(Y)

shinbutsu-konkō　a mixture of Buddhism and Shinto-ism.　The polytheistic nature of Shintoism not only tolerated the introduction of Buddhism into Japan but also established harmony between the old and new religions.　People enshrined both Buddha and Japanese native gods in the same place on the basis of a doctrine identifying Buddha and Buddhist saints with the ancient gods and goddesses of Shintoĭsm.　According to the doctrine (*honji-suijaku-setsu*), Buddha and Buddhist saints appear in the guise of familiar deities to work for the salvation of Japanese people.　They could, therefore, worship both Buddhist and Shintoist deities at the same time without bothering about consistency in their faith.　This belief dating from the eighth century was generally accepted and remained popular for centuries, until separation of Shintoism and Buddhism was strongly advocated during the Meiji period (1868–1912).　(S)

shinjū　a double or multiple suicide.　The most usual case is that of a man and a woman committing a double suicide when they believe that their love for each other cannot be fulfilled in this world.　Their reasons for doing so may vary from case to case, although class disparity is perhaps the most common.　Other cases may involve a family suicide as the result of the parents' financial failure in business.　In such cases, parents apparently believe that their children would be happier to die together with them rather than be left alone

神仏混淆　　土着の宗教である神道は多神教的性格を持っていたために，仏教の日本への伝来に対してあまり抵抗を示しませんでした。このため，古い宗教と新しい宗教の間に調和が生まれました。仏陀や菩薩を神道の古代の神々と同一視する教義に基づいて，仏陀と日本古来の神々は同じ場所に祭られました。この教義（本地垂迹説）によれば，仏陀や菩薩は日本人を救済するために，よく知られた神々に変装して現われるということです。だから，日本人はその信仰上の矛盾を気にかけることなく，仏と神とを同時に崇拝することができたのです。8世紀に起こったこの考えは，それ以来長い間一般に信じられてきましたが，明治時代になると，神道と仏教の分離が強く主張されました。

心　中　　最も一般的なケースは，男女2人の場合で，この世で成し遂げられそうもない愛の行方に悲観して一緒に自殺するものです。これほどまでに思いつめる理由はいくつかあります。一番多いのは社会的理由で，例えば，家族の社会的背景が違うといったことがあります。他のケースでは，一家心中があります。親の商売上のやりくりがつかなくなり，子供を道連れにしようとするのです。親にしてみれば，子供は後に残されるよりも死を共にしたほうが幸せと考えるのでしょう。中には，家名を守るためには一家心中しかないと考える人もいます。

without parental care. Some people might also resort to a family suicide to protect their family honor if they believe this is the only recourse. (K)

Shinkansen   the New Trunk Line for a "bullet" train. Always hailed here and abroad as representing Japan's technological advancement, it is a railroad system for super-express passenger trains. The Japanese National Railways has three *Shinkansen* systems in operation now. The *Tōkaido Shinkansen* goes from Tokyo via Kyoto and Osaka southwest to Hakata, Fukuoka Prefecture, Kyushu, covering a distance of 1,069 kilometers (664 miles) in 6 hours and 40 minutes. The *Tōhoku Shinkansen* and *Jōetsu Shinkansen* run from Tokyo northeast to Morioka (465 km or 289 mi) and north to Niigata (270 km or 168 mi) respectively. The most popularly used line is that between Tokyo and Osaka on the *Tōkaido Shinkansen*. Completed in 1964 as the first priority project in the whole *Shinkansen* network, it serves the nation's most industrialized area on the Pacific coast for a distance of 500 km (311 mi) in 3 hours and 8 minutes with a maximum speed of 210 kilometers per hour or 130 mph. (HO)

shinkyū   acupuncture and moxibustion. More popularly known as *hari*, acupuncture is one of the Oriental medical methods for killing pain by insterting fine needles at varions therapeutic points of the human body. This technique has been long accepted in Japan for eliminating small pains such as stiff shoulders and a backache. In China, a more modernized method of acupuncture through the use of electricity has

新幹線　　弾丸列車用の特別鉄道です。国内外で日本の技術発展の象徴と称賛されています。国鉄は現在のところ3本の新幹線システムをもっています。東海道新幹線は，東京から京都，大阪を通って南西の博多まで行きます。全長1,069km（664マイル）で，6時間40分で行きます。東北新幹線は東京から東北の盛岡（465km，289マイル）まで，そして上越新幹線は東京から北の新潟（270km，168マイル）まで行きます。もっとも利用度の多い区間は東海道新幹線の東京―大阪間です。この線は新幹線ネットワークの最優先プロジェクトとして1964年に完成しました。これは，日本でもっとも産業化が進んだ太平洋沿岸の500km（311マイル）を3時間8分で走ります。最高時速は210km（130マイル）です。

鍼　灸　　一般にハリと呼ばれるものは，東洋医学の一つで，身体の特定な部分に針を刺すことにより苦痛を和らげる治療方法です。日本では，肩こりや背中の痛みをとり除く治療法として，長年人気があります。中国では，電気を利用した，さらに近代化したハリ治療が，外科手術の麻酔法として開発されています。また，お灸も良く知られた治療法で，ひとつまみのもぐさを身体の一部にのせ，火をつけて燃やすことにより，循環系統や神経系統

been developed for anesthesia in operations. Familiarly called *o-kyū*, moxibustion is another widely known treatment for improving the health by kindling a small amount of moxa on certain therapeutic points to heal the circulatory and neural troubles. Acupuncture and moxibustion are popular ways of maintaining good health among the elderly, especially in those cases where Western medical treatment has not been effective. (K)

Shintō Shinto or Shintoism. Shinto is Japan's native religion. It is based on the Providence of *Kami* (God), the laws of nature, and ancestor worship. Historically, it existed from the dawn of Japanese civilization, but it became more clearly defined after Buddhism entered Japan in the middle of the sixth century. According to Shinto mythology, Amaterasu-ōmikami, the goddess of the sun, was born to rule in Takamaga-hara (the Plain of High Heaven). The misbehavior of her younger brother upset her so much that she hid away in a cave, leaving the universe in complete darkness and chaos. Many gods enacted a lot of merrymaking to bring her out. Finally she came out and shone again, thereby restoring order. Six generations after her, Jinmu became Japan's First Emperor. This legend supported the hegemony of the Imperial family over other ancient great families, and thus Shintoism became part of the emperor system (tennoism) of Japan. With the Meiji Restoration in 1868, Shinto became the state religion promoting the authority of the emperor, and shrines were supported by the Government. The state-religion union took on a nationalistic tone. Especially in the

に適度な刺激を与えて，健康の回復をはかるのです。鍼灸はお年寄りの間で，健康を維持する方法として人気があり，特に西洋医学では効果の少ない場合に使われています。

　　神　道　　神道は日本固有の宗教であり，神の摂理，自然の法則，そして祖先崇拝などを説いています。歴史的には，日本の文明の誕生以来存在していますが，6世紀中頃の仏教の伝来にともなって，よりはっきりした教義を持つようになりました。神道の神話によると，太陽の女神である天照大神が高天原の主神として生まれました。女神は弟の不品行に業を煮やして洞穴へと身を隠してしまいました。そのために世界中が暗闇の大混乱に陥ったのです。そこで，多くの神々はお祭り騒ぎをして，女神を呼び出そうとしました。ついに女神は現われ，地上に光が戻り，世の秩序も回復したというのです。女神から6世代たって，神武が日本の最初の天皇になりました。この伝説は，皇族の他の豪族に対する支配権を裏付ける役割をはたしました。したがって，神道は天皇制の一部に組み込まれました。1868年の明治維新にともなって，神道は天皇の権威を助長する国家宗教となり，神社は政府の管轄下に置かれました。国家と宗教の合体は国粋主義的な気風をもたらしました。特に，1930年代の愛国主義の時期には，国家神道が広く普及しました。しかし，第2次大戦後，国家との関係が断ち切られ，神社神道と宗派神道のみが残ったわけです。今日，人々は祈願成就や参拝に神社に出かけます。

jingoistic decade of the 1930s, "State Shintoism" was prevalent. But after World War II, it was disbanded, and only "Shrine Shintoism" and "Sect Shintoism" remained. Today people visit a Shinto shrine to pray for the materialization of their wishes and to attend certain self-purification services. (K)

shippō   cloisonné. *Shippō* is ornamental work in which various colors of enamel are used to produce beautiful designs on a base of metal or ceramic objects. The term *shippō* literally means seven treasures, which, according to a Buddhist sutra, are gold, silver, lapis lazuli, crystal, giant clam, coral, and agate. *Shippō* articles such as vases, plaques, and personal ornaments have won worldwide fame for their exquisite beauty. However, the origin of *shippō* is scarcely known; it is considered to have been introduced from China around the seventh century. In those early days the art of *shippō* was not practiced for very long, and it was discontinued for several centuries of its history. In the seventeenth century it was revived and improved remarkably, particularly by a craftsman who came from a village near Nagoya. The village was later named Shippō in honor of his great contribution to modern cloisonné. (T)

shiro   a castle. It was made of heavy stucco and thick timbers set on a stone foundation surrounded by a moat. Castles in Japan originally served as military fortresses designed to defend the lords from possible enemy invasions. In feudal ages, they served both as a residence and as a seat for

七 宝　さまざまな色のガラス釉を金属や陶器の素地に焼き付けて美しい図案を作り出す装飾工芸です。七宝という語は文字通りに7つの宝の意味で，ある仏典によれば，金，銀，瑠璃，水晶，しゃこ，さんご，めのうとされています。花びん，額，装身具などの七宝焼は，精巧な美しさで世界的な名声を博しています。しかし，七宝の起源はほとんどわかっていません。7世紀ごろ中国から伝わって来たと考えられています。伝来当初は七宝の技術はあまり長く続かず，その歴史に数世紀の空白期間があります。17世紀になって復活し，とりわけある工芸家のおかげで著しく進歩しました。その工芸家が出た村は名古屋に近く，後に近代の七宝に対する多大な貢献を記念して七宝村と名付けられました。

城　城は堀にかこまれて，石垣の上に丈夫なモルタルと分厚い材木を用いて築き上げられました。日本の城は当初，外敵の侵入から領主を守るために軍事的要塞として使われました。封建時代になると，領主の住居としてだけではなく，領内の統治，権勢の象徴としても機能しました。城の周囲には城下町が栄えまし

military and political power of the lords. Towns developed around castles. At first these communities were small, consisting merely of a castle surrounded by powerful followers' dwellings, merchants' stores, and artisans' workshops. These castle towns have developed into the present cities of Tokyo, Osaka, Nagoya, Himeji, Kanazawa, and many others. Today castles in these cities provide some of the most attractive tourist spots in Japan. (K)

shiruko   sweet bean soup.   *Shiruko* is a hot sweet soup made of cooked red beans (*azuki*).   It has been a favorite with the Japanese as a traditional snack or dessert in winter. Many kinds of traditional Japanese sweets contain sweet bean paste made from boiled *azuki* red beans.   When the paste is pureed, thinned with water, and a certain amount of sugar is added, it becomes the *shiruko* soup.   It is always served hot in a small lacquer ware bowl, and usually a few small pieces of grilled *mochi* (rice cakes) are added.   A pair of chopsticks is used for the *mochi*, and the soup itself is drunk directly from the bowl. (O)

shō-chiku-bai   pine-bamboo-plum. This word consists of three Chinese characters which mean "pine, bamboo, and plum", respectively.   Since these three plants are all very hardy against the cold, they were appreciated during winter and came to be used for a symbolic decoration on happy occasions such as New Years, weddings, commencements, etc. They are always used together as a set.   Real trees, branches, leaves, or blossoms of *shō-chiku-bai* are often used as a

た。最初は，家臣の住居や商店，職人の仕事場などからなる小さい町でした。これらの城下町はやがて，現在の東京，大阪，名古屋，姫路，金沢などの大都市へと発展していったのです。今日，これらの都市に残存する城は観光の名所になっています。

汁　粉　　あずきを煮て甘い汁にしたものです。汁粉は日本の伝統的なおやつやデザートとして，特に冬に好まれます。日本の多くの伝統的なお菓子には，あずきを煮て作ったあんこが入っています。あんをきれいに漉して水で薄め，砂糖を加えて作るのが汁粉です。熱くして小さな塗りのお椀によそい，焼いた餅をいくつか加えて出します。餅を食べるのには箸を使いますが，汁粉は直接お椀からすすります。

松竹梅　　これは松，竹，梅という
3つの漢字から成り立っています。こ
れらの3種類の植物は寒さに対してと
ても強いところから，冬の間に珍重さ
れます。そして，お正月や結婚式や卒
業式といった喜びのときに，その象徴
的な飾りとして使います。いつも3種
を合わせて使います。普通は本物の松

ceremonial decoration, but a picture or a figure of these three may also serve the same purpose. (O)

shōchū a traditional Japanese distilled spirit. It is made from sweet potatoes, buckwheat, molasses, barley, rye, rice, corn, sugar cane, carrots, tomatoes, sesame, strawberries, or even coffee beans. The *shōchū* of Okinawa is made from millet and is called *awamori*. The popularity of *shōchū* is now becoming more and more conspicuous, because the price is more reasonable than any other kinds of alcoholic beverages due to lower liquor taxes. As its alcoholic content is very strong (25-50%), *shōchū* is generally drunk with hot or cold water. It is also mixed with soda (called *chū-hai*), soft drinks, or various kinds of fruit juice. It is perfect to mix with tomato juice for a bloody Mary, with orange juice for a screw driver, or with grapefruit juice for a salty dog. (HO)

shochū-mimai an inquiry after a person's health in the hot season. Many years ago, it was customary to visit relatives and friends to inquire after their health in the heat of mid-summer. This practice still remains common in rural areas especially among the older generations. Today writing letters is more popular than making visits. People use postcards to inquire as to whether their relatives and friends are keeping well in the hot summer and to express the sincere wish that they take the best of care of themselves. (K)

shodō calligraphy or the art of producing fine and elegant writing. This visual art is characteristic of countries

竹梅の木や枝や葉を儀式用の飾りとして使いますが，これらを絵に画いたものを使うこともあります。

　焼　酎　　焼酎は昔から日本にある蒸留酒で，さつまいも，そば，黒糖，麦，ライ麦，とうもろこし，さとうきび，人参，トマト，ゴマから，あるいはコーヒー豆からも作ります。沖縄の焼酎は粟から作られ，アワモリと呼ばれます。最近，焼酎の人気はうなぎのぼりです。酒税法の関係で値段が安いからです。焼酎はお湯か水で割って飲むのが一般的です。ソーダや，ソフトドリンクや，いろいろなジュースともよく合います。ソーダで割ったのをチューハイといっています。トマトジュースで割ればブラディメアリー，オレンジジュースで割ればスクリュードライバー，グレープフルーツジュースで割ればソルティドッグになります。

　暑中見舞　　昔は，夏の暑い盛りに，親戚，知人などの安否を気遣って訪問するのが習わしでした。地方に行くと，年輩者の間では今でも行われています。一般には，手紙で用を済ませる方が普通です。葉書で親戚，知人などに安否を問うとともに，十分健康にも留意してほしい旨を書き添えます。

　書　道　　この視覚芸術は漢字を使用する国々に特有のものですが，それは漢字がその性格から審美的対象になるからです。唐

where people use Chinese characters (*kanji*), which can be, by nature, an object of aesthetic delights. As early as the ninth century when Japanese nobles had great esteem for the culture of the Tang-Dynasty China, they regarded calligraphy as an important part of their education. The invention of Japanese characters (*kana*) in the ninth century forwarded the development and popularization of calligraphy. It is now a required subject for elementary school and junior high school students, and also one of their most popular extra-curricular activities. Writing brushes (*fude*) and India ink (*sumi*) are used in writing. More importance is attached to concentration of the mind than to dexterity of the hand. Calligraphy is then often considered to be a way of cultivating the mind as well as of attaining skillful penmanship. (S)

shōgatsu   the first month of the year, or historically the first month of the lunar calendar. The word *shōgatsu*, however, more often means a particular period of the New Year, especially the first three days or the first week of January, rather than the month itself. The customs prevailing during this festive season originated in the religious observances performed by the ancients, who prayed at year's beginning for the favor of their ancestoral deities and for an abundant crop for the year. However, the religious implication has been lost, and people now follow the time-honored customs simply in celebration of the New Year. Spiced *sake* (*toso*) and rice cakes boiled with vegetables (*zōni*) are what characterize the breakfast taken on the morning of New Year's Day. Some people start the New Year with new

の文化を日本の貴族が高く評価していた9世紀には，早くも書道は貴族の重要な教養の一部とみなされていました。9世紀の仮名文字の発明は書道の発達をさらに促進しました。現在では，書道は小中学生の必修課目ですし，人気のある課外活動でもあります。書くには，毛筆と墨が必要です。手先の器用さよりも精神の集中に重きが置かれます。能筆になる技術を習得すると同時に，精神の修養にもなると考えられているのです。

　　正　月　　　正月とは歴史的には太陰暦の最初の月ですが，月そのものよりも，新年の特定の期間，特に1月の最初の3日間または最初の週を指すことが普通です。この祝祭時に行われる一般的な習慣は，古代人の宗教的行事に由来するもので，彼らは年の始めにあたって祖霊の庇護や豊作を祈ったのです。しかし，宗教的意味合いは今日ではなくなり，新年を祝う意味でただ昔からの習慣が守られています。元旦の朝食にでるものは屠蘇と雑煮です。ある人は年頭の決意を立てて新年を迎えます。というのは，諺にもいうように，一年の計は元旦にありだからです。この日に束になって配達される年賀状を見て友人の消息を知るのも大変楽しいものです。多くの人々は，神社や仏閣に初詣でに出かけます。有名な神社は，信心深い人もそうでない人も含めて老若男女で非常に混雑しますので，群衆を整理するために警察が動員されるほどです。子供はお年玉をもらい，凧あげ，こままわし，羽根つ

resolutions, since New Year's Day is, as the proverb says, the day to make one's plans for the year. People enjoy reading New Year's cards (*nenga-jō*), often delivered in a batch on this day, and see how friends and relatives are getting along. Many people pay the year's first visit to temples and shrines. Some famous shrines are so thickly thronged with the multitude—with men and women, the young and the aged, the pious and the indifferent—that the police are needed to handle the crowds. Small children are given good luck gifts (*otoshidama*) and enjoy playing what are the traditional games for the *shōgatsu* season, such as kite-flying (*tako-age*), top-spinning (*koma-mawashi*), Japanese badminton (*hane-tsuki*), and card games (*karuta-tori*). Younger children usually enjoy *iroha-karuta* (cards of the Japanese syllabary), whereas older children and teenagers may take more interest in playing *hyakunin-isshu* (cards of one hundred famous short poems). On January 7 some people eat rice porridge with seven kinds of spring herbs (*nanakusa-gayu*), which was believed in ancient times to be capable of preventing and curing every known disease. The custom which marks the end of *shōgatsu* is the cutting and eating of the New Year's rice cakes (*kagami-mochi*) offered on the household altar. On January 11, or in some districts on January 20, those round mirror-shaped rice cakes are cut or broken to pieces, toasted, put into heated sweet red-bean soup (*shiruko*), and then eaten by the whole family. (S)

shōgi   Japanese chess. Having been introduced to Japan in the late eighth century, it followed a quite different

き，カルタとりなどの伝統的な遊びをして正月を楽しみます。子供はたいていいろはがるたをしますが，少し大きくなると百人一首のほうに興味を示します。1月7日には七草がゆを食べる人がいますが，これは昔は万病を防ぎ治す効果があると信じられていました。正月の終りを示す行事は，神棚にそなえられた鏡餅を割って食べることです。1月11日，また地方によっては20日に，鏡餅を細かく切ったり割ったりして焼き，お汁粉にして家族みんなで食べます。

将 棋　8世紀後半に日本にもたらされた将棋は，中国の将棋とはまったく異なる発展をしました。このゲームは，それぞれ

development from that of Chinese chess. The game is played on a chessboard of 81 squares (9 files by 9 ranks) by two players with 20 chessmen each (11 pieces and 9 pawns). Chessmen are made of wooden pieces, longish pentagonal in shape, and on their faces are written Chinese characters that designate their functions. Each player has, beside pawns (*fuhyō*), seven different kinds of pieces, some of which are similar in function to those of Western chess; the pieces are *ōshō* (king), *hisha* (rook), *kaku* (bishop), *kinshō, ginshō, keima* (knight), and *kyōsha*. The game is played in much the same way as that of Western chess. The differences are that chessmen which are captured can be used again by the opposing player and that not only pawns but also all pieces (except *ōshō* and *kinshō*) can be promoted to *kinshō*. A game ends when one of the players checkmates the opponent's *ōshō*. This is called *ōte-zume*. (S)

shōji   a paper sliding door. It is a door made of checkered panes of thin, white paper, fastened on a wooden frame fixture between rooms. It originated in the eighth century and served for dividing one room into two smaller rooms. Even today, it is commonly seen in Japanese-style houses. Since translucent Japanese papers are used, *shōji* is often set at the windows facing outside to control direct sunlight. In this case, it is used as a curtain. (O)

shōjin-ryōri   vegetable dishes. Absolutely no meat or fish is included in a *shōjin-ryōri* meal. Nuts, seaweed, and various kinds of vegetables and vegetable products such as

20のコマを持った2人によって，（縦横9列の）81の正方形の描かれた将棋盤の上で行われます。コマは長細い五角形の木片でできていて，その上にその働きを示す漢字が書かれています。それぞれの対戦者は歩兵の他に7種類のコマを持ちますが，そのいくつかは西洋のチェスの動き方に似ています。それらをあげると，王将，飛車，角，金将，銀将，桂馬，香車です。ゲームはチェスとほぼ同じやり方で行われます。違いは，取ったコマを使えるということ，歩兵だけではなく王将と金将を除いたすべてのコマが金将に成れるという点です。1人が相手の王将を詰めれば勝負は終りです。これを王手詰めといいます。

障　子　薄い白い紙を格子のある木の枠に張ったもので，部屋と部屋との仕切りとして，また戸外からの明りとして使います。8世紀に考案され，一部屋を2つの小部屋に分けるために使われました（襖障子）。今では明り障子が日本式家具ではあたりまえになっています。半透明の和紙を使うところから，外に面する窓につけられ，直射日光を制御する役割をはたします。この場合はカーテンの代わりをするわけです。

精進料理　精進料理には肉や魚は一切含まれません。木の実，海草，いろいろな種類の野菜と，野菜から作られる豆腐や油揚げやこんにゃくなどを料理し，上手に組み合わせて，和風のや

tōfu (soybean curd), *age* (fried soybean curd), and *konnyaku* (devil's tongue jelly) are cooked and cleverly combined and served in Japanese style. This eating style was originated by ancient Buddhist priests who tabooed meat eating. Some Buddhist temples have inherited their own recipe. They often prepare their *shōjin-ryōri* dishes for secular gourmets. People today customarily have a *shōjin-ryōri* meal on the day of a funeral and during the mourning period. A vegetarian diet followed for other purposes may also be called *shōjin-ryōri*. (O)

shōyu   soy sauce. It is the most important basic seasoning in Japanese cuisine. Generally a brown salty sauce, it is made from soybeans, grain (wheat or barley), brine (salt and water), and mold. A mixture of boiled soybeans ·and grilled grain is crushed or ground and put in a barrel with salt, water, and mold. It is allowed to ferment and brew for one or two years. Then the liquid is drained off, strained, and pasteurized. *Shōyu* was brought to Japan in the ninth century from China, and by the fifteenth century Japan began producing its own type of soy sauce, employing its own unique techniques. Much more wheat is used for making Japanese soy sauce, which tastes sweeter and less pungent than Chinese soy sauce. Generally, it is clearer in color and thinner than the Chinese-style. (O)

shūgaku-ryokō   a school excursion. Specifically this trip refers to the very special outings which take place during the final year of elementary, junior high, and senior high

りかたで出します。この食べ方は，昔，僧侶が肉食を禁じられた
ことから生まれたものです。お寺ではその寺特有の調理法を受け
ついでいるところがあります。一般の食道楽の人々のために料理
してくれるところもあります。今日では，葬式の日や忌中には精
進料理を食べる習慣があります。別の目的をもつ菜食主義者の食
事も精進料理と呼んでよいでしょう。

しょう油　　日本料理の中で最も重要な基本的調味料です。た
いがい褐色の塩辛いソースで，大豆と小麦か大麦の粒，塩水，こ
うじから作られます。ゆでた大豆と煎った麦をまぜ合わせて細か
くすりつぶし，樽に入れて塩と水とこうじを加えます。発酵して
醸造するのに1年か2年かかります。そして，水気を切って取り
出した液体を漉して殺菌します。しょう油は9世紀に中国から伝
わりましたが，15世紀までに日本では，独自の技術を使って，日
本独特のしょう油を製造するようになりました。日本のしょう油
を作るときにはたくさんの麦を使うので，中国のしょう油よりも
甘い味がして辛みも少ないのです。一般に日本製は中国製よりも
透明でさらっとしています。

修学旅行　　この旅行は特別なものとされていて，小学校，中
学校，高等学校の最終学年の時に行われます。生徒は，日本の歴
史，文化，産業にとって重要な意義のあるいろいろな場所を見学

schools. Students visit various places of the nation's historical, cultural, or industrial significance. It is a trip which includes overnight stays. The trip for elementary school children usually lasts one night and two days. At the junior high school level, the trip is three to four days, and it is about one week at the senior high school level. *Shūgaku-ryokō* is intended to provide the students an opportunity to see different parts of the country, and also to experience group living.　(O)

shūgi　a congratulatory gift presented on a festive or joyous occasion. *Noshi* or a decoration made of folded pieces of paper and thin strips of dried abalone is usually attached to these gifts. If the gift is money, it is put in an envelope with *noshi* printed on it. A gratuity given to entertainers, servants, or loyal followers is also called *shūgi*. In this case there is less formality in the presentation ritual.　(S)

shūkanshi　a weekly magazine. Various kinds of weekly magazines are available at newsstands and bookstores throughout the country. The readers are usually white-collar workers (called *sararīman* after salaried man), who read them just to pass the time on commuter trains, or even in bookstores. Those weeklies also serve as a cheap source of information and knowledge, if superficial, providing good topics for conversation with friends and colleagues. Written in plain language, they are easy to read. Geared to average readers, they deal with all topics of human interest ranging from current hot news of international and domestic politics, economics, and social events to those of the entertainment

します。泊まりがけの旅行になります。小学生は普通1泊2日くらいです。中学生の場合は3，4日で，高校生は約1週間くらいです。修学旅行の目的は，生徒に国内のいろいろなところを見せること，そして集団生活を経験させることにあります。

祝　儀　　祭事やめでたい行事のときに贈るお祝いのことです。贈り物には熨斗，つまり乾燥したのしあわびを細かく切ったものと折った紙片からできた飾りを付けます。贈り物が金銭のときには，熨斗が印刷された封筒に入れます。芸人やお手伝いや忠実な部下などに与える感謝の心づけも祝儀と呼ばれます。この場合には，贈り方にそれほどあらたまった形式はとりません。

週刊誌　　あらゆる種類の週刊誌が全国の新聞売場や書店で手に入ります。読者の大半がサラリーマンで，通勤のバスや電車の中，または本屋で時間つぶしに読むのです。これら週刊誌は値段も手頃な上に，若干内容の希薄さはあるものの，社交上必要な話題提供の源でもあります。わかりやすいことばで書かれ，読みやすくなっています。取り扱うテーマは一般の読者にあわせて幅広い分野をカバーし，最新の国内外の政治・経済・社会問題に関するニュースから，さまざまな種類の娯楽物にまでわたります。また，ほとんどの週刊誌は読者の目をひくように見出しを工夫しています。最近では，女性，中年，青少年と特定の読者層にねらいを定めたものもはやっています。

world. Their provocative, eye-catching headlines arouse readers' curiosity. More specialized magazines, those directed toward specific readers such as women, middle-aged men, young adults, and so forth, are also flourishing. (Y)

soshina   a small gift. *Soshina* is a term used in a humble manner for a small gift in general. While the semiannual gift-giving tradition, known as *chūgen* (the midsummer gift) and *seibo* (the year-end gift), is customarily practiced on a rather formal basis, the exchange of *soshina* gifts is popularly practiced in a cordial and casual fashion for multiple purposes. It is mostly used just as a token of a person's gratitude for a service given. It can also play a vital role as a greeting gift when the person wants to make acquaintance with people in his new surroundings. Furthermore, it can function as a return present. The *soshina* exchange, after all, is an important gift-giving custom for the establishment of a new and harmonious relationship between people. It is a useful lubricant in Japanese society where people are expected to display much consideration for others in an exquisite manner. (Y)

soroban   an abacus. The *soroban* is an instrument used for arithmetic calculation. It has beads on a certain number of vertical rods traversed by a horizontal bar and is fixed in a rectangular frame. Each rod has five (or six in the old type) beads on it, one of which in the upper division represents five units, while each bead in the lower division represents one unit. Each vertical rod is worth units ten times

粗　品　　他人への贈り物をへり下っていうことばです。ほとんど慣例化している夏の中元と冬の歳暮が儀礼的である一方，粗品のやりとりは重宝がられて多目的に役立っています。一般に粗品は，受けた行為に対するお礼のしるしとして贈られますが，新居地での挨拶がわりや，お返しとしても贈られます。粗品のやりとりは，新しいスムーズな人間関係を生み出すためのものです。おたがいに細かな気くばりが要求される日本社会では，潤滑油として有効な機能を持っています。

算　盤　　算術計算をするための道具です。横長の長方形の枠内に，上下を仕切る左右の梁と，梁を上下に貫く多数の細い桁があり，それぞれの梁の上部には5単位を表わす1個の珠がはめ込まれています。梁の下部にはそれぞれ4個の珠がはめ込まれており，1

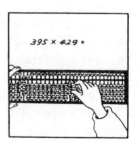

greater than those on the rod immediately to the right. The *soroban* was introduced to Japan from China around the thirteenth century. In the present age of electronic calculators and computers, many children still go to private schools to learn how to use the *soroban*. Regular and systematic exercises in *soroban* can develop mental calculation skills as well. It is also believed that manual work in *soroban* operation will activate the general brain capacity. (Y)

suibokuga India-ink painting. *Suibokuga*, also known as *sumie*, is an art form in which everything is depicted in black India ink. This style of painting was introduced into Japan from China together with Zen Buddhism, and perfected by the painter and priest Sesshū (1420-1506) in the fifteenth century. As in many other Japanese arts and traditions such as *haiku* poetry and tea ceremony, the deep-rooted preference for simplicity and subtlety is seen in *suibokuga*. It abhors superfluous strokes of the brush and unnecessary splashes of ink. It is interested in the essence of the subject matter, usually mountains, rivers, plants, animals, etc. Various shades of black and gray on the white background stimulate the imagination of the viewer far more than real colors. The white space left untouched does not represent emptiness in its literal sense but embodies all meaning and possibility, thus playing as important a part as the painted object itself. (T)

sukiyaki a pot dish of meat and vegetables. It is a popular Japanese dish cooked in a pan usually at the table. The name *sukiyaki* originally meant "grilling on the blade of a

つの珠が1単位を表わしています。縦の桁は右から左に進むにつれて10単位ずつ増します。算盤は13世紀ごろ中国より伝わりました。この電算器機の時代にも，子供のための算盤塾は大流行です。算盤を規則的にそして組織的に練習すると暗算に強くなるといわれています。また，このような手作業は脳の活性化にも役立つといわれています。

水墨画　　墨絵とも呼ばれ，すべてのものを墨で描く美術です。この画法は禅とともに中国から日本に伝えられ，15世紀に，画家で禅僧の雪舟によって完成されました。俳句や茶道など多くの日本の芸術や伝統の場合と同様に，水墨画においても，簡潔と微妙さに対する深い好みが見られます。水墨画では，余分な筆の運びや不要な墨のはねを嫌います。この手法で題材の山や川，植物や動物の本質に迫ります。白地を背景にした黒とグレイの濃淡さまざまな色合いは，実際の色よりもはるかに見る者の想像力をかきたてます。手をつけないままの余白は，文字通り空白を表わすのではなく，あらゆる意味と可能性を示しています。それゆえ，余白は描かれている事物と同じくらい重要な役割をはたしています。

すき焼き　　すき焼きはだれもが好む料理で，普通，食卓の上に鍋を置いてつくります。すき焼きという名前の由来は，鋤の刃の上で肉を焼くという意味で，民間語源説によると，畑で農作業

plow", and according to folk etymology it originated from a dish cooked by farmers working in the field. The most common ingredients are thinly sliced beef, *tōfu* (soybean curd), and vegetables such as green onions, mushrooms, bamboo shoots, etc. A pan or a skillet set on a small stove on the table is greased and heated. Slices of beef are cooked first, and then, a mixture of soy sauce, sugar, *sake* (rice wine), and water is added. When this mixture boils, the rest of the ingredients are put in the pan. Raw eggs are served in small individual bowls. Before eating, the cooked meat and vegetables are dipped in the beaten egg, which cooks slightly when it contacts the hot food. Since eating from the same pan fosters intimacies among the diners, *sukiyaki* is very often enjoyed at parties. (O)

sumō traditional Japanese wrestling. *Sumō* is one of the most popular national sports in Japan. Many fathers teach their young sons how to play it. Sponsored by the Japan *Sumō* Association with a subsidy from the Ministry of Education, fifteen-day professional *sumō* tournaments are held in Tokyo, Osaka, Nagoya and, Fukuoka in odd-numbered months every year. Professional *sumō* has a long history. As the present system was fixed about 300 years ago, *sumō* society has many old-fashioned and feudalistic elements, such as topknots (*chon-mage*), loincloths (*mawashi* or *fundoshi*), stables (*heya*), and the master-disciple relations. The first time Commodore Perry landed in Japan in 1853, his crew was shocked to see *sumō* wrestlers so fat and big. But, in recent times, several stables have admitted some American hopefuls,

をしているお百姓さんが料理したものといわれています。最も一般的な材料は，薄切りの牛肉，豆腐，ねぎやしいたけやもやしなどの野菜，そしてしらたきなどです。卓上のコンロに浅い鍋をのせ，油をひいて熱します。まず，牛肉を鍋にいれて，醬油と砂糖と酒と水を混ぜ合わせたものを加えます。この調味料が沸騰したら，残りの材料を鍋に入れます。生卵をかきまぜて，煮えた肉や野菜を浸して食べます。生卵は熱い材料とまじり合って半煮えになります。同じ鍋の料理を食べるということは，食事をする人たちの親近感を強めるので，すき焼きは会合などで大変喜ばれます。

　　相　撲　　相撲は日本国内で最も人気のあるスポーツの一つです。父親はたいがい息子に相撲を教えます。日本相撲協会は文部省の助成を得て，毎年，奇数の月に，東京，大阪，名古屋，そして福岡で，年に6回，15日間のトーナメントを開催します。プロの相撲には長い歴史があります。現在の制度はおよそ300年前に確立されたものなので，相撲社会には昔風の，あるいは封建的な要素がたくさん見うけられます。例えば，ちょんまげ，まわし，部屋制度，師弟関係などです。1853年にペリー提督が黒船で初めて日本を訪れたとき，乗組員たちは力士の大きいのに驚いたそうです。今では，将来性のありそうなアメリカ人を受け入れている相撲部屋もあり，現に彼らは人気者になっています。

and they too have become popular *sumō* wrestlers.　(K)

sunomono　salads with a vinegary dressing. *Suno-mono* (literally "vinegared foods") can be described as the equivalent of Western-style salads.　Normally the ingredients of *sunomono* include a mixture of vegetables (fresh, or some-times parboiled and cooled) and seafood, such as seaweed, kelp, squid, octopus, crab meat, etc. The ingredients are sprinkled with or tossed with a thin vinegary or lemony dressing which is commonly a mixture of rice vinegar, sugar, soy sauce, and broth (*dashi*).　Only a small portion is served in an elegant bowl and set beside the main dish.　Unlike Western salads, *sunomono* is eaten along with the main dish. (O)

supōtsu-shinbun　a sports newspaper.　Sports news-papers are specialized papers which are chiefly devoted to the coverage of all kinds of national sporting events.　Like weekly magazines and comic magazines, they have a relative-ly large readership among salaried men, who buy and read them on the way to and from their work on commuter trains to pass the time.　These newspapers also devote space to show business news and stories.　In addition, they usually offer all other kinds of distractions, such as cartoons, pornog-raphic features, serialized erotic stories, and news of publicly-operated gambling events (horse, bike, and boat races, and lotteries).　(Y)

suribachi　an earthen ware mortar. *Suribachi* and

酢のもの　　酢を使った食べ物という意味ですが，洋食のサラ
ダと同じようなものです。酢のものの材料は，生か固ゆでにして
冷ました野菜と海草や，いか，たこ，かになどの魚貝類を混ぜ合
わせたものです。材料を酢やレモンのドレッシングで和えます
が，ドレッシングは米酢，砂糖，醤油，そしてだし汁を合わせた
ものです。ほんの少量をすてきな小鉢に盛って主菜のわきに置き
ます。西洋のサラダと違って，酢のものは主菜と一緒に食べま
す。

　スポーツ新聞　　国内の主だったスポーツニュースを報道する
ことを主目的とする新聞です。週刊誌や漫画雑誌のように，スポ
ーツ新聞も読者の大半がサラリーマンで，通勤の車中で時間つぶ
しに読まれます。スポーツ記事の他に芸能ニュースや特集記事も
のせています。その他，大衆好みの娯楽ものはすべてあつかって
います。例えば，漫画，ポルノ，ギャンブル，そして宝くじとい
ったぐあいです。

　すり鉢　　すりこ木とともに，ごまなどの種子をすりつぶすた

wooden *surikogi* (a pestle) are used for crushing and grinding seedy materials such as sesame seeds. *Suribachi* is a pottery bowl the inside of which is grooved in a crisscross pattern. The average size of this cooking utensil is about 9 inches in diameter. Recently plastic grinding bowls have become available, but the traditional pottery *suribachi* remains popular because of its appropriate weight. (O)

sushi   a traditional Japanese raw-fish cuisine. There are several kinds of *sushi*. *Nigiri-zushi* is the most popular of all. It is a bite-sized raw fish slice atop a small oblong rice ball. Rice (called *shari* in the *sushi* jargon) is seasoned with sugar and vinegar. After it is hand-formed into a small oblong ball, it is surfaced with a dab of Japanese horseradish (*wasabi*). The kinds of fish or fish parts used for *nigiri-zushi* are numerous. Here is a representative list.

aji (saurel)	*akagai* (arkshell)
amaebi (sweet shrimp)	*anago* (sea eel)
aoyagi (trough shell)	*awabi* (abalone)
ebi (shrimp)	*hamachi* (young yellowtail)
ika (squid)	*ikura* (salmon roe)
iwashi (sardine)	*kaibashira* (scallop)
kaki (oyster)	*karei* (flat fish)
kazunoko (herring roe)	*maguro* (tuna)
mirugai (surf clam)	*saba* (mackerel)
sake (smoked salmon)	*sayori* (hemiramph)
shako (giant clam)	*suzuki* (sea bass)
tai (sea bream)	*tako* (octopus)
torigai (cockle)	*toro* (fatty tuna meat)

めに使います。すり鉢は陶器の鉢で，内側には櫛ですいたような形の溝があります。大きさはだいたい直径９インチほどのものです。最近はプラスチック製のすり鉢もありますが，陶器のすり鉢のほうが適当な重さがあるために今でも好まれています。

寿司・鮨　　すしにはいろいろな種類があります。にぎりずしが最もポピュラーで，これは，一口サイズに切った新鮮な生魚を，小さな長方形ににぎったすしめしの上にのせたものです。すしめし（すし用語でシャリと呼ばれます）は砂糖と酢で味つけがなされており，小さな長方形ににぎったところで，ワサビを少しつけます。すしに使う魚はたくさんあります。次にその代表的なものをあげましょう。

あじ（鯵）	あかがい（赤貝）
あまえび（甘海老）	あなご（穴子）
あおやぎ（青柳）	あわび（鮑）
えび（海老）	はまち（䰣）
いか（烏賊）	いくら
いわし（鰯）	かいばしら（貝柱）
かき（牡蠣）	かれい（鰈）
かずのこ（数の子）	まぐろ（鮪）
みるがい（海松貝）	さば（鯖）
さけ（鮭）	さより（細魚）
しゃこ（蝦蛄）	すずき（鱸）
たい（鯛）	たこ（蛸）
とりがい（鳥貝）	とろ
うに（雲丹）	

uni (sea urchin)

Maki-zushi is a long rice roll, which is wrapped with a toasted sheet of dried sea weed (*nori*). It contains various kinds of foodstuff in the middle. Here is a representative list of *maki-zushi*.

ikura-maki
(salmon roe roll)

kampyō-maki
(gourd roll)

kappa-maki
(cucumber roll)

nattō-maki
(fermented soybean roll)

o-shinko-maki
(pickle roll)

shiso-maki
(shredded *shiso* roll)

tekka-maki
(tuna roll)

In addition, there are, among others, *inari-zushi* (*aburage*-enveloped seasoned rice) and *chirashi-zushi* (a big bowl of seasoned rice covered by raw fish slices). The most popular way to enjoy this traditional cuisine is to visit a *sushi* bar and order the variations of your choice. The freshly made *sushi* is handserved directly by the cook on the bar in front of you. Pick it up with your fingers and dip it in soy sauce (called *murasaki*) on the fish side. Remember that *sake* is the best friend of *sushi*. (HO)

suteteko   men's long drawers. Middle-aged and old men usually wear a *suteteko* above underpants to prevent sweat from wetting their trousers. It is particularly effective in hot and humid summer. In informal households, men may be seen in an undershirt and a *suteteko* watching TV or working in the yard. (HO)

巻きずしは，すしめしを細長くしたもので，海苔で巻きます。まん中にはいろいろなものを入れます。次にまきずしの代表的なものをあげます。

いくら巻き　　　　かんぴょう巻き
かっぱ巻き　　　　納豆巻き
お新香巻き　　　　しそ巻き
鉄火巻き

ほかにも，いなりずし（すしめしを油揚に入れたもの），ちらしずし（丼にすしめしを入れ，その上に生の魚の切身をのせたもの）など，いろいろあります。この伝統的な料理をおいしく食べるのには，おすし屋さんのカウンターにすわり，お好みのものを注文するのが一番です。板前さんがにぎりたてのすしを目の前においてくれます。手でつまんで，魚の方にしょう油（むらさき）をつけて食べます。すしには燗をしたお酒が合うことをお忘れなく。

ステテコ　　中年以上の男性は普通パンツの上にステテコという長い下着をはきます。ズボンが汗でぬれないようにするためです。むし暑い夏に特に効果的です。気軽な家庭では，男の人はシャツとステテコ姿でテレビを見たり庭仕事をしたりすることがあります。

tai　a sea bream.　Since the sound of this fish's name is similar to the word *medetai* (happy), the sea bream has been regarded as a high-class fish and served accordingly.　Because of its significant name, its attractive shape, and its reddish-pink color, which is considered a lucky color, it is served completely whole from head to tail especially on festive occasions.　The custom of serving the fish whole was derived from a belief that the full and perfect shape will bring good luck to the diner.　*Tai* is usually served broiled with salt or boiled in soy sauce.　(O)

takarakuji　a public lottery.　Some of the nation's famous public lotteries started immediately after World War II to deal with the depressed economic conditions and to give an additional source of income to both the national and local governments.　However, since 1954 only local governments have been authorized to hold public lotteries in order to subsidize community projects.　The lotteries provide less than one percent of local government revenue.　The result of the nation's most popular New Year lottery is usually announced on December 31, now a traditional event in the New Year holidays.　The first prize was 50 million yen in 1985.　(K)

takeuma　a stilt.　*Takeuma* (literally, "bamboo horse") is composed of a pair of bamboo poles to which wooden footstands are attached at right angles.　It is a traditional activity toy for boys.　They walk on *takeuma* or enjoy such games as stilt races, stilt wrestling, and stilt acrobatics.　Boys themselves used to make their own stilts in old times, but

鯛　この魚は「めでたい」ということばに似ているため，高級な魚とみなされ，おめでたいときに食べます。名前も良いし，形も魅力的で，赤っぽいピンク色もおめでたい色と考えられているので，お祭りのときなどにはお頭つきでだします。鯛をもとの形のままで食べると運に恵まれるといわれています。鯛は塩焼きか煮付けが普通です。

宝くじ　有名な宝くじのうちのあるものは，終戦直後，経済不況の中で，国と地方が財源不足を補うために始まりました。しかし，昭和29年（1954年）以降は，都道府県のみが公共事業の助成を目的とした宝くじを主宰することができることになりました。宝くじによる収益は，地方自治体の歳入の1パーセント以下です。国内で最も人気の高い新年の宝くじの結果は，大晦日に発表され，今や新年を迎える数々の伝統的行事の一つになっています。昭和60年（1985年）度の1等賞金は5,000万円でした。

竹　馬　2本の竹に木の足台を付けた男の子用の遊び道具です。それに乗って歩いたり，競走したり，格闘したり，曲芸をしたりします。むかし男の子は自分で竹馬を作ったものですが，今の子供はたいてい作り方を知り

today very few children know how to make them. Steel or plastic stilts are available at toy shops. The word *takeuma* can be read *chikuba*. Thus *chikuba-no-tomo* ("a stilt friend") refers to a friend of childhood days. （HA）

tamago-yaki　　rolled fried-eggs. Rolled fried-eggs and scrambled eggs (*iri-tamago*) are egg dishes both of which are cooked with the same seasonings—sugar, soy sauce, and *sake* (rice wine), or soup stock. The egg mixture for *tamago-yaki* is poured into a well greased, heated frying pan. When it sets slightly, it is rolled or folded in many layers with chopsticks. It requires much skill to roll this fried egg mixture into an attractive oblong shape. It is said that if a cook succeeds in this dish, his promotion is assured. A square frying pan made specifically for this dish is available. *Tamago-yaki* is served hot or cool for breakfast and is often added to a box lunch. （O）

tanabata　　the Star Festival. *Tanabata* originated from an old Chinese star festival, which was introduced to Japan in the eighth century. It celebrates the annual rendezvous of the Herdsman (Altair) and the Weaver (Vega), symbolized as a couple of lovers, in the Milky Way on the night of July 7. The festival was named after a Japanese mythological goddess who was very good at weaving. Over a period of many centuries, it became customary on this evening to offer vegetables and fruits of the season to the stars, and to decorate branches of a cut bamboo with strips of paper on which poems or proverbs have been written. Colored threads are also hung

ません。スチール製かプラスチック製の竹馬が，おもちゃ屋で手に入る時代なのです。竹馬はチクバとも読み，竹馬の友とは幼友達のことです。

卵焼き　卵焼きというり卵はどちらも，砂糖，醤油，そして酒かだし汁の調味料を加えて料理します。卵焼きを作るには，卵と調味料を混ぜたものを，十分に熱して油をしいたフライパンに流し入れます。半熟になったら，箸で巻き込みながら何層かにたたんで焼きます。巻き込みながらきれいな長方形にととのえるには技術が必要です。料理人がこれを上手にできるようなれば，昇進は確実といわれています。この料理を作るために特別の四角い焼き器があります。卵焼きはよく朝食やお弁当に使います。できたてでも冷えていてもおいしいものです。

七夕　七夕は古代中国の星祭りから起こったもので，8世紀に日本へ伝えられました。恋人どうしにみたてられた牛飼い（アルタイル）と織姫（ベガ）が年に1度だけ7月7日の夜に天の川でランデブーをすることを祝ったお祭りです。七夕という名前は，日本の神話にでてくる機織りのじょうずな女神の名前からつけられました。何世紀もたつうちに，七夕の夜には季節の野菜や果物を星に供えるのが習慣となりました。そして，切りとった竹の枝に，詩や諺を書いた短冊をつるして飾りとします。色糸も竹の枝につるします。飾りをつけた竹の枝は家の戸口にしばりつけます。竹飾りの習慣は，詩や諺を短冊に書いて星に供えると習字がじょうずになるという言い伝えから生まれました。色糸を供

on the bamboo branches. The decorated bamboo is fastened to the doorway of the house. The custom of decorating a bamboo arose from the belief that if you wrote poems or proverbs on strips of paper and offered them to the stars, you would acquire good penmanship skills. Offering colored threads is believed to make you a good weaver and a good seamstress. The *Tanabata* Festival held in Sendai (Miyagi Prefecture) is one of the most famous festivals in Japan. (O)

tanuki   a raccoon dog. The *tanuki* are badger-like creatures that have lived all over Japan since prehistoric days. Their meat and fur have long been used for food and brushes. They frequently appear as tricksters in Japanese folktales. By transforming themselves into other forms, they play many tricks and cheat human beings. Hence *tanuki-neiri* means someone pretending to be asleep when circumstances become difficult. *Tanuki-oyaji* (a raccoon father) or *furu-danuki* (an old raccoon) refers to a crafty old person. *Tanuki-babā* (a raccoon grandmother) is a shrewd old woman. Since *tanuki* are also regarded as cute animals, these expressions have some humorous connotations. (K)

tasuki   a sash used to hold uptucked sleeves. *Tasuki*, just like *hachimaki* (a headband), has both a practical and spiritual significance. It is a sash or cord to tuck up the sleeves of *kimono* which hinder the wearer from working briskly. Hence wearing a *tasuki* often implies bracing oneself up for an effort. Today the original use of *tasuki* has almost disappeared because very few women wear *kimono* in their

えるのは，機織りや裁縫がじょうずになると信じられているから
です。仙台の七夕祭りは日本で最も有名なお祭りの一つです。

狸　　有史以前より日本全国に生息
する，穴熊に似た動物です。肉と毛皮
は長い間，それぞれ食用とブラシ用に
されてきました。また，日本の民話
に，いたずら好きの動物として登場し
ます。そして，いろいろな物に化け，
人間をからかったり騙したりします。
だから，狸寝入りは，不利な状況にお

かれた者が眠っているふりをすることを意味し，狸おやじや古狸
は，悪賢い大人を指すのです。狸ばばあとは，悪知恵の働く年と
った婦人のことです。狸はひょうきんな動物ともみられることか
ら，これらの表現にはユーモラスなひびきがあります。

たすき　　たすきには，はちまきと
同様に，実用的な意味と精神的な意味
があります。たすきは，着物の袖が機
敏に働くのに邪魔になるため，それを
たくし上げておくひもです。それで，
たすきがけという表現には，何かに励
み，身を引き締める様子という比喩的
な意味もあります。今では日常で着物

295

daily lives. Instead, the word *tasuki* is more often used to refer to a white sash worn over one shoulder. It is customary for candidates on the election campaign to wear *tasuki* and white gloves, and for workers on a strike or demonstration to wear *hachimaki* and *tasuki*. （T）

tatami　a straw mat. Traditional Japanese rooms have, as a floor-covering, *tatami* mats. They are made of straw and rush. Since a *tatami* mat is always of a designated size （roughly 6 by 3 feet）, it also serves as a unit of measurement for the size of a room. Rooms that have 4.5, 6, or 8 *tatami* mats are most common. Most houses now have both Western rooms and traditional *tatami* rooms. Elder people prefer to sit and relax on the *tatami*, while youngsters find themselves more comfortable on chairs or sofas. Traditional arts such as the tea ceremony and flower arrangement are almost always practiced on the *tatami*. （K）

taue　rice-planting. *Taue* is the transplantation of the seedlings of rice plants from the nursery to the rice paddies. This is the most important as well as the busiest work in the entire rice-making process. Some schools in rural districts close for about a week, when children are expected to help parents with this aspect of the farm work. The work starts around the end of May, and it lasts for about one month during the rainy season. The rains during this period are indispensable to a good rice crop. First, farmers plow the paddy into a mire in preparation for transplanting the seedlings. Then, they bed out a bundle of three or four seedlings in lines in the

を着る女性が非常に少ないため，たすきの元来の使われ方はほとんど見られません。代わって，肩から斜めにかける白い布を指すことが多くなりました。選挙運動中の候補者は，このたすきをかけ白手袋をはめ，ストやデモ中の労働者は，はちまきとたすきをするのが慣例です。

畳 日本式の部屋の床には畳が敷いてあります。畳は藁と藺草_いでできています。畳は，その大きさが一定（縦約180 cm，横約90 cm）であるところから，部屋の広さを表わす単位としても用いられます。4畳半，6畳，8畳が最も一般的な部屋の広さです。現在，ほとんどの家には洋間と和室があります。年輩の人は畳の上に座るほうがくつろげるのに対して，若い人は椅子やソファのほうが落ち着くようです。伝統的芸術であるお茶や生け花は畳の上で行われます。

田植え 苗代で育てた稲の苗を水田に移し植えることです。米作りでは最も重要な，また忙しい作業です。ある地方では田植えの時期に学校も休みとなり，子供たちが田植えの手伝いに駆り出されます。5月末頃から始まり，梅雨時期にあたる約1ヵ月間続きます。この時期に降る雨が稲作にとって不可欠であることはいうまでもありません。稲作の手順としては，まず，本田を代_{しろ}かきでやわらかい泥田にします。次に3～4本の苗を1株として一線上に植えていきます。1坪当り約70株植えるのが普通です。一般に，秋の天候が不順な東北地方では田植えや収穫の時期が早くなります。暖地では二毛作も行われます。

paddy. About 70 bundles per one *tsubo* (3.3 square meters) are usually planted. Rice-planting and rice-reaping usually take place earlier in the northern part of Japan where the growing season is shorter. In the warm districts, double cropping can be observed. (Y)

tengu   a mountain spirit. The typical figure of *tengu*, as described in literature, paintings, and other arts since the Middle Ages, is a winged novice monk with a reddish face and a prominent nose ; he usually carries a fan in his hand. According to folk belief, this spirit has extraordinary power and control over the mountains. This belief is based on the awe primitive people experienced toward certain mysterious mountains. It also comes from the fact that villagers found mountain people mysterious, as they lived and behaved differently and as they seemed adept at dealing with fearful natural phenomena. (K)

tennō   an emperor. According to Japanese mythology the First Emperor Jinmu established his reign in the "land of the rising sun" in 660 BC. Assumedly a direct descendant of this line, the present Emperor Hirohito is said to be the 124th. In recent history, there have been two great changes in the definition of the role and status of the Imperial family. The Meiji Constitution, proclaimed in 1889, restored to the Emperor political power which had been in the hands of the successive shogunates since the ninth century. Inevitably, the military too came under his control. After Japan's defeat in World War II, the New Constitution of 1947 stipulated that the

天　狗　中世以降の文学，絵画など に描かれている天狗の格好は，翼の ある山伏のようで，赤ら顔で鼻が高 く，手にはいつもうちわを持っていま す。民話では，天狗は山々を自由自在 に飛び回れる神通力を持つといわれて います。これは，太古の人々が山々に 対して抱いていた畏敬の念から生れま
した。また，村人が山人のことを神秘的に考えたことにもよりま す。山人は，村人とは生活の様式も行動の様式も異なり，恐ろし い自然現象に対処する方法を知っていたからです。

天　皇　日本の神話によると，初代の神武天皇は紀元前660 年に，日出ずる処で即位したとされています。その直系の子孫で あるとされている現在の天皇裕仁は，124代目にあたります。現 代史において，皇室の役割と地位をめぐって大きな変化が2回あ りました。まず，明治22年（1889年）に公布された大日本帝国憲 法では，9世紀以来将軍の手中にあった政治権力が天皇の手に戻 されました。必然的に，政治権力は軍事権力にも及びました。第 2次大戦の敗北後，昭和22年（1947年）に施行された新憲法で は，天皇は国の元首ではなく，国と国民統合の象徴であると定め られました。現在，天皇の国事に関する責任は，外交儀礼と形式 的行事に限定されています。

Emperor was not the head of the state, but "the symbol of the state and of the unity of the people". Now his responsibility for state affairs is limited to protocol and formalities. (K)

tenpura   a deep-fried dish. Although it is regarded as a typical Japanese dish, it was introduced by the Portuguese in the late sixteenth century. In the course of its history, *tenpura* has evolved to suit Japanese tastes. The common ingredients of this dish are white fish, squid, shrimp, shellfish, etc., and vegetables such as eggplant, sweet potato, onion, green pepper, etc. The cooking time for *tenpura* is short—about four to five minutes. Prepared ingredients, sliced to about bite-size, are dipped into a lumpy flour-and-water batter, and deep fried in hot vegetable oil. It is eaten with a dipping sauce comprised of a mixture of soy sauce, sweet rice wine (*mirin*), and soup broth (*dashi*). Grated white radish (*daikon-oroshi*) is often served to garnish the sauce. (O)

tera   a Buddhist temple, where an image of Buddha is enshrined and Buddhist priests live together. Temples were first built by powerful clans in the sixth century soon after the introduction of Buddhism into the country. As they gradually increased in number, the Imperial Court protected them and even raised some of them to the status of national temple. In the course of time, the Japanese temple took on a variety of forms—public and private temples, monasteries and nunneries, for instance. In the seventeenth century, the Tokugawa Government, banning Christianity, introduced the *danka* (Buddhist parishioner) system and set up ranks among

天ぷら　　天ぷらは日本独特の料理とされていますが，16世紀末にポルトガルから伝えられたものです。時を重ねるうちに，天ぷらは日本人の嗜好に合うように変化しました。材料は，白身の魚，いか，えび，貝類などと，なす，さつまいも，たまねぎ，ピーマンなどの野菜類です。天ぷらの一品を料理する時間は短く，約4，5分です。材料を一口サイズに切り，小麦粉を水でといたころものなかにひたし，熱したサラダオイルにいれてあげます。食べるときは，醤油とみりんとだし汁で作った天つゆにつけます。天つゆには大根おろしを添えます。

寺　　仏像が安置され僧侶が共同生活をする寺院は，日本に仏教が伝来した直後の6世紀に，有力な豪族によって最初に建てられました。その数が次第に増えるにつれて，朝廷は寺院を保護し，そのいくつかを国寺に昇格させました。やがて日本の寺院はさまざまな形をとるようになりました。例えば，官寺と私寺，僧院や尼寺などです。17世紀に，徳川幕府はキリスト教を禁止し檀家制度を取り入れ，重要度に従って寺院を格づけし，それぞれの宗派の本山を定めました。朝廷は19世紀に再び政権をとり，信教の自由を保証し，政府の寺院支配を廃止しましたが，これらの制度の大半はその後も影響を受けずに残りました。建物は最初は大陸の寺院の様式に従って設計されました。古い大きな寺院には，

temples in order of importance, appointing a head temple for each sect. Though the Imperial Court, taking over the government again in the nineteenth century, guaranteed freedom of faith and abolished the government control of temples, these systems have mostly remained intact. The architecture was originally planned after the style of the continental Buddhist temple. Old and big temples have inside the spacious grounds a set of several buildings such as gates, a pagoda, main hall, lecture hall, bell tower, and the priests' living quarters. Small temples have only the main hall and living quarters. The chief priest in charge of a temple is called *jūshoku* or *oshō*. (S)

tera-meguri   a pilgrimage to Buddhist temples. Pilgrimages made for religious purposes are called *henro* or *junrei*, the most popular of which is the pilgrimage to the eighty-eight sacred places in Shikoku. It is generally known as *Shikoku hachijūhakkasho*, and these eighty-eight temples are all associated with Kūkai or Kōbō-Daishi (774–845), the founder of the Shingonshū sect of Buddhism. This ancient custom originating in the medieval times is still maintained today by devout believers of Kūkai. Pilgrims travel from temple to temple, ringing bells and chanting Buddhistic hymns. The names of the temples they visit are stamped on their white clothes or on the notebooks they carry with them during the travel. The pilgrimage to the eighty-eight sacred places is believed to make one happy both in this world and in the next world. There are also many people who make a *tera-meguri* tour of famous temples in Kyoto, Nara, and elsewhere. They

広大な敷地内に門，塔，本堂，講堂，鐘楼，僧房などの建物があります。小さな寺院は，本堂と庫裏だけです。寺の長である僧侶は住職または和尚と呼ばれます。

寺巡り　　宗教的な目的の寺巡りは，遍路または巡礼といわれますが，そのうちでも最も広く行われているのは，昔からある四国の88の聖地への巡礼です。これは一般に四国八十八ヵ所として知られているもので，この88の寺院はすべて真言宗の開祖である空海または弘法大師にゆかりのある所です。中世に始まったこの古い風習は，空海の熱心な信者によって今日でも行われています。巡礼者は鈴を鳴らし，御詠歌を歌いながら寺から寺へと旅をします。訪れた寺の印が，彼らの着ている白衣や，巡礼中に携行する帳面に押されます。八十八ヵ所への巡礼によって，現世でも来世でも幸福になれると信じられています。京都，奈良などの有名な寺院へ寺巡りの旅をする人も多くありますが，それは主として観光が目的です。

enjoy their trips mostly for purposes of sight-seeing.　(S)

teruteru-bōzu　a fine-weather doll.　*Teruteru-bōzu* is a very simple doll made of white paper or cloth, which is popularly believed to have a magic power to bring fine weather.　Children hang it from the eaves or on the outside of a window on the eve of their school excursion or sports day. If the following day happens to be fine, they are very happy and thankful.　If not, they learn that not everything turns out as they wish.　In either case, they have fun with their *teruteru-bōzu*.　In Japan, spring and autumn, though ideal seasons for outdoor activities, have frequent rainfalls and possibly a few typhoons.　Consequently, *teruteru-bōzu* is a familiar sight. The custom of praying to it for good weather has long been practiced, though its origin is not known at all.　Although it is a childish superstition, many people invariably associate it with their happy and innocent childhood days.　(T)

tōfu　soybean curd.　It is a soft custard-like food made from soybeans.　Having originated in China over 2,000 years ago, it soon spread throughout the Far East.　To make *tōfu*, dry soybeans are cooked in water for a short while. They are mashed into milk-like liquid.　With the addition of a specified amount of calcium sulfate, the curdy liquid congeals into a very soft custard-like substance.　The mixture is poured into a square frame over the bottom of which a straining cloth has been attached.　Gentle pressure is applied to squeeze off the excess liquid until the custard is about half of its original volume.　The remaining "curd" is *tōfu*.　It is

てるてる坊主　　白い紙か布で作る
たいへん簡単な人形で，晴天をもたら
す魔法の力があると俗に信じられてい
ます。子供たちは遠足とか運動会の前
日に軒先や窓の外にてるてる坊主をつ
るします。もし翌日が晴天ならば，子
供たちは喜び，感謝します。もし雨天
になれば，物事はすべて思い通りにな

るとは限らないのだと知ります。いずれにしても子供たちはてる
てる坊主に興じます。日本では春と秋が戸外活動に最適の季節で
すが，雨が多く，台風が来ることもあります。したがって，てる
てる坊主をよく見かけます。てるてる坊主に晴天を祈願する風習
は昔からありますが，その起源はまったくわかりません。たわい
ない迷信ですが，てるてる坊主は多くの人々に楽しく無邪気な子
供時代を思い起こさせるものです。

豆　腐　　豆腐はやわらかいカスタードのような食べ物で，大
豆から作られます。2千年以上も前に中国で作られ，すぐに極東
全体にひろがりました。豆腐を作るには，まず乾燥大豆をしばら
くのあいだ水にひたします。その後，すりつぶしてミルクのよう
な液体にします。カルシウム硫酸塩を適量加えると，どろどろの
液体はやわらかなカスタード状の物質に凝固します。それを，し
ぼり布をのせた四角い枠の中にそそぎ入れます。圧力をゆるやか
に加えると余分な水分がしぼり出され，カスタードは始めの分量
の約半分位の大きさになります。この残った凝乳が豆腐です。豆
腐は高蛋白質，高カルシウムですが，低カロリーです。食べ方
は，そのまま食べる冷やっことか，湯の中で煮て調味料をつけて

305

high in protein and calcium, but low in calories. It can be eaten fresh as *hiyayakko*, or cooked in hot water and served with seasonings as *yudōfu*. It can also be served in soup with traditional seasonings such as soy sauce or *miso* (soybean paste). (O)

tōki ceramic ware. Pottery in Japan has a long history, with the earliest example of earthenware ever found going back approximately ten thousand years. As an art form, greatly influenced by China and Korea, it has developed its own techniques and tastes. Today Japan is the main center of ceramics in the world. The tea ceremony and the art of flower arrangement stimulated the aesthetic aspect of pottery. Japanese table setting requires a great number and variety of specially designed vessels. Probably no other people in the world use such varied ceramic ware in daily life as the Japanese. Many places in Japan are blessed with clay suitable for pottery and produce their own types of ceramic ware. Seto City on the outskirts of Nagoya is particularly famous as the home of Japanese ceramics, so much so that *seto-mono* (literally, Seto goods) is often used as a general term for all kinds of ceramic ware. (T)

tokonoma an alcove in a Japanese-style room. It is said to have originated in the fourteenth century from the household altar room of a Buddhist priest's house. It is a space used for hanging a scroll (*kakejiku*) and displaying ornaments or arranged flowers (*ikebana*). A room with a *tokonoma* often serves as guest room, since this recessed part,

食べる湯どうふがあります。また，すまし汁にもみそ汁にも入れます。

陶　器　　日本の陶器類には長い歴史があり，これまでに発見された最も古い土器は約1万年前のものとされています。日本の陶器は芸術として，中国や朝鮮からの大きな影響を受けながら，独自の技巧や趣向を発達させてきました。今日の日本は世界の陶磁器の中心地になっています。茶道や生け花は陶器の美的側面の発達を促しました。日本人の食卓には，料理によってそれぞれ決まった食器が数においても種類においても豊富に必要とされます。おそらく，日本人ほど日常生活で多種の陶器類を使う国民は他にないでしょう。日本各地に焼き物に適した土が採れる場所があり，その地方独特の陶器を生産しています。名古屋近郊の瀬戸市は特に日本の陶器の本場として有名で，そのため瀬戸物という言い方をしばしば陶器の総称として使っています。

床の間　　床の間の起源は，14世紀のある僧侶の家の仏間であったといわれています。床の間は，掛け軸を掛けたり，装飾品を置いたり，生け花をいけたりする場所です。床の間はたいてい銘木でできた床柱と床框で区切られ

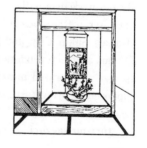

usually marked by an alcove post and a front edge-beam made of precious wood, gives stateliness to the room. A seat near the *tokonoma* is considered to be the top seat (*kamiza*), which the host occupies when he sees a visitor in the room, unless the latter is higher in social position than the former. (S)

tokoroten   cold jelly. *Tokoroten* is a jelly-like food made from red seaweed called *tengusa*. Made into thin strips by being pushed out from small holes of a special wooden instrument which works like a hand pump, *tokoroten* is eaten with vinegar-flavored soy sauce. It is known that *tokoroten* has been eaten for more than one thousand years. It used to be one of the typical cold snacks in summer, but nowadays it is not as popular among young people as soft drinks or ice cream. However, to the older generation it is a food reminiscent of the good old days. (T)

tori-no-ichi   a rooster-day festival. The old Japanese lunar calendar marks several "rooster" days (*tori-no-hi*) every month. The rooster-day festivals are held on those days of November at many Ōtori shrines of Shinto belief. These shrines were originally dedicated to the gods of victory in war, but later to the gods of good luck in general. The fairs in Osaka's Sakai City and Tokyo's Asakusa district are most famous. Street vendors (*yashi*) set up their stalls and sell specially decorated miniature lawn rakes (*kumade*) that are supposed to bring fortune. (HO)

tori-no-saezuri   birds' twitterings. The songs of birds

た入り込んだ空間で，部屋に品格を添えるので，床の間のある部屋はよく客間として使われます。床の間に近い席が上座とされ，客が主人より社会的に地位が高くないかぎり，主人がその席に座って客に会います。

ところ天　　ゼリーのような食物で，寒天と同様に，てんぐさという赤い海藻で作ります。ところ天は，手押しポンプのように動く特別の道具を使って，先の小さな穴から押し出し，細い短冊状にしてから，酢じょう油をかけて食べます。ところ天は1千年以上も昔からあり，以前は夏を代表する冷たいおやつでしたが，今では清涼飲料やアイスクリームほどには若い人に好まれていません。しかし，古い世代の人にとっては昔なつかしい食物です。

酉の市　　酉の市は，神道系の大鳥神社で，11月の酉の日に開かれます。これらの神社はもとは武運の神様をまつったものですが，のちに幸運の神様をまつるようになりました。大阪の堺市や東京の浅草で開かれる酉の市は特に有名です。香具師と呼ばれる行商人が露店を開き，幸運を呼ぶとされる熊手を大声で売っています。

鳥のさえずり　　鳥の鳴き声は自然の主な魅力の一つです。そ

constitute one of the chief charms of nature. They announce daybreak, nightfall, and the changes of the four seasons. The bush warbler (*uguisu*), which is considered a herald of spring, and the little cuckoo (*hototogisu*), which sings in summer, are among the most highly prized by those who love birds' songs. The medieval priest Dōgen (1200-1253) composed a poem about the beauty of the four seasons, choosing the cuckoo's song as representative image of summer. It goes, "In the spring, cherry blossoms,/in the summer the cuckoo./ In autumn the moon, and in winter/the snow, clear, cold." (translated by Edward G. Seidensticker) There are many different onomatopes in Japanese reproducing the warbling sounds associated with birds of various kinds. Since birds' twitterings can be very noisy sometimes, *saezuri* also means "prattling". (S)

tōrō   a lantern. Lanterns vary greatly in size, form, and material. Standing stone lanterns and hanging metal lanterns are commonly seen at temples and shrines. These are for offering candles to Buddhist and Shintoist deities as well as for illuminating the grounds. Garden lanterns mostly made of stone are placed for the beauty they add to gardens in Japanese style. A garden lantern is not so much an illuminator as a sculptural decoration. In some districts the custom prevails of offering small wooden lanterns afloat on the water on the last evening of the Bon Festival. This custom is called *tōrō-nagashi* or *mandō-nagashi*. It was originally intended as a ceremony for sending off ancestral souls back to their world, which was believed to lie beyond the sea. (S)

れは，夜明けや夕暮れや四季の移り変わりを教えてくれます。春の先ぶれをつげる鶯と，夏に鳴くほととぎすは，鳥の鳴き声の愛好者がもっとも珍重するものです。中世の僧侶である道元は四季の美しさについて歌をよんでいますが，夏の代表的イメージとしてほととぎすの鳴き声を選んでいます。それは，「春は花夏ほととぎす秋は月／冬雪さえて冷しかりけり」（エドワード・G・サイデンステッカー英訳）というものです。多くの種類の鳥の鳴き声を表わす擬声語が日本語にはたくさんあります。鳥のさえずりは時には非常にやかましいこともあるので，さえずりはおしゃべりの意味にもなります。

灯　籠　　灯籠は大きさも形式も素材も非常に多様です。石造りの立ち灯籠や金属製の吊り灯籠は，寺院や神社でよく見られます。これらは境内を照らすとともに，神仏に灯明を献じるためのものです。庭園の灯籠はたいてい石でできていて，和風の庭園の景観を引き立てる役割をはたします。それは

照明具であるよりも彫刻の装飾なのです。地方によっては，お盆の最後の夕方に，小さな木製の灯籠を水に流す風習があります。この風習は灯籠流しとか万灯流しとか呼ばれています。もともとこれは，海のかなたにあると信じられていた霊界へ先祖の霊を送る儀式として始まったものです。

tororo   grated yam. Various kinds of yams are popular ingredients in Japanese cuisine. Those used for *tororo* (grated yam) are beige, hairy mountain yams, including *nagaimo* and *jinenjo*. The yam is peeled, finely grated and churned with a *surikogi* (wooden pestle) in the *suribachi* (large pottery mortar). Very often a raw egg and clear soup seasoned with soy sauce are added to the grated sticky yam to make it tasty and smooth to the tongue. Boiled rice with *tororo* on it is very refreshing especially after heavy dishes. It is also served in combination with many other foods, for example, with sliced raw tuna fish. (T)

tsukemono   pickles. Pickles have been an important part of the Japanese-style meal closely associated with boiled rice. Some Japanese say that a meal of rice, *miso* soup, and pickles is enough for their breakfast. In northern Japan pickles are also enjoyed with green tea between meals. There is a wide variety of pickled foods, preserved in various ways often varying from region to region, and from home to home. The most common pickle is *takuan* (pickled white radish), which is made with salted *kome-nuka* (rice bran) in a stone-weighted barrel. Every home used to make *takuan* with its own flavor and aroma. Nowadays many homes buy professionally made pickles because they have neither the time to spare nor a dark, cool place suitable for storing barrels. Vegetables as commonly pickled are *hakusai* (Chinese cabbage), cucumber, and eggplant. *Umeboshi* (soft pickled plum) is also an important pickle which most Japanese cannot do without as a condiment for *o-musubi* (rice balls). (T)

とろろ　　日本料理ではごく普通の材料としてさまざまな種類の芋があります。とろろ料理に使う芋は，表面がベージュ色で，毛のような根が生えている山芋です。長芋とかじねんじょがこれに属します。芋の皮をむき，すり鉢の中にすりおろして，すりこぎでよくすります。ねばっこいとろろに，生卵とすまし汁を加えると，味がよくなり，舌ざわりも滑らかになります。温かい御飯にとろろ汁をかけたものは，特にしつこい料理の後では，大変さっぱりしておいしいものです。とろろはまた，他の食物と組み合せて，例えばまぐろのさしみにかけて食べることもあります。

漬　物　　漬物は，御飯と密接な関係をもつ和食の中で重要な地位を占めています。日本人の中には，御飯と味噌汁と漬物があれば朝食としては十分だという人さえいます。北日本では漬物をおやつとして緑茶といっしょに楽しむこともあります。漬物には非常に多くの種類があり，地方によって，また家庭によって，それぞれ違った漬け方で保存されています。最も一般的な漬物はたくあんで，たるの中で塩を混ぜた米ぬかに大根を漬け，石で重しをして作ります。以前はどの家庭も特有の味と香りを持つたくあんを漬けたものです。今日では，漬物を作る暇も，たるを貯蔵するのに適した冷暗所もないため，専門店が作った既製の漬物を買う家庭が少なくありません。漬物にする野菜としては，白菜，きゅうり，なすが一般的です。梅干もまた重要な漬物で，おむすびを作るときにはどうしても欲しいものです。

tsukimi   a moon-viewing party. This custom is usually held around the middle of September. It originated from farmers' religious observances ensuring a good harvest. People offer *tsukimi-dango* (dumplings) and *satoimo* (taros) with *susuki* (Japanese pampas grasses) and *hagi* (bush clovers) to the full moon and pray for the realization of their wishes.   (K)

tsuru-kame   a crane and a tortoise. In Japan there is a popular saying : "*Tsuru* (a crane) lives one thousand and *kame* (a tortoise) ten thousand years." These two creatures, referred to as *tsuru-kame* like one word, immediately remind every Japanese of long life. The use of them as symbols of longevity and prosperity is said to have been introduced into Japan from China and Korea in ancient times. It has taken such deep root in Japanese life that both *tsuru* and *kame*, especially the former valued for its dignified beauty, are very often employed as patterns or decorations for festive occasions. For example, the postage stamp specially issued for happy events has a crane design. Various forms of traditional Japanese music and drama, such as *koto* music and *nō* drama, have a piece entitled *Tsuru-kame*, which is often performed by way of well-wishing compliments.   (T)

tsuya   a wake. Prior to a funeral service, mourners spend the evening together keeping a watch over the dead on the eve of the funeral. Originally this custom was practiced by the family of the deceased, but it has become a religious ceremony at which condolence callers express their sympathy

月　見　　この年中行事は通例9月中旬に行われます。昔，農民が豊作を願って行った行事に由来します。月見団子と里芋にすすきと萩を添えて満月に供え，願いが叶うことを祈ります。

鶴　亀　　日本には「鶴は千年，亀は万年」という格言があります。この2種の生き物が鶴亀と1語のようにいわれると，日本人はだれもが長寿を連想します。長命と繁栄の象徴として鶴と亀を使うことは，古代中国と朝鮮から日本に伝わって来たといわれ，日本人の生活の中に深く根をおろしています。鶴と亀の両方，とりわけ鶴は，品がある美しい姿のため重んじられて，お祝いごとの図案や装飾によく使われます。例えば，慶事用に特に発行された切手には鶴が描いてあり，贈物はしばしば鶴の模様で飾ります。琴とか能のような日本の伝統的な音楽や劇には「鶴亀」という題の作品があり，これを祝辞の代わりに演じることがあります。

通　夜　　葬式の前夜に喪家は死者を見守って夜を明かします。もともとこの習慣は遺族によって行われていましたが，今では弔問客が喪家に対して哀悼の意を表わす宗教的儀式となっています。葬儀の祭壇が設けられ，その家が仏教徒であれば，僧侶が読経をします。通夜の礼拝は夜の早い時刻に行われ，葬儀ほど形

315

for the bereaved family. The altar for the funeral is set up and if the family is Buddhist, sutras are chanted by a priest. The service of *tsuya* is held in the early hours in the evening, and there is a slight touch of informality as compared with the funeral. (S)

uchi-soto   insiders and outsiders. Japanese people recognize that they are good at intra-group communication, but not at inter-group communication even within the framework of Japanese society. They have developed a fine in-group semiotic system (verbal and nonverbal) that contributes to the reinforcement of a shared set of the communalized assumptions. Yet this system simply is not made to be shared by out-group members. The phenomenon emanates from a peculiar mode of group distinction Japanese people have traditionally sustained. In-group members maintain a common sense of identity and solidarity. They thereby develop a familial feeling of relatedness that is characterized by sympathy, interdependence and mutual benefit. The concomitant result can be a socio-psychological distance that in-group members tend to take toward out-group members. This can be witnessed in the relations of employees of one company to those of another. It is also the case in Japanese attitudes toward *gaijin* (foreigners) domestically, and refugees internationally. (HO)

ue-shita   the relationship between a superordinate and a subordinate. One of the important patterns that Japanese people are expected to recognize in human interaction is

316

式ばらない儀式になります。

うち・そと　　日本人はグループ内のコミュニケーションはじょうずですが，グループ間のコミュニケーションはへたであると感じています。これは日本社会のわく組みのなかでもそうなのです。日本人はグループ内にのみ通じる精巧な意味体系を発達させました。そのおかげで，多くの文化的前提を共有するようになりました。しかしこの体系は，グループ外の人々が利用するようにはできていないのです。この現象は，日本人が伝統的に維持してきた独特の集団識別法に由来します。グループ内の人々は共通の存在意識ならびに連帯意識をつちかいます。このことによってお互いが家族のように関係し合っているという意識を持つようになるのです。それは，思いやり，相互依存，相互扶助といったことで示されます。その結果，グループ内の人々はグループ外の人々に対して，社会的にも心理的にも一定の距離を持つようになります。このことは，ある会社の従業員が他の会社の従業員に対して持つ関係に表われています。また，日本人が国内で外人に対してとる態度，あるいは国際的には難民に対してとる態度にも表われているといえるでしょう。

うえ・した　　日本人が人間関係で気をつけなければならないとされている最も重要なものの一つは，上下関係です。下位の人は上位の人に対して敬意を表わし，上位の人は下位の人に対して愛

the relationship between a superordinate and a subordinate. A subordinate is supposed to be respectful to a superordinate and the latter caring in a paternal manner for the former. The relationship used to demand absolute obedience and loyalty on the part of the subordinate to the superordinate, and special favors and privileges given by the latter to the former. But it has recently lost its traditional significance and has apparently become largely a matter of honor and politeness. There are various verbal and nonverbal means to express delicate shades of those relationships. Superordinate positions are held by those who are longer in experience in a situation (such as a company), older in age, and more competent. How these criteria interact and what is more important among these criteria can vary situationally. For example, in a school or company situation, a younger but senior member can generally claim, or be politely granted, a superordinate position over his older but junior member (often referred to as a *senpai-kōhai* relationship). Where there exist criterion incongruencies, there certainly will emerge adaptation problems. (HO)

ujigami   originally a guardian god of a family or of a tribe. As it has gradually become the community deity protecting the inhabitants of a particular parish or a village, people living away from their native places may have more than one *ujigami* to worship. Parishioners (*ujiko*) of the shrine enshrining their *ujigami* celebrate an annual festival and hold services on various occasions, offering prayers for the peace and prosperity of the family. Devout believers feel that they are under the protection of *ujigami* throughout their lives,

情を示すものとされています。この関係は，かつては，下の者に対して上の者への絶対的服従と忠誠を，上の者に対しては下の者への特別の温情を求めるといったぐあいでした。しかし現在では，その伝統的意味合いは薄れ，主として体面上あるいは礼儀上のことがらになっています。言葉づかいでもそれ以外でも，これらの関係の微妙なところを表現するさまざまな方法があります。どんな人が上位の立場を占めるかというと，状況（会社など）において経験年数の高い人，年上の人，あるいは能力のある人です。これらの基準の相互関係，あるいはどの基準がより重要であるかといったことは，状況によっていろいろ変わります。例えば，学校や会社では，若くても経験年数の多い者が，年をとっていても経験の少ない者に対して上位の立場を主張できますし，また礼儀としてそれが与えられることがあります。この関係は先輩・後輩関係ともいわれます。基準に一貫性が見あたらないところでは，いろいろと適応の問題が生じることになります。

氏　神　　本来は家族や氏族の守護神だった氏神は，次第に，村落や地域の住民を保護する地域の神となりました。故郷から離れて生活している人は崇拝する氏神が2つ以上あることもあります。氏神をまつっている神社の氏子は，さまざまな機会に礼拝を行い，家内の安全と繁栄を祈願します。熱心な信者は一生を通じて氏神の保護を受けていると感じ，折にふれて神社に参拝し，誕生や成人や結婚や遠くへの旅行など，人生に起こる重要な行事や変化を氏神に報告します。

and they occasionally pay a visit to the shrine and inform their guardian god of important events or changes occurring in their lives such as birth, coming of age, marriage, or travels to distant places. (S)

ukai   cormorant fishing. *Ukai* is a unique way of fishing with large black seabirds called *u* (cormorants). This fishing, which has a history of more than 1,200 years, is now practiced in several parts of Japan only as a tourist attraction. The most famous is that on the Nagara River in Gifu Prefecture, where each skillful fisherman in traditional costume manipulates from his fishing boat twelve cormorants with long ropes tied to them. The cormorants, after receiving two or three years' training, can dive into the water, catch *ayu* (sweet fish) and return to their master to give away their catches without swallowing them. The scenes, enacted with the fishermen's characteristic shouts, and fishing fires burning brightly against the darkness of night, make an impressive pageant of water and fire. In summer, tourists can enjoy viewing it from a pleasure boat floating down the river. (T)

ukiyo-e   genre pictures and woodblock prints. *Ukiyo-e* started and flourished during the Edo period (1603–1867) as a conspicuous example of urban merchant culture quite distinct from that of the ruling *samurai* (warrior) class. It is very popular even today, and to the West it is the best-known style of traditional Japanese painting. *Ukiyo-e* literally means pictures of the fleeting world, that is, this secular world, and their favorite subjects largely were stylish courtesans, *kabuki*

320

鵜　飼　　鵜と呼ばれる大きな黒い海鳥を操って行う珍しい漁法です。鵜飼には1,200年以上の歴史がありますが，今は観光客向けに，国内の数カ所で行われているにすぎません。最も有名なのは岐阜県の長良川の鵜飼です。ここでは，伝統的な服装をして漁船に乗り込んだ鵜匠が，長いなわにつないだ12羽の鵜を操っています。鵜は2，3年の訓練を受けると，水中にもぐり，鮎を捕えて，それを飲み込まずに鵜匠のところへ戻り，吐き出すようになります。夜の暗闇を背景に，かがり火が赤々と燃え，鵜匠が独特のかけ声をあげながら演じる鵜飼風景は，印象深い水と火のページェントです。夏になると観光客は川を下る観覧船からこの眺めを楽しむことができます。

浮世絵　　江戸時代には，支配階級である武士の文化とはまったく違った特徴を持つ都市の商人文化が発達し栄えましたが，浮世絵はその顕著な例です。浮世絵は今日も大変人気があり，日本の伝統的な絵画の中で西洋に最もよく知られています。浮世絵は文字通りには，浮世すなわちこの俗世を描く絵を意味します。よく用いられる題材は，粋な遊女，歌舞伎役者，力士，名所風景などです。18世紀中頃に多色刷が発達して，さらに浮世絵の人気が高まりました。有名な浮世絵師の中でも，歌麿は美人画で，北斎

actors, *sumō* wrestlers, and places of scenic interest. The development of multicolored printing in the mid-eighteenth century led to the still greater popularity of *ukiyo-e*. Among many famous painters, Utamaro (1754–1806) is especially noted for his portraits of beauties, Hokusai (1760–1849) for his views of Mt. Fuji, and Hiroshige (1797–1858) for his 'Fifty-three Stages on the Tōkaidō Highway'. Perhaps *ukiyo-e* is in part responsible for the general, often misleading image abroad of Japan as the country of Mt. Fuji and *geisha* girls. (T)

umeboshi　　a pickled plum. *Umeboshi* are round, red, sour pickles which are kept at almost all Japanese homes. Making *umeboshi* started in the thirteenth century. When Japanese plums (*ume*), a species of apricot, turn yellow in June, the unripe fruits are harvested, soaked in salted water, packed with *shiso* (perilla) leaves, which dye the plums red and give them better flavor, and left to mature in a large jar for a couple of months. Then, the plums and *shiso* leaves are taken out of the jar, squeezed to remove excess liquid, and dried in the hot summer sun. They are returned to the jar to further mature for another month. When *umeboshi* are ready to eat, they are packed in a smaller container. They keep indefinitely at room temperature. When they have nothing around the house to cook, many Japanese will be happy to have some rice balls and *umeboshi* pickles. (O)

umeshu　　plum liqueur. *Umeshu* is made from the hard, green, unripe fruit of the *ume* (Japanese plum). The tight-

322

は富士山の風景画で，そして広重は「東海道五十三次」で特に知られています。浮世絵のおかげで日本は富士山と芸者の国というイメージで海外に広まったのかもしれません。もちろんこのイメージは真の日本を正しくとらえているとはいえません。

　　梅干し　　丸くて赤い色をした酸っぱい梅のつけもので，日本のほとんどの家庭にあります。梅干し作りは13世紀に始まりました。日本の梅はアプリコットの一種で，6月に黄色になります。熟しきる前の実をとって塩水にしたし，しその葉と一緒につけこみます。しそは梅を赤く染め，味に風味をそえます。大きなビンにいれて2ヵ月間待ちます。それから，その梅としその葉をビンから取り出し，余分な水分をとって，夏の強い日光で干します。そして再びビンにもどし，さらに1ヵ月ほどねかせます。梅干しが食べられるようになると，小さなうつわにいれます。室温でいつまでも保存できます。たいがいの日本人は，何も作るものがないときは，おにぎりと梅干しがあれば満足します。

　　梅　酒　　梅酒は，固く緑色をした未だ熟していない梅の実で作ります。固い梅の実を1つずつていねいにふき，砂糖と焼酎と

fleshed *ume*, carefully wiped one by one, are put in a large glass jar with sugar and *shōchū* (spirits distilled from rice, sweet potatoes, etc.), and then stored in a dark, cool place. The beautiful amber-colored liqueur can be enjoyed in two or three months, but it tastes even better as it matures. It is not only a pleasant drink in summer, but also popular for its considerable medicinal benefits for intestinal disorders. *Umeshu* is certainly far more commonly made in Japanese homes than any other kind of fruit wine. (T)

unagi an eel. Since eels have long been considered to be an energizing food, it is customary to eat them on *ushi-no-hi* (literally, the day of the ox) during the hottest period of summer called *doyō*. These names come from an old way of reckoning days. *Unagi* is indeed very nutritious, and therefore, effective for those who tend to lose their appetite due to the heat and humidity characteristic of Japanese summer. Boiled rice served with *unagi* which has been broiled over charcoal fire and specially seasoned with a thick, sweet soy sauce is most people's favorite dish, though it is too expensive for them to enjoy frequently. (T)

uranai fortune-telling. While the horoscope, floral language, and zodiac are all popular means of foreseeing the future throughout the world, *tesō* (palmistry), *ninsō* (physiognomy), and *seimei-handan* (onomancy) seem to have taken root in the Japanese society as successful businesses. These fortune-tellers practice their business at night, scattered here and there on the street corners of big cities. *Omikuji* (a

いっしょに，大きなガラスのびんに入れて，冷暗所へ保存しておきます。2，3カ月で美しい琥珀色の液体を楽しむことができますが，熟成すればさらにおいしくなります。夏の快適な飲物であるばかりか，胃腸障害にかなりの薬用効果があるため，人気があります。日本の家庭では他のどの種類の果実酒よりも梅酒をよく作ります。

うなぎ　うなぎは昔から精力をつける食品と考えられています。古い暦で土用の丑の日と呼ばれる夏の日にうなぎを食べる習慣があります。実際，うなぎは栄養価が高く，日本特有の暑さと湿気のため食欲を失いがちの人に効果的です。炭火で付焼きにしたうなぎと御飯の料理は，たいていの人が大好物にしています。ただし値段が高くて，あまりたびたび食べるわけにはいきません。

占 い　星占いや花ことば，そして十二宮図などは世界各地で見られますが，手相，人相，姓名判断などは日本でのみ商売として繁盛している占いのように思われます。これらの占い師たちは夜の盛り場であちこちに見られます。おみくじには，引いた人の運・

written oracle) tells what kind of fortune the lottery drawer can expect ranging from an excellent fortune to a singular ill fortune. *Omikuji* are generally obtained at shrines and temples. People enjoy having their future told. But most of them, unless they are exceptionally superstitious or in serious trouble, do not believe the words written on the slips, but rather read them just for fun. (Y)

yagō the name of a store. A store is usually named after the founder or the location of the establishment. This custom originated in the Muromachi period (1392–1573). In old days, merchants considered their *yagō* extremely important as it was the symbol of their reputation. When they allowed some of their apprentices to branch out and become independent store owners, they let them use their *yagō* for the newly-opened businesses. Today well-known *yagō* include those of the first-class department stores, such as Matsuzakaya, Mitsukoshi, and Takashimaya, and those of the giant business conglomerates, such as Mitsui, Mitsubishi, and Sumitomo. Incidentally, *kabuki* families also have *yagō*-like names. Otowaya, Naritaya, and Narikomaya are several of the more famous ones. (K)

yakitori chunks of grilled chicken on a bomboo stick. It is usually a speciality of a *nawanoren* (rope-curtained) or *aka-chōchin* (red-lanterned) drinking place. It usually refers to chicken chunks charcoal-grilled with green onion slices on a bamboo skewer (*kushi*). It is served either sprinkled with salt (*shio*) or dipped in the house-special barbecue soy sauce

不運が書かれており，神社やお寺にあります。日本人は自分の運勢を占ってもらうのが好きなようです。しかし，迷信深い人や大変な悩みごとのある人を除いては，おみくじに書かれていることばを信じる人は少なく，たいていの人はただ楽しんでいるだけです。

屋　号　　商店の名前は普通，創設者または創業地の名にちなんでつけられます。この習慣は室町時代にさかのぼります。昔，商人は屋号を非常に大切なものと考えました。屋号は商人の名声の象徴だったのです。奉公人が独立して開業するときなど，主人は元奉公人の新しい店に自分の屋号を使うのを許可しました。今日，有名な屋号としては，一流デパートの松坂屋，三越，高島屋，その他，大複合企業の三井，三菱，住友などがあります。また別に，歌舞伎役者にも，屋号に似た名前があります。有名なものでは，音羽屋，成田屋，成駒屋などです。

焼　鳥　　焼鳥は，縄のれんとか赤ちょうちんと呼ばれる一杯飲み屋の名物です。鳥肉の小切れをねぎと一緒に竹串にさして炭火で焼きます。塩焼きとたれ焼きがあります。また，豚や牛の臓物の場合（もつ焼き）もありますが，食べ方は同じです。もつ焼きには独特の用語があります。タン（舌），ハツ（心臓），レバ（肝臓），ガツ（胃袋），シロ（小腸），テッポウ（直腸），カシラ

(*tare*). It also often refers to various entrails and parts of pork or beef cooked and served in the same way (*motsuyaki*). There is a jargon for each part such as follows: *tan* (tongue), *hatsu* (heart), *reba* (liver), *gatsu* (stomach), *shiro* (small intestine), *teppō* (rectum), *kashira* (head), *nankotsu* (gristle), *kobukuro* (womb), *zui* (spinal cord), *chire* (spleen), etc. (HO)

yakudoshi　a critical age. According to a Japanese popular belief, a person is apt to fall ill or to experience other misfortunes at a certain age during his life span. At what age a person is believed to encounter such calamities varies regionally and historically. The common saying now is that men are doomed to enter a critical stage at age 42 and women at age 33. The popular belief in these particular ages as *yakudoshi* may be based on the physical conditions of men and women in ancient times. It is also said that these two digits are phonetically unlucky numbers. 42 can be read as *shini*, homophonous with the word for death. Likewise, 33 can be pronounced as *sanzan*, interpreted as meaning a miserable state. Men and women of those *yakudoshi* ages are supposed to invite relatives and friends to a gorgeous dinner to implicitly ask them to shoulder the unlucky burden together. They may also pray at temples and shrines for the elimination of an evil spirit. The year before the *yakudoshi* is called *maeyaku* and precaution is called for. Similarly, the year after is called *ato-yaku* and prudence is advised. (HO)

yakuza　a gangster. Following the behavior patterns of feudal-age street toughs, the *yakuza* claim to act out the

（頭），ナンコツ（軟骨），コブクロ（子宮），ズイ（脊髄），チレ（脾臓）などです。

厄　年　民間信仰によれば，人間は一生のうち何歳かの時に病気になったり他の不幸にみまわれたりするものだそうです。何歳でこのような災難にあうかは，地域的にも歴史的にもいろいろといわれています。最も普通の言い方では，男性は42歳，女性は33歳が危険な年だそうです。これらの年齢を厄年とするのは，昔の男女の健康状態からきたのでしょう。また，これらの2ケタ数は音のうえでアンラッキー・ナンバーとなっています。42はシニとも読め，死という語と同音です。同じように，33はサンザン（散々）と発音され，非運の状態を意味します。これらの厄年をむかえる男女は，親戚や友人にごちそうするものとされています。この不運をみんなで分かち合うようにお願いするためです。また，神社やお寺に行って，悪霊の退散を祈ります。厄年の1年前は前厄とよばれ，要注意です。同様に，厄年の1年後は後厄とよばれ，自重するものとされています。

ヤクザ　ヤクザは，封建時代に街道筋の暴れ者といわれた連中の行動をまね，義理と人情を生活信条にかかげています。浪花

traditional codes of *giri* (mutual obligations) and *ninjō* (human feelings). They also are often depicted as anti-establishment heroes or self-disciplined truth seekers in old-fashioned *naniwabushi* stories. But they are actually under-world outcasts who live by gambling and racketeering. Of little worth as individuals, they organize into family groups (*kumi*), in which the leaders are called *oyabun* (boss) and the others *kobun* (henchmen). The *oyabun* support the *kobun* economically. The *kobun* reciprocally do whatever they are told to do by the *oyabun* or for the sake of the *oyabun*. If they fail, they have to sever joints from their little fingers to make up for uncompleted missions or broken promises. The *yakuza* sometimes distinguish themselves by tatooing their bodies from neck to calves. Their tatoo (for example, a dragon) is their image of value (strength). Now often described as the Japanese Mafia, the *yakuza* have become an organized crime syndicate with various international connections. (HO)

yamato-damashii   the Japanese spirit. It usually means bravery and purity, and is often symbolized by the ephemeral beauty of cherry blossoms. This concept original-ly developed centuries ago to counteract the influence of Chinese culture through emphasis of the practical wisdom that was believed to be inherent in Japanese civilization. It soon took on the contemporary meaning. During the war, this spirit became the slogan of the ultranationalistic military government in its support for the Emperor. Today this word does not necessarily convey such a nationalistic implication. Business people sometimes draw inspiration from it before

節などでは，反体制の英雄とか，自律心のある正義の味方など
と，表現されています。しかし実際は裏街道を歩くはずれ者で，
賭博と恐喝の常習犯です。1人では何もできないので，家族制度
的な組をつくって行動します。主領格は親分と呼ばれ，子分を従
えます。親分は経済的に子分の面倒をみます。子分はお返しに親
分のいうことを何でもきき，親分のためなら何でもします。仕事
に失敗したり約束を破ったりすると，小指をつめねばなりません。
ヤクザの中には全身に入墨をしている者もいます。入墨（例えば
竜）は彼らの価値観（例えば力）を表わします。最近は日本のマ
フィアなどと呼ばれ，さまざまな国際的コネクションを持った犯
罪シンジケートにのしあがっています。

大和魂　　普通，勇敢で純粋であることを意味し，しばしば桜
の花のはかない美しさに象徴されます。本来この概念は，数百年
前，中国文化の漢才に対して，和才すなわち日本文化に固有のも
のとされた実利的な英知を強調するところから発展しました。し
かし，すぐに今のような意味になりました。戦時中には，天皇制
を利用する超国家主義的軍事政権のスローガンとなりました。今
日では，このことばは必ずしもそういった国家主義的な意味合い
を持つとは限りません。ビジネスマンは，困難な仕事にぶつかっ
たときなど，心を引き締めるためにこのことばを使うことがあり
ます。係長は，優柔不断で生産性の上がらない部下をみると，
「大和魂はないのか，当たって砕けろだ」などということがあり

undertaking a difficult task of some sort. A section chief may shout to an indecisive and unproductive subordinate : "Don't you have *yamato-damashii* ? Get up and go for it." (K)

yamato-nadeshiko the Japanese women. Though very few young Japanese today use the word *yamato-nadeshiko*, it used to be very often employed as a synonym for a Japanese woman. It was the case especially when emphasis was put on her traditional virtues of modesty, obedience, patience, and moreover, bravery and determinedness when she was faced with difficulties. *Yamato* is another term for Japan, and is more connotative of characteristics peculiar to Japan ; *nadeshiko* (a pink) is a plant well known for its lovely flower and slender, yet rather strong stalk. Therefore, *yamato-nadeshiko* came to mean a typically Japanese woman, or rather an ideal Japanese woman for conservative men. Until the end of World War II, girls were told by their parents and teachers to be *yamato-nadeshiko*. However, Japanese women now are not what they were supposed to be a few decades ago. They are becoming more and more independent and individualistic. *Yamato-nadeshiko* seem to have almost disappeared both in name and reality, to the regret of older generations. (T)

yasegaman endurance for the sake of pride. *Yasegaman* is a combination of *yaseru* (to become skinny) and *gaman-suru* (to endure). It literally means "to endure until one becomes emaciated". Ruth Benedict, in her famous book *The Chrysanthemum and the Sword*, once said that Japanese culture is based on shame while American culture is based on

ます。

大和なでしこ　　今日では大和なでしこということばを使う若い人はほとんどいませんが，日本女性の同意語として非常によく用いられたものです。特にそのときは，つつましさ，従順，忍耐，さらに，困難に直面したときの勇気と強い意志など，日本女性の伝統的美徳が強調されました。大和は日本の別名で，日本独自の特徴をより強く暗示している語です。なでしこは，かれんな花と，細いけれども意外に強い茎を持つことでよく知られた植物です。それで，大和なでしこが，典型的な日本女性，あるいは，保守的な男性にとって理想の女性を意味するようになりました。第2次世界大戦末までは，女の子は大和なでしこになるように両親や先生から教えられました。しかし，日本女性はもはや数十年前に期待された女性とは違います。独立心を持ち，個性をたいせつにする傾向にあります。古い世代の人々は，大和なでしこは名実ともにいなくなったようだと残念がっています。

やせ我慢　　やせ我慢とは，やせると我慢するをいっしょにしたことばです。直訳すると，やせるほど我慢するということです。ルース・ベネディクトは『菊と刀』の中で，アメリカの文化は罪に基づいているのに対し，日本の文化は恥に基づいているといいました。恥を規準にした社会においては，体面を失うことは全人格を失うことにもなります。昔，武士は非常にプライドが高

a sense of sin or guilt. In a shame-oriented society, for persons to lose face is to have their ego destroyed. In olden days, *samurai* warriors were proud people. When they were too poor to have anything to eat, they held a toothpick in their mouth to pretend that they had just eaten a meal. In this way, they maintained their honor and independence. Actually, to save face or maintain dignity, some people would do anything, however absurd or painful it might be. (K)

yatai a stand set up on a street. Ordinary people enjoy a quick drink in the evening at a red-lanterned *yatai* set up on a street corner. Typically, all *yatai* stalls provide some kinds of alcoholic drinks, but each specializes in *rāmen* (Chinese noodles), *oden* (hotchpotch), and *yakitori* (chunks of grilled chicken), etc. On a festival day, fun seekers enjoy lines of open-air *yatai* shops where many curious things are on sale. (HO)

yobikō a preparatory school for entrance examinations. Since educational experience is perhaps the most valuable asset for careerists in Japan, young people crowd to enter prestigeous universities. The situation surrounding the competition in entrance examinations for high-ranking Japanese universities is so stressful that it is often called "examination hell" (*shiken jigoku*). Many senior high graduates who have failed in their first trial enter a prep school to prepare for the second attempt. *Yobikō* students are often called *rōnin* (lordless *samurai*) because they have no meaningful place to belong to. Although *rōnin* students are often

334

く，お金が無くて食べ物が買えないときでも，楊子をくわえ，満腹を装うなどして，名誉と自立心を守ろうとしました。事実，人によっては，体面や名誉を保つためなら，いくら不合理なことでも，いくら辛いことでもするかもしれません。

屋　台　　夕方，通りの一角に店びらきした赤ちょうちんの屋台で，いっぱいひっかけるのを楽しみにしている人がたくさんいます。普通，どの屋台でも何らかのアルコール飲料を出します。また，それぞれラーメン，おでん，焼鳥などのどれかを専門にしています。お祭りでは，娯楽を求める町の人々が屋台（露店）を楽しみにしています。おもしろそうな品物がたくさん並ぶからです。

予備校　　日本では学歴が仕事のうえで最も価値ある資産となっているため，若者は有名大学に殺到します。一流大学の入学試験は厳しいので，試験地獄などといわれています。多くの高校卒業生は第1回目の大学入試に失敗すると予備校に入り，次回を期します。予備校生はよく浪人といわれます。浪人とは，主君を失った侍を指す昔のことばです。予備校生も，所属するところがないのでこう呼ばれるのです。多くの高校生は，自分の望む大学に入るためには1年か2年浪人するのを何とも思っていません。しかし，浪人は灰色で単調な生活を送り，ただひたすらに試験勉強をしているというイメージがあります。最近，こういった傾向はますます激しくなりました。小学生や中学生も試験地獄にまきこ

described as leading a grayish, monotonous life cramming for admission tests, many senior high students take it for granted that they will become *rōnin* for a couple of years in order to get to the university of their first choice. The current trend in this direction is intensified by the fact that more and more elementary and junior high pupils are getting trapped in the "examination hell". After school, young children go to extra-curricular private schools (*juku*). They work with tutors (sometimes until midnight!) for entrance examinations of "good" junior and senior high schools. (HO)

yōkan　　sweet bean jelly. It is a typical Japanese sweet confection, a slice of which is often served with strong powdered green tea. Since the fourteenth century, it has been closely associated with the tea ceremony. A mixture of red-bean paste, sugar, and Japanese gelatin is either kneaded or steamed, and formed into a narrow rectangular bar approximately 8 inches long. Some districts produce *yōkan* with chestnut, dried persimmon, or some other local specialities. A wide selection is available at Japanese-style confectionaries. (O)

yome-shūto　　the relationship between mother-in-law and daughter-in-law. In Japan the strained relationship between mother-in-law and daughter-in-law is an old and new problem. Similar problems do exist in other countries, too. For example, advice columns in American newspapers often take up complaints from women against their mothers-in-law or daughters-in-law. In Japan, however, conflicts between in-

まれているのです。放課後，たくさんの子供が塾に行きます。そして，「良い」中学校や高校の入学試験を受けるため，時には深夜まで勉強しています。

　　羊　羹　　羊羹は日本の代表的なお菓子で，濃い抹茶と一緒にいただきます。14世紀以降，羊羹は茶道と深く結びついてきました。あずきをつぶしたものと砂糖と寒天を混ぜ合わせたものを練ったり蒸したりして，8インチほどの長さの細長い長方形の木箱へ入れて形を作ります。地方によっては，胡桃や干柿や他の材料をいれた羊羹を作ります。和菓子屋ではいろいろな種類の羊羹が売られています。

　　嫁　姑　　日本では嫁姑の緊張した関係は古くて新しい問題です。似たような問題は他の国にもあります。例えば，アメリカの新聞の人生相談欄はしばしば姑や嫁に対する不平不満をとりあげています。しかし日本では，嫁姑間の争いが非常によく起こり，しかも深刻であるため，日本の家庭の特徴であるとさえ考えられています。この理由の一つは，核家族化が進んでいるものの，若夫婦が夫の親と同居している家庭の割合が欧米よりもはるかに大

laws have been so common and so serious that they are even thought to be a common characteristic of Japanese households in general. One reason for this is that, despite a growing number of nuclear families, the proportion of homes where the young couple live with the husband's parent(s) is far larger in Japan than in Western countries. A proverb says, "Don't feed the autumn eggplant to your son's wife." It means that eggplants in autumn are considered to be too great a delicacy to give to daughters-in-law who are on bad terms with their in-laws. Such tense relations have been a favorite theme in novels, dramas, or comic strips. The TV series drama *Oshin*, depicting the eighty-year life of a woman, got amazingly high audience ratings in 1983, partly because its author thoroughly described the merciless treatment of the heroine Oshin by her mother-in-law. Under the prewar Japanese family system, the young wife was often regarded not as an individual, but as part of her husband's family to whom she had to devote most of her life, under her mother-in-law's strict, or even cruel supervision. The young wife in turn tended to assume the same harsh attitude toward her son's wife. Hence the popular expression *yome-ibiri* (daughter-in-law abuse). Since the new Constitution and Civil Code abolished the old family system soon after World War II, tremendous changes have taken place in the family. Some people say that the relationship between mother-in-law and daughter-in-law has been almost reversed. Elderly people are no longer in the position to treat their daughters-in-law as their subjects. (T)

yūgen　　quiet beauty or elegant simplicity. It is one of

きいことです。「秋なすは嫁に食わすな」という諺があります。これは，秋なすは非常においしいものとされているため，姑と仲が悪い嫁に与えるわけにはいかないという意味です。このような緊張した関係は，小説，ドラマ，漫画などが好んでテーマにとりあげています。1人の女性の80年の生涯を描いた連続テレビドラマ『おしん』が1983年に驚異的な高視聴率を得ましたが，その理由の一部は，主人公おしんに対する姑の情容赦のない扱いを作者が徹底的に描き出したからです。戦前の日本の家族制度のもとでは，嫁は個人として認められず，夫の家族の一部とみなされ，姑の厳格な，あるいは残酷でさえある監督を受けて，夫の家族に一生のほとんどを捧げなければならないこともありました。そのような嫁は，今度は自分の息子の妻に対して同じように厳しい態度をとったものです。嫁いびりという慣用表現もあります。第2次世界大戦後まもなく，新しい憲法と民法が古い家族制度を廃止して以来，家族に大きな変化が起こりました。嫁姑の関係はほとんど逆転したとさえいわれています。老人はもはや以前のように嫁を召使のようにあつかう地位にはいません。

幽　玄　　幽玄とは，落ち着いた美しさ，または趣きが深い簡

the traditional aesthetic concepts of Japanese poetry, and often regarded as a term for ideal beauty pursued particularly by poets and novelists of the medieval times. The poet Fujiwara-no-Shunzei (1114-1204) used the word *yūgen*, meaning quiet, elegant, and stately beauty, which he believed was the soul of *waka* poetry (poems of 31 syllables). According to Kamo-no-Chōmei (1155-1216), another poet and essayist of this age, *yūgen* is a sentiment or a vision not explicitly expressed in words but symbolically suggested by imagery. It was also associated with *nō* drama, since the *nō* playwright and actor Zeami (1363?-1443) often emphasized that quiet and elegant beauty was the supreme goal of artistic expression. Later it became a kind of critical term used for discussions of Japanese classical literature, and it has since acquired various interpretations. It has now several different shades of meaning—the subtle and profound, the simple and elegant, or the tasteful and graceful. *Yūgen* sounds a little too literary to give it colloquial currency. (S)

yukata an informal *kimono* for summer wear. It was originally called *yukatabira*, a cambric *kimono* worn by a person at his or her bath. Later it became a kind of cotton bathrobe worn after a bath. In the nineteenth century, people began to wear *yukata* in the hot season both at home and in the streets. It now generally refers to an unlined cotton *kimono* for casual wear. It is usually starched and has floral or simple geometrical patterns dyed or printed on its white or deep blue ground. It is also used as nightclothes and often worn in bed. Most Japanese-style hotels (*ryokan*) have *yukata* available for

潔さを意味します。和歌の伝統的な美的概念で，特に中世の詩人や文学者が追究した理想美を指すものとみなされています。歌人藤原俊成は幽玄という語を，静かで優雅で壮麗な美を表わすのに用いました。彼はそれが和歌の魂であると考えました。この時代のもう一人の歌人で随筆家の鴨長明によれば，幽玄とは，ことばであからさまに表現されるのではなく，イメージによって象徴的に暗示される情趣のことです。能作者であり能役者であった世阿弥も，幽玄が芸術的表現の最終目標であるとたびたび強調したので，幽玄は能とも関連づけられました。後にそれは日本の古典文学論に使われる一種の批評用語となり，いろいろに解釈されるようになりました。今では，微妙で深遠なこと，簡素で優雅なこと，あるいは趣きがあって上品なことなどさまざまなニュアンスがあります。しかし，文学的にすぎる響きがあり，口語ではあまり使われません。

浴 衣　もとは湯帷子と呼ばれて，入浴のときに着る麻地の着物でした。後にそれは入浴後に身につける一種のバスローブとなりました。19世紀には，暑い季節に家でも外でも浴衣を着るようになりました。現在では一般に，木綿の単衣の普段着の着物を指します。たいていは糊がきかせてあり，

白または紺地に花模様や単純な幾何学模様が染めたり印刷したりしてあります。寝衣として着ることもあります。旅館ではたいて

the guests. (S)

yutanpo a hot-water bottle. It is kept in the bed as a foot warmer, especially for infants, the sick, and the aged. It is a flat oval-shaped bottle, made of galvanized iron (or plastic today) and holding about half a gallon of hot water. It has several advantages over *anka*, another type of foot warmer containing a charcoal fire. It is more economical, safer, and easier to handle than *anka*. The electric blanket is a modern invention serving the same purpose, and it has spread throughout the country. Many people, however, prefer to use *yutanpo*, because they like the genial warmth it generates through heat conduction. The warmth of the *futon* (a thick bedquilt) heated by *yutanpo* makes one comfortable and drowsy—makes him feel like an infant nestling in its mother's bosom. (S)

wabi a simple and austere type of beauty. The word *wabi* is a noun derived from the verb *wabu* (to lose strength) and the adjective *wabishi* (lonely). Originally it meant the misery of living alone away from society. Later, however, it gained a positive aesthetic meaning: the enjoyment of a quiet, leisurely, and carefree life. Some medieval priests and poets found a solitary life attractive and blessed with opportunities for enjoying freedom from materialism and for cultivating the sense of oneness with nature. They valued a simple, austere type of beauty and a transcedental attitude toward life. It is the key concept in the appreciation of the tea ceremony and various forms of traditional poetry. Noted poets Saigyō

い宿泊客のために浴衣が用意してあります。

湯たんぽ　特に幼児や病人や老人のために，足を温める目的で寝具に入れます。平たい楕円形のトタン製（今日ではプラスチック製）の容器で，約1.8 l の湯が入ります。炭火を入れる足温用具であるあんかと比べて，湯たんぽにはいくつかの利点があります。湯たんぽはあんかよりも経済的で，安全で，扱いやすいのです。今では電気毛布が，就寝中に暖を取るものとして全国に普及しています。しかし，熱伝導によって湯たんぽが発する快い暖かさのために，多くの人々は湯たんぽのほうを好みます。湯たんぽで暖められた蒲団に入ると，母親の胸に抱かれた幼児のように，気持ちよい眠気がおとずれます。

わ　び　わびは，わぶ（動詞）とわびしい（形容詞）に由来する名詞です。この語は，もともと世間から離れて独り住むことのわびしさを指していました。それが後に，「世事に煩わされずに閑居の日々を満喫する境地」という，より肯定的で美的な意味合いを獲得したのです。中世の僧侶や歌人はそのような独り住いの生活にひかれ，それが，実利主義から解き放たれた自由を享受し，自然との一体感をはかることのできる境遇であると考えました。こうして，素朴な美と人生に対する超越的な態度に価値を見出していったのです。だから，茶の湯とか連歌・俳諧の類を味わううえで，わびの趣きはことのほか重要です。詩人の西行と心敬と芭蕉はわびの境地に従い，また茶人の武野紹鷗と千利休もこれを重んじました。彼らは，貧しさの中に豊かさを，簡素の中に美

(1118-1190), Shinkei (1406-1475), and Bashō (1644-1694) followed the life style of *wabi*, which was also stressed by the two great tea masters, Takeno Jōō (1502-1555) and Sen-no-Rikyū (1522-1591). They all pursued "richness in poverty and beauty in simplicity". (HA)

wagakki   traditional musical instruments of Japan. Japan's most popular traditional musical instrument, especially among women, is the *koto*, a kind of horizontal harp, made of wood about 6 feet long and 1 foot wide, with 13 strings, which is laid on the floor when played. The general name for music played on the *koto* is *sōkyoku*. The *shamisen* is a banjo-like instrument with three strings and played with a plectrum (*bachi*), and used for accompanying the *bunraku* puppetry and the *kabuki* theater, as well as other narrative kinds of folk music. The *shakuhachi* is a sort of flute made of a hollow bamboo stem about 1 foot 8 inches long with five finger holes. The *koto*, *shamisen*, and *shakuhachi* are called the trio of instruments for traditional Japanese music. Besides these, the *biwa* (a big mandolin-like lute with a bent neck), the *fue* (flute), and the *taiko* (drum) are also used in Japanese classical music. (Y)

wairo   a bribe. People in business and politics seek social links with their associates and clients. They exchange moderate gifts simply to make human relations function more smoothly. Exchanges of gifts among businessmen, merchants, and social acquaintances in summer (*chūgen*) and at the end of the year (*seibo*) are popular practices exercised

しさを求めたのです。

和楽器　　日本古来の楽器の総称で
す。中でも最も人気のあるのは琴（右
図）で，特に女性に好まれています。
長さ180cm，幅30cmほどの木製の細長
い胴の上面に13本の弦が張ってあり，
床に置いて爪弾きます。琴で演奏する
曲は箏曲と呼ばれます。三味線は西洋
のバンジョーに似た3弦楽器で，弾く

ときはばちを用い，文楽や歌舞伎の伴奏やその他の邦楽に使われ
ます。尺八は竹製の縦笛の一種で，5つの指穴があり，1尺8寸
の長さです。琴，三味線，尺八は一般に邦楽を代表する3楽器と
呼ばれています。これらの他に，マンドリンを大きくしたもので
首元の折れている琵琶，そして笛や太鼓などが，日本の古典音楽
で用いられています。

賄　賂　　実業家や政治家は，同僚や得意先と社会的つながり
を求めるものです。彼らは人間関係を円滑にするために，適度な
贈り物をやりとりします。会社関係者，商人，一般の社会人の間
で行われる夏（中元）と年末（歳暮）の贈り物の交換は，日本中
でみられる一般的な習慣です。この贈り物の習慣は時として，必
要以上に高価な物や，場合によっては現金を贈って人を買収する

throughout the country. Unfortunately, this gift-giving custom has, at times, been used to influence or bribe others, in which cases unnecessarily expensive gifts or, as is often the case, money are given. Occasionally, the difference between a gift given as a token of friendly business relationship and a gift offered as a bribe is so subtle that it is difficult to distinguish one from the other. In politics, interest groups may try to bribe their representatives. Many people seem to regard this trend as inevitable as politics is an evil in and of itself. They tend to believe that there is no politician who will not succumb to *wairo* manipulation. (K)

wasabi Japanese horseradish. *Wasabi* is a plant unique to Japan and its root serves as one of the strongest spices in Japanese cooking. Without a dab of finely grated pale green *wasabi*, typical Japanese dishes such as *sushi* and *sashimi* (sliced raw fish) cannot be fully enjoyed. *Soba* (buckwheat noodles) is bland and uninteresting if a little bit of *wasabi* is not added to the dipping sauce. There are many other kinds of spice, a dab of which stimulates the appetite and enhances the flavor of Japanese dishes. For example, grated *shōga* (ginger root) added to *daikon-oroshi* (grated Japanese white radish) makes the dipping sauce for *tenpura* even more delicious. (T)

zen Zen Buddhism. A school of Mahayana Buddhism. Zen Buddhism was founded in the sixth century by Bodhidharma in India. It was soon introduced into China, where it achieved further development. It was brought to Japan late

のに悪用されます。仕事上の親しい関係のしるしとしての贈り物と買収のための贈り物との違いは実に微妙であるため，時として区別しにくいことがあります。政治においては，さまざまな利益集団が彼らの代表を買収しようとします。多くの人々はこの傾向を必然的なものと考えているようです。それも，政治そのものが邪悪なものだからです。政治家はみな賄賂に屈するものと思っているのです。

わさび　わさびは日本特有の植物で，その根は日本料理において最も刺激の強い薬味として使われます。ほんの少量でいいのです。すりおろした淡い緑色のわさびがなかったら，すしや刺身などの代表的な日本料理はもの足りなくなります。そばも，つけ汁に少量のわさびを加えなかったら，ピリッとせず，ものたりない味になってしまいます。わさびの他にも，ほんの少量で食欲をそそり，日本料理の風味をよくする薬味がいろいろあります。例えば，すりおろしたしょうがを大根おろしに加えると，天ぷらのつゆはいっそうおいしくなります。

禅　大乗仏教の一宗派である禅宗は，6世紀にインドの菩提達磨によって始められました。それはすぐに中国に伝えられ，さらに発展しました。禅宗は，平安末期に，臨済宗の開祖である栄西によって，また鎌倉時代に，曹洞宗の開祖である道元によって

in the Heian period (794-1185) by Eisai (1141-1215), the founder of the Rinzaishū sect, and again in the Kamakura period (1192-1333) by Dōgen (1200-1253), the founder of the Sōtōshū sect. In addition to these two sects, the naturalized priest Ingen (1592-1673), coming from China, founded the Ōbakushū sect in the Edo period (1603-1867). Zen Buddhism teaches self-discipline, deep meditation, and attainment of enlightenment or spiritual awakening. It is characterized by its emphasis on *kenshō, zenkai*, and *samu. Kenshō* means direct intuitive insight into transcendent truth beyond all intellectual conception. In other words, it is to see with one's mind's eye and recognize the Buddhahood inherent in oneself. Zen Buddhism derived its name from silent meditation (*zenjō*), which is a means of attaining this self-realization. Sitting in silent meditation is known as *zazen. Zenkai* is the Buddhist commandments characteristically interpreted by the Zen sects which hold that the commandments are what an enlightened person would naturally and spontaneously practice. *Samu* means labor, especially physical work in every day life, in which, according to the teachings, transcendent truth can be found. Zen Buddhism has exerted a great influence on the shaping of Japanese culture, especially on such arts as flower arrangement and the tea ceremony. Since Suzuki Daisetsu (1870-1966) introduced it to America, it has probably become the most popular Buddhist school among Westerners. (S)

日本に伝えられました。これらの2つの禅宗に加えて，江戸時代には中国からの帰化僧隠元が黄檗宗を開きました。禅宗は自己規律と瞑想と悟道を説きます。その特質は，見性と禅戒と作務を強調することにあります。見性は，理知的には把握できない超越的真理を直観的に洞察することです。いいかえれば，自己の内にある仏性を心眼で認識することです。禅宗の名称は静かな瞑想（禅定）に由来していますが，それはこの自己認識を達成する手段なのです。静かに座って瞑想することを座禅といいます。禅戒というのは，禅宗特有の解釈による仏教の戒律のことです。禅宗では，戒律というものは悟りを開いた人が自然に自発的に実行するものであると説いています。作務は，労働，特に日常生活の身体労働のことですが，教えによれば，その中にこそ超越的真理が見出されるということです。禅は，日本文化，特に生け花や茶の湯などの芸術の形成に大きな影響を及ぼしました。鈴木大拙が禅をアメリカに伝えて以来，これは西洋人の間で最もよく知られた仏教の宗派のようです。

索　引（太字は見出し項目）
（Index）

i

索 引 (Index)

ii

索 引 (Index)

v

索 引 （Index）

索 引 (Index)

索 引 (Index)

編者紹介（Editors）

本 名 信 行（ほんな　のぶゆき）

　　　　1940年生
　　　　青山学院大学大学院卒業
　　　　現在　青山学院大学教授
　　　　専攻　英語学，社会言語学，異文化間コミュニ
　　　　ケーション，アメリカ研究
　　　　テキサス・キリスト教大学客員研究員，トリニ
　　　　ティ大学客員教授などを歴任，豊富な渡米経験
　　　　をもつ。編著書，翻訳，論文多数

Bates Hoffer（ベイツ・ホッファ）

　　　　1939年生
　　　　テキサス大学大学院卒業（Ph. D.）
　　　　現在　トリニティ大学教授
　　　　専攻　英語学，社会言語学，異文化間コミュニ
　　　　ケーション，日本研究
　　　　東京電機大学客員研究員，ハワイ大学客員教授
　　　　などを歴任，豊富な来日経験をもつ。編著書，
　　　　論文多数

日本文化を英語で説明する辞典

昭和 61 年 5 月 30 日　初版第 1 刷発行
昭和 61 年 9 月 10 日　初版第 5 刷発行

定価 1,600 円

編　　者　　　　本　名　信　行
　　　　　　　　ベイツ・ホッファ

発 行 者　　　　江　草　忠　敬

　　　　〒101 東京都千代田区神田神保町 2-17

発 行 所　　　株式 有 斐 閣
　　　　　　　会社

　　　　　　　電　話　03-264-1311
　　　　　　　振替口座　東京 6-370 番
　　　京都支店〔606〕左京区田中門前町 44

印刷　暁印刷株式会社　製本　稲村製本所
Printed in Japan
ISBN 4-641-07492-5